Griffin, Keith B
　　The political economy of agrarian change : an essay on
the green revolution / Keith Griffin. — Cambridge, Mass. :
Harvard University Press, 1974.

　xv, 264 p. : ill. ; 23 cm.

　Includes bibliographical references and index.
　ISBN 0-674-68531-8

The Political Economy of Agrarian Change

THE POLITICAL ECONOMY OF AGRARIAN CHANGE

AN ESSAY ON THE *GREEN REVOLUTION*

Keith Griffin

Harvard University Press
Cambridge, Massachusetts
1974

Library of Congress Catalog Card Number 74-80154

ISBN 0 674 68531 8

First published in the United Kingdom in 1974 by
The Macmillan Press Ltd.
London and Basingstoke

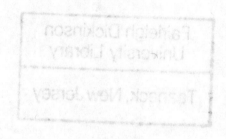
Printed in Great Britain

To Mother

Contents

Preface

This book is about technical change in the agricultural sector of underdeveloped countries. It is concerned specifically with the economic, social and political implications of introducing new, high yielding varieties of rice and wheat in the rural areas of Asia and, less prominently, of Latin America. Thus it is an essay on what is widely known as the 'green revolution'.

The volume is divided into eight chapters. The first chapter is introductory. In it the new varieties are described, the extent of diffusion is indicated, estimates are presented of trend rates of growth, and the demographic context in which technical change occurs is discussed. A theory of resource allocation in the rural areas of underdeveloped countries is developed in Chapter 2. Our major hypothesis is that economic and political power are concentrated in a small group and, as a result, factor markets are highly imperfect. That is, many members of the rural community have restricted access to the means of production, and this affects the methods of cultivation that are used and the efficiency of the system. In Chapter 3 we demonstrate how biased technical change, market imperfections and government policy combine to ensure that the benefits of the 'green revolution' accrue largely to the more prosperous regions and the more prosperous landowners. In other words, it is suggested that technical change in agriculture is resulting in greater income inequality and a polarization of social classes.

The empirical material in Chapters 2 and 3 comes primarily from monsoon Asia. In Chapter 4 we briefly illustrate the argument with data from two countries in Latin America — Mexico and Colombia — in order to show that the analysis is quite general and has worldwide implications.

The next two chapters are concerned not with methods for increasing production but with the methods by which production is disposed of. Chapter 5 is devoted to the domestic market and shows how the marketable surplus of agricultural commodities is in practice intimately related to a transfer of real resources from rural to urban areas. It is argued that a major policy goal of most governments has been to extract resources from agriculture and to transfer these to urban areas where they have been used to increase public and private consumption and industrial investment. We describe the various mechanisms which have been used to facilitate a resource transfer, comment on the efficiency of these devices and indicate how the 'green revolution' helps to perpetuate the system.

Chapter 6 explores some of the international implications of the introduction of high yielding varieties of wheat and rice and especially the effect of the 'green revolution' on the international division of labour. It is noteworthy that in each of the three countries which has participated most actively in the 'revolution' – India, Pakistan and the Philippines – the government has introduced high support prices for foodgrains and the question thus arises as to whether these countries can produce rice and wheat competitively. The new seeds have encouraged many countries to attempt to reduce their imports of food, but so far this has been possible only by subsidizing both inputs and output.

The final two chapters are concerned with policy issues. Chapter 7 raises some fundamental questions about the objectives of government, the organization of social forces and the circumstances under which technical change produces cumulative disequilibrating movements. Chapter 8 contains a summary of the argument of the book and a discussion of specific policy measures that could be taken by governments anxious to ensure that the 'green revolution' contribution to faster growth and diminished inequality.

What, briefly, has been the contribution so far of high yielding varieties of foodgrain to development? It is not possible to claim that the new seeds and the accompanying technology have increased agricultural production per head or reduced malnutrition. The most that can be claimed is that the introduction of high yielding varieties, along with other changes, enabled some countries to maintain existing levels of per capita production and nutrition in a context in which population was increasing rapidly and arable land was becoming ever more scarce. Since the rate of growth of agricultural output has not accelerated, it cannot be argued that the new seeds have contributed to a faster rate of growth of national income per head. The direct, quantitative effects of the new technolgy have, therefore, been rather modest at the aggregate level.

The indirect and qualitative effects, however, have sometimes been significant, particularly when one focuses on specific regions or localities. The new technology has led to changes in crop pattern and in methods of production. It has accelerated the development of a market oriented, capitalist agriculture. It has hastened the demise of subsistence oriented, peasant farming. It has encouraged the growth of wage labour, and thereby helped to create or augment a class of agricultural labourers. It has increased the power of landowners, especially the larger ones, and this in turn has been associated with a greater polarization of classes and intensified conflict.

Changes in status and class alignments have been accompanied by changes in the distribution of income. Profits and rents have increased absolutely and relatively. The share of wages has declined, and in some instances real wage rates or the number of days worked, or both, have declined. This has occurred most notably when the introduction of high yielding varieties has been accompanied by labour displacing mechanization, but it has also occurred when the rise in employment has been less than the increase in the labour force attributable to demographic expansion and migration. In other words, inequality has increased in most areas and poverty has increased in some areas.

The new seeds have been used in many countries in order to attain self-sufficiency in food. To the extent that this strategy of import substitution in agriculture succeeds, the growth prospects of traditional grain exporting nations will be adversely affected. But in the countries in which innovation occurs, a new stimulus for industrial growth also will be created. This arises from the fact that high yielding varieties are relatively intensive in their use of chemical and mechanical inputs, and this provides an opportunity for the industrial sector to supply these products to agriculture. Thus new links between industry and agriculture can be, and in a few cases have been, established.

Agricultural innovation, however, has been encouraged by considerable subsidies, in the form of domestic price support programmes for wheat and rice and in the form of cheap credit and low prices for machinery and agro-chemicals. There is a danger that these subsidies to particular commodities and particular inputs will lead to the creation of an inefficient and capital intensive agriculture which is incapable of producing an adequate livelihood for the mass of the rural population. If agriculture of the 1970s follows the path of industry in the 1960s, and fails to provide productive employment for the rapidly increasing labour force, the drift to the cities will continue unabated and the growth of unproductive employment in petty services may become explosive. If this occurs, the standard of living of large numbers of people is likely to fall.

In summary, an old system of agriculture, slowly or swiftly, is in the process of being destroyed by the advance of contemporary technology. This technology contains a positive potential for economic and social development. But if used unwisely, it can aggravate tendencies already discernible and contribute to further inequality and poverty. It is not inevitable that it will do so; nor is it inevitable that it will not.

This study has arisen from a project financially supported by the United Nations Development Programme and the United Nations Research Institute for Social Development and executed by the United Nations through its Office of Technical Cooperation and UNRISD. The views expressed in this study, however, do not necessarily reflect the views of these organizations. The study is based largely upon work carried out by the author while employed under a special service agreement with UNRISD, under the UNDP Global research project entitled 'The Social and Economic Implications of the Large-Scale Introduction of High-Yielding Varieties of Foodgrain'. An earlier version of Chapters 2–6 of the present volume has been circulated by the Institute as a work in progress report, under the title *The Green Revolution: An Economic Analysis*.

My colleagues at UNRISD, Andrew Pearse, Antonio Barreto, N. D. Abdul Hamed and Ingrid Palmer, were a continuous source of suggestions and assistance. Randolph Barker, of the International Rice Research Institute (IRRI) in the Philippines, is an unusually generous scholar. He spared no effort to provide me with data and material, to arrange field trips and to facilitate introductions to other knowledgeable persons; I am much indebted to him for the courtesy and hospitality he showed me on the two occasions I visited IRRI. G. A. Marzouk, of ECAFE, and Professor Shigeru Ishikawa, of Hitotsubashi University, shared their knowledge of Asian agriculture with me. Carmel Budiarjo was helpful on Indonesia and Raymond Apthorpe on Taiwan. The conversations I had with R. A. Berry increased my understanding of what is happening in Colombia and the kindness of Wayne Thirsk, in allowing me to read and use some data from a draft of his Ph.D. thesis, enabled me to document several important points. Cynthia Hewitt de Alcantara was a delightful guide in Hermosillo, Mexico and Luise Pare did all that was possible on a rather hurried trip to Puebla. To these people, and the many others in India, Sri Lanka and elsewhere who took the trouble and the time to help me, I am most grateful.

K. B. G.

Magdalen College, Oxford
October 1973

CHAPTER 1

Introduction

It was not so many years ago that serious and informed observers of the international scene were predicting prolonged famine in large parts of the underdeveloped world, particularly in Asia.[1] Such predictions rarely are heard today – and rightly so. Food supplies in relation to population are more satisfactory now than they were in the crisis years of the mid 1960s and, with the possible exception of Africa, there does not appear to be any secular tendency for the per capita availability of food to decline, although cyclical catastrophes can be expected to occur with distressing frequency. Our tentative and rather qualified optimism that there has been a reduction in the likelihood of acute food shortages is due in part to the presence of economic forces (e.g. an improvement in some countries in the internal terms of trade of the agricultural sector), in part to government policy decisions (e.g. a greater allocation of investment expenditure to agriculture) and in part to the development of high yielding varieties of foodgrains and the accompanying technical changes (i.e. to the 'green revolution').

---

[1] For a vision of catastrophe read René Dumont and Bernard Rosier, *Nous Allons a la Famine*, (Éditions du Seuil, 1966). Lester Brown, in *Increasing World Food Output* (Washington, USDA Foreign Agricultural Economic Report No. 25, 1965), also feared it would not be possible to halt the decline in food output per head. Five years later, in *Seeds of Change* (London: Pall Mall Press, 1970), he predicted food surpluses. Also see William and Paul Paddock, *Famine – 1975* (Boston, 1967), George Borgstrom, *The Hungry Planet: The Modern World at the Edge of Famine* (New York, 1965) and P. P. Ehrlich, *The Population Bomb* (New York, 1968).

A. Rhetoric and Reality

Alarms about the possibility of famine were a response to the failure of the monsoon in South Asia for two successive years. There is no doubt that the food situation, particularly in India, was extremely critical in 1965—66 and 1966—67, but the likelihood of permanent mass starvation never was very great. Hunger and malnutrition are indeed chronic in many parts of the world, but famines tend to be temporary phenomena associated with major wars or natural disasters. The crisis of agriculture in the underdeveloped world is a silent one; only rarely does the misery of most of mankind become dramatic.

Today one hears a great deal about the 'green revolution' and there is a danger of becoming complacent about the state of food and agriculture in poor countries. The expression 'green revolution' is a loaded term, a political slogan.[2] It suggests there has been a major breakthrough in agricultural production, that this has been done in a peaceful context without the need for institutional reform, and indeed, that technical change is an alternative to political change. As we shall see, all of these suggestions are misleading. Reality is quite different from current rhetoric.

The expression 'green revolution' has been used to mean two different things. Some writers use it when referring to a broad transformation of the agricultural sector in under-developed countries, to a reduction in food shortages and undernourishment, and to the elimination of agriculture as a bottleneck to overall development. Others use it when referring to specific plant improvements, notably, the development of high yielding varieties of rice and wheat. In this latter context the vocabulary of propagandists sometimes is enriched by the addition of yet another misleading phrase: 'miracle rice'.[3] Evidently, those who use the term 'green

[2] As far as can be determined, it was first used in its present context by William Gaud, at the time Administrator of the U.S. Agency for International Development, in a speech before the Society for International Development in Washington, D.C. in 1968. The speech was entitled 'The Green Revolution: Accomplishments and Apprehensions'.
[3] Perhaps it is not surprising that the phrase 'miracle rice' originated in the Philippines, a country where the government encourages the Catholic populace to wait for miracles and desist from action.

revolution' in its narrow sense do not necessarily wish to imply that there has been a broad transformation of agriculture, but there is an observable tendency in the literature on the subject for those who believe that output of foodgrains has markedly increased to believe also that the rural problems of the Third World are on the way to being solved. Let us now examine the data to see whether in either a broad or a narrow sense there has in fact been a 'green revolution'.

B. Where is the 'Green Revolution'?

At a recent international conference on the Place of Agriculture in the Development of Underdeveloped Countries a well known Indian economist began his paper with the following statement: 'No one seriously doubts that the Green Revolution or the use of High Yielding Varieties (HYV) is resulting in a substantial increase in output and employment in agriculture in the developing countries.'[4] It may be true, of course, that few people have 'doubts', but if so, their lack of scientific scepticism should be deplored. There is, in fact, very little evidence that there has in recent years been a reversal of the trend rate of growth of food and agricultural output. Indeed, the opposite may be the case.[5]

Following a method first used by T. N. Srinivasan on Indian data,[6] we have calculated exponential trend rates of growth of output for the pre-green revolution period of 1955–1965. We then added to our original data observations for five more years, 1966 through 1970, the period when the 'revolution' is supposed to have begun, and recalculated the

[4] C. H. Hanumantha Rao, 'Employment Implications of Green Revolution and Mechanization in Agriculture in Developing Countries: A Case Study of India', paper presented at a conference on the Place of Agriculture in the Development of Underdeveloped Countries, Bad Godesberg, West Germany, 26 August–5 September 1972, mimeo., p. 1.
[5] Data on food and agricultural output in underdeveloped countries are not always reliable and no significance should be attached to small changes in the level or trend of production. Throughout this study we have tried to illustrate our argument with quantitative evidence, but the reader is warned that this evidence is not as trustworthy as one would wish.
[6] T. N. Srinivasan, 'The Green Revolution or the Wheat Revolution?', Indian Statistical Institute, Discussion paper No. 66, 1971.

trend for the entire 16 years, 1955–1970. By comparing the
two trends we should be able to detect whether there has
been an acceleration in growth in the last half decade. This
method will not enable us to determine what is the true trend
since 1965 – which in any case is impossible given the
volatility of agriculture and the small number of observations – but it should allow us to test the hypothesis that
there has been no increase in trend. That is, if the trend rate
of growth for 1955–1970 is significantly greater than the
trend for 1955–1965, we can be fairly confident that an
acceleration in the growth of output has occurred since 1965.

The data we have used were obtained from various issues
of FAO, *The State of Food and Agriculture*. In the tables
below the trend rates of growth are presented for four
underdeveloped regions:[7] Latin America; Africa, excluding
South Africa; the Near East, i.e., the area extending from
Libya and the U.A.R. to Afghanistan, excluding Israel; and
the Far East, i.e., the area from Pakistan to Korea, excluding
China and Japan. The estimating equation we have used is of
the type $y = ae^{bt}$.

Growth of food and agriculture

Let us begin by examining whether there has been an
acceleration in the rate of growth of total agricultural
production, i.e. in both food and non-food agricultural
commodities. If the 'green revolution' in its widest sense has
been successful, one would expect to find a breakthrough on
a broad front, and this should be reflected in the indexes of
total production. The estimated trends are presented in the
table below.

It is obvious from the data in Table 1.1 that in none of the
major underdeveloped regions of the world has there been an
acceleration in the growth of agricultural output. Indeed in
each case the inclusion of data from recent years lowers the
trend rate of growth. Moreover, these trends, in a statistical

[7] When assessing these growth rates it would be wise to remember that
the rate of demographic increase in all four regions is between 2.6 and
2.9 per cent per annum. Per capita growth rates are presented in
Chapter 7. See especially Table 7.2.

Table 1.1
Rates of Growth of Total Agricultural Production, 1955–1970

	Percentage annual rate of growth	R^2	T value of regression coefficient
Latin America			
1955–65	3.10	0.98	19.8
1955–70	2.74	0.98	26.2
Africa			
1955–65	2.86	0.97	16.9
1955–70	2.49	0.97	23.0
Near East			
1955–65	3.42	0.96	13.9
1955–70	3.11	0.98	23.7
Far East			
1955–65	2.90	0.98	19.0
1955–70	2.77	0.98	25.4

sense, are highly significant: both the coefficients of determination (R^2) and the T values of the regression coefficients are exceptionally high. Thus one can be confident that there has been no breakthrough yet in overall agricultural output.

From a nutritional point of view, however, the crucial variable may be food production, rather than agricultural production as a whole. Commodities such as jute, sisal, cotton and timber may be expanding slowly while food output may be increasing rapidly, perhaps as a result of a transfer of land from non-food to food crops. The reverse, of course, also could occur. Our estimates of the trends in food output are contained in the table which follows.

Again the results are unambiguous. In no region has there been an acceleration in food production. The rate of growth of food output has remained essentially constant in Latin America and in the other areas, if anything, the trend may have declined. As in the previous case, the R^2s and T values indicate an unusually good statistical fit. Except in Africa, food production exceeds population growth, although the margin sometimes is rather slight. Thus, in general, the Third World is not drifting toward famine, but neither is it

Table 1.2
Rates of Growth of Food Production, 1955—1970

	Percentage annual rate of growth	R^2	T value of regression coefficient
Latin America			
1955—65	3.02	0.97	18.7
1955—70	3.05	0.99	35.1
Africa			
1955—65	2.49	0.95	13.5
1955—70	2.15	0.96	19.5
Near East			
1955—65	3.10	0.94	11.9
1955—70	2.89	0.97	22.3
Far East			
1955—65	2.94	0.97	17.3
1955—70	2.80	0.97	22.4

advancing rapidly to a state of abundance and adequate nourishment.[8]

Growth of wheat and rice
There has been a breakthrough in plant breeding which has enabled biologists to produce high yielding varieties of foodgrains, but so far this breakthrough has been confined to essentially two crops: wheat and rice. Improved varieties of maize, millet and even coffee have been developed, but the progress achieved has been relatively modest and their impact on world agricultural supplies has not been substantial. Research is underway to improve the yields of other crops, e.g. potatoes, but for the time being those who use the term 'green revolution' in its narrow sense really are referring to the introduction and cultivation of high yielding varieties of wheat and rice.

The new wheat seeds were developed originally in Mexico in the 1940s and 1950s and soon occupied most of the wheat

[8] Simple estimates of rates of growth of per capita food and agricultural output since 1950 are presented in Chapter 7; see especially Table 7.2. Estimates for several Asian countries can be found on p. 61, Table 3.3.

area in that country. It was not until the mid 1960s, however, that high yielding varieties of wheat were adopted in other countries. Today the improved seeds account for a high proportion of the total wheat area in Pakistan, Nepal and India, and they have been adopted on a small scale in parts of the Middle East and North Africa, but elsewhere their impact has been negligible. This can be seen in Table 1.3.

Table 1.3
Rates of Growth of Wheat Production, 1955–1970

	Percentage annual rate of growth	R^2	T value of regression coefficient
Latin America			
1955–65	2.21	0.17	1.3
1955–70	1.28	0.15	1.8
Africa*			
1956–65	2.25	0.14	1.1
1956–70	2.19	0.23	2.0
Near East			
1955–65	1.93	0.58	3.5
1955–70	2.23	0.81	7.8
Far East*			
1956–65	3.48	0.72	4.5
1956–70	5.06	0.75	6.3

* In Africa and the Far East no data were available on wheat production in 1955.

The trends in wheat production in Latin America and Africa are not clear. Superficially, it would appear that the trend has not increased in either area. On the other hand, the estimated trend line does not fit the data very well and the *T* values are low in both periods in both regions. Thus it is very difficult to say what is the true trend. Nonetheless, there is no positive evidence that there has been a wheat revolution in this part of the world. The Near East is somewhat more difficult. On the surface there appears to have been an increase in trend, but the confidence interval for the first period extends from 0.68 to 3.18 and straddles the confidence interval of the longer period (1.6 to 2.8) and thus we cannot be certain that there has been a true change in behaviour. In the Far East, in contrast, there has been a clear — even dramatic — increase in the rate of growth of the production of wheat. There certainly has been a breakthrough in this crop.

Consider now the situation in rice, which in terms of the number of people who rely on it for subsistence (especially in the Far East, of course) is far more important than wheat. The first semi-dwarf indica variety was developed by plant breeders in Taiwan in 1956. This variety is known as Taichung Native 1, and it is on this plant material that most of the subsequent research has been built. This is especially true of the work done at the International Rice Research Institute in Los Baños, Philippines (IRRI).

IRRI was established by the Ford and Rockefeller Foundations at an initial capital cost of $7.4 million. Serious research on the Institute's 80 hectare farm started in 1962 and by 1965 many genetic lines had been developed. The best of these lines have double the yield potential of traditional rice varieties. They are short and therefore are less inclined to fall over or 'lodge': the new varieties are about 100 centimeters tall as compared to 160—180 centimeters of the local varieties. The high yielding varieties have short, upright leaves, which enables sunlight to penetrate; they have a heavy tillering capacity; they are only mildly sensitive to length of day, and therefore can be planted at any time of the year; and they have a grain to straw ratio of 1.0 as compared to 0.6 or 0.7 of the indigenous varieties. Under ideal conditions the maximum yield of these HYVs is over 10 metric tons per hectare, and even in the cloudy, monsoon season yields can exceed 5 tons per hectare. In comparison, the average yield of rice in the Third World, using mostly local varieties, is less than 2 tons per hectare.

In November 1966 the first of the IRRI varieties was released for general use, IR—8. This was followed in 1967 by IR—5. Then came IR—20 (perhaps the best high yielding variety of rice now available) and IR—22 in 1969. Lastly, ‾24 was released in 1971. Thus over a period of six years five new varieties of rice were developed for the market by IRRI alone. In addition, of course, scientists in other countries, e.g. Sri Lanka and India, were attempting to develop improved local varieties, and they encountered some success. Nonetheless, the impact of all this effort on rice production has been relatively modest. There certainly has been no breakthrough in monsoon Asia, as can be seen in the table which follows.

Table 1.4
Rates of Growth of Rice Production, 1955—1970

	Percentage annual rate of growth	R^2	T *value of regression coefficient*
Latin America			
1955—65	6.30	0.95	12.8
1955—70	4.85	0.92	13.1
Africa			
1955—65	2.50	0.83	6.6
1955—70	3.40	0.91	12.1
Near East			
1955—65	5.94	0.70	4.6
1955—70	5.49	0.84	8.7
Far East*			
1956—65	3.30	0.77	5.2
1956—70	2.84	0.85	8.5

* In the Far East no data were available on rice production in 1955.

The trend in rice production appears to have declined in the Far East and Latin America. At best it has remained roughly constant in the Near East. Only in Africa is there evidence that the tempo of rice output has accelerated, and rice in Africa accounts for less than 10 per cent of total cereal production, so the breakthrough there is of little significance. Thus the conclusion is inescapable: despite the development of high yielding varieties of rice there has been no increase in the trend of production in the Third World as a whole, i.e., there has been no 'green revolution' in rice.

Big gains in small areas

Although there does not appear to have been a 'green revolution' in either the broad or the narrow sense when one looks at the major underdeveloped regions of the world, this does not imply that no localities have experienced rapid agricultural or cereal growth in the last few years. Several clearly have. Indeed one of the characteristics of recent agricultural development is that accelerated progress has been limited to only a small number of countries. Those nations which depend on crops other than wheat or rice to provide the basic subsistence for their population have been largely excluded from the fruits of technical change. This includes most of Black Africa (which depends on millets, cassava and yams) and a large part of Central and South America (which depends on potatoes and maize). Moreover, even within the rice and wheat producing areas, only those countries — or, more accurately, parts of countries — which are endowed with fairly good irrigation facilities have been able to exploit the opportunities which high yielding varieties create. It is for this reason that even in countries where the new seeds have been introduced only a fraction — usually less than half — of the land devoted to wheat or rice is cultivated with high yielding varieties. This is evident from Table 1.5.

It is important to maintain a sense of perspective. By 1971, in the non-socialist countries of the Third World exclusive of Taiwan and Mexico, only 17.2 per cent of the wheat area and 10.2 per cent of the rice area was planted to high yielding varieties. Expressed as a proportion of all foodgrains, high yielding varieties of wheat and rice occupied only 6.7 per cent of the land devoted to cereals. Clearly, the 'green revolution', from a global point of view, is still a very small phenomenon. In some areas, however, very big gains in yields have been achieved. This has occurred, for example, in the Punjab of Pakistan, in the wheat growing areas of northwest India, and in large parts of the Philippines. In several of the chapters which follow we shall examine the economic and social implications of the changes which have occurred in areas such as these.

Even in regions where the new seeds have not been utilized on a wide scale, however, technical changes are occurring.

Table 1.5
Percentage of Crop Area Under High Yielding Varieties, 1970—71

	Rice	Wheat
Afghanistan	—	7.8
Bangladesh	3.3	7.7
Burma	4.0	—
India	14.7	32.9
Indonesia	11.3	—
Laos	7.0	—
Nepal	5.8	49.1
Pakistan	41.7	48.7
Philippines	50.3	—
South Vietnam	19.3	—
Sri Lanka	4.5	—
Syria	—	10.1
Thailand	2.1	—
Tunisia	—	14.0
Turkey	—	5.8
West Malaysia	24.5	—

Source: USDA, *Imports and Plantings of High-Yielding Varieties of Wheat and Rice in the Less Developed Nations*, Foreign Economic Development Report No. 14, February 1972; Table D, p. 51. The wheat figure for Nepal was obtained from FAO.
Note: High yielding varieties are defined in the report as varieties originating or directly descended from those developed at IRRI and CIMMYT and thus exclude locally improved varieties. This is particularly important in the case of Sri Lanka.

For example, one frequently observes a greater use of mechanical equipment in tropical areas, and the tools of analysis developed in this study can be used to assess the likely implications for rural livelihood. In some respects the most fundamental change that has occurred or is about to occur in many tropical regions is the termination of the land frontier and the consequent inability of several countries to expand production at a high rate merely by increasing the area under annual cultivation. For many years, especially in sparsely populated countries, agricultural growth has been able to proceed at a sustained pace without the necessity of raising yields. Rice output in Thailand, for instance, has expanded considerably during the last 50 years, yet yields in

1963—67 were no higher than in 1923—27.[9] In future, however, rising yields must become a source of growth. In the Philippines, rice yields remained constant from 1923 to 1962 at 11.7 quintals per hectare, but they began to increase thereafter in response to rising population density and greater difficulty of increasing the gross area under cultivation.[10] Even in India and Pakistan, until about 1965 half of the increase in agricultural output can be attributed to an increase in the area under cultivation.[11]

As land becomes more and more scarce the source of agricultural growth should switch from expanding area to rising yields, and accordingly investments in such things as irrigation, fertilizer, improved seeds, weed and pest control should become more important.[12] In some countries, however, the deceleration in the rate of growth of the gross area under cultivation may be greater than the acceleration in the rate of growth of yields. Where this occurs the rate of increase of agricultural production will decline, and in extreme cases may fall below the rate of increase of the population. In other words, the transition to a more intensive agriculture may be far from smooth.

Increasing scarcity of land in an agrarian community may aggravate social tension. This is particularly likely to happen, first, if changes in the degree of land shortage are inversely associated with the growth of agricultural output and, second, if income earning opportunities outside agriculture do not expand sufficiently fast to absorb productively a significant fraction of the increase in the rural labour force. Under these circumstances tension is likely to erupt into conflict and violence whenever established sources of author-

[9] Thai rice yields were 18.6 quintals per hectare in 1923—27 and 16.3 in 1963—67. See United Nations, Department of Economic and Social Affairs, *1970 Report on the World Social Situation*, 1971, Table 3, p. 9.
[10] *Ibid.*
[11] For data covering the period 1948 to 1963 see U.S. Department of Agriculture, *Changes in Agriculture in 26 Developing Countries*, Foreign Agricultural Economic Report No. 27, 1965.
[12] For an interesting model in which demographic expansion induces technical change in agriculture see E. Boserup, *The Conditions of Agricultural Growth*.

ity and power are weakened. Often conflict will be concentrated in regions where population densities are high and resources per head are low, as in Northeast Thailand, Central Luzon, Philippines and the island of Java in Indonesia.[13] In other cases, however, the inhabitants of densely settled regions may migrate to more sparsely inhabited areas, and in doing so they may encroach upon the livelihood of people of a different tribe, ethnic group or religion. The indigenous population can be expected to resist the loss of territory, and violence is a likely result. This process can be observed on the island of Mindanao in the Philippines and possibly too in the tribal area of northeastern India.

Clearly, the processes of change in agrarian communities are highly complex. As long as land is abundant, and population increase is relatively slow, agricultural growth occurs by expanding the gross cultivated area. As population density rises, however, land becomes increasingly scarce and this induces technical change, more intensive cultivation and higher yields. But new methods of cultivation may not be introduced fast enough to compensate for the falling rate of increase of crop acreage, and consequently, the rate of growth of agricultural production may decline. That is, paradoxically, the rate of agricultural expansion may begin to slow down precisely during a period when the rate of

[13] It is still widely believed that the 1965 massacre in Indonesia was a result of ideological conflict between communists and non-communists. This is a very misleading way of viewing the events of that tragic year. The basic problem arose from the fact that roughly 90 per cent of the villagers in central and southern Java do not own the land they cultivate, and in return for their labour the peasants receive only 33—40 per cent of the harvest. Moreover, the real income of this enormous mass of population was slowly declining. Unrest increased among the landless in response to the frustrations arising from the slow implementation of the promised land reform, and this was matched by the fears of landowners that eventually they would be deprived of their source of wealth, power and status. The violence began around October 20th 'in the Klaten area of Central Java, an area where serious agrarian tension had prevailed. ... The killing was soon extended to areas where ... land reform had interfered with the interests of wealthy, mainly Muslim, landowners...' (Gerrit Huizer, *Peasant Mobilization and Land Reform in Indonesia*, Institute of Social Studies, The Hague, Occasional Paper no. 18, June 1972, p. 52).

innovation and technical change is accelerating. When this occurs, social tensions, always present to some degree in rural areas, are likely to be accentuated. One will then discover an apparent correlation between technical change and agrarian unrest. This unrest will be further intensified if agricultural expansion falls below the rate of demographic increase (so that poverty rises absolutely) or if the new technology (because of its inherent characteristics or the way it is introduced) results in greater inequality and social differentiation. On the other hand, tension will be assuaged if it is possible for the peasantry to escape the poverty and inequality of the countryside by shifting to industrial employment and migrating to urban areas.

In summary, the actors in our drama are (*i*) the pace of demographic expansion, (*ii*) the rate of increase of the area under cultivation, (*iii*) the rate of yield-increasing technical innovation, (*iv*) the direction of change of income distribution, (*v*) the extent to which social differentiation occurs and the ease with which groups with common interests can be organized, and (*vi*) the rate of growth of non-agricultural employment opportunities. The interplay of these actors determines the outcome of the drama, and there is no reason to expect that the final act will be the same in each country. Indeed the only safe generalization is that one cannot generalize. One can, however, scrutinize the data, build an analysis upon them and point out trends which seem to be common in apparently diverse situations. This is what we have tried to do in the chapters which follow.

PART ONE

Economic Aspects of Technical Change in the Rural Areas of Asia and Latin America

CHAPTER 2

Factor Prices and Methods of Cultivation

A. Factor Prices

A basic feature of the agricultural sector of almost all underdeveloped countries is that access to factors of production is much easier for some groups than others. That is, factor markets are highly 'imperfect', and in consequence market prices diverge considerably from social opportunity costs. In many instances, in fact, there is a multiplicity of markets within a locality for a single factor of production, e.g. credit. In these instances there may be no such thing as 'the' price of an input; different groups may pay different prices for the same input. In other cases there may be no market for certain inputs. For example, in many regions of the world land is seldom bought or sold; transfer is usually through gift or inheritance. Moreoever, in some regions there may be no rental price of land, although producers will, of course, operate in terms of implicit or subjective prices. Thus the rural areas of underdeveloped countries are characterized both by a scarcity of factor markets and by an abundance of small, fragmented markets. This market structure affects the allocation of resources within agriculture, the methods of production adopted by the farmer, the readiness to innovate and the distribution of income.

There are many explanations for the high degree of market imperfection in rural areas. Resources are immobile, means of communication are poor, accurate information is sparse. Probably the two most important explanations, however, are government policies, which are systematically biased in favour of certain groups, and the monopoly power possessed by the relatively wealthy and prosperous members of the

farming community. These two phenomena tend to re-en-
force each other. Wealth, particularly landed wealth, is often
accompanied by political influence,[1] and this in turn may be
strengthened by the inherited status that accompanies a tribal
chief, the village headman or the landed gentry. In other
words, status, political influence and economic power are
often joint attributes of an individual or family, and these
can be used to ensure privileged access to the scarce means of
production.

Land ownership

In rural areas the most important means of production is
land, and the only way to ensure access to it is to own it. Yet
in many underdeveloped countries the majority of rural
inhabitants either own no land or possess less than one
hectare each. Often a major reason for this is the high density
of population per unit of land. In Taiwan, for example, 66.4
per cent of the farms are of less than one hectare, and in
Indonesia the proportion is even higher, viz. 70.1 per cent. In
these countries, and in Bangladesh, farms are typically small,
and there are many landless labourers, because the ratio of
agricultural labour to land is very high.

   Even in countries where population densities are not high,
however, the majority of people have restricted access to
land. In many nations — particularly in Latin America, North
Africa, the Middle East and the Philippines — the most
prominent characteristic of the rural economy is the concentration of landownership. The majority is deprived of land
because most of the land is possessed by a tiny minority.
Cases can be found where 5 per cent of those active in
agriculture possess 60 per cent or more of the cultivable
surface,[2] and 10 per cent of all landowners may account for

[1] In India in 1972, for example, 45 out of 64 members of the Punjab
Assembly were big landowners, in Haryana, 30 out of 52, and in
Madhya Pradesh, 96 out of 220. (See Wolf Ladejinsky, 'New Ceiling
Round and Implementation Prospects', *Economic and Political Weekly*,
30 September 1972, p. A-129.)
[2] The best data on the distribution of landownership among members of
the rural population are from Latin America. The evidence is summarized in Keith Griffin, *Underdevelopment in Spanish America*,
Chapter 1.

half or more of the land. Moreover, this land is usually the most fertile and the most conveniently located with respect to irrigation, transport and marketing facilities. In a particular village, locality or region the monopolization of land may be acute. Indeed, there are numerous cases of one individual owning an entire village and its adjacent fields.

The distribution of land in India is not as unequal as in some countries. None the less, 23 per cent of the rural population own no land at all, while the top 7.7 per cent own over half the cultivated area. This can be seen in Table 2.1 below.

Table 2.1
Distribution of Landownership Among the Rural Population of India, 1954—55

Amount of land owned (acres)	Percentage of rural households	Percentage of area owned
0.00	23.09	0.00
0.01—5.00	51.64	16.32
5.01—15.00	17.55	31.18
15.01—30.00	5.12	22.05
More than 30	2.60	30.45

Source: Compiled from data published in K. N. Raj, 'Ownership and Distribution of Land', *Indian Economic Review*, April 1970, Table 1, p. 3, who cites the National Sample Survey, *Reports on Land Holdings.*

Across the border, in the Punjab of Pakistan, the degree of land concentration is even greater. Indeed, the largest 0.6 per cent of landowners possess 21.5 per cent of the land, and this is the richest region of the country. The top 21 per cent of landowners account for about 68 per cent of the land. Large numbers of peasants, of course, are utterly landless.

Inequality in the distribution of land in the Philippines is comparable to that in Pakistan or Latin America. For example, a study of coconut farms in the provinces of Quezon and Laguna indicates that the top 5.6 per cent of the farms account for 36.9 per cent of the land. The bottom 55.5 per cent of the landowners, in contrast, possess only 13.4 per

Table 2.2

Distribution of Land Among Landowners in the Pakistani Punjab, 1959

Area (acres)	Percentage of landowners	Percentage of cultivated area
Less than 10 acres	78.7	31.8
10—99	20.7	46.7
100—499	0.5	11.2
500 acres and above	0.1	10.3

Source: Government of West Pakistan, *Report of the Land Reform Commission for West Pakistan*, 1959.

cent of the land. A single farm accounted for nearly a quarter of the land in the sample data reproduced in Table 1.3.

Equally dramatic is the distribution of land under rice cultivation. A study of 101 landowners in the provinces of Bulacan and Nueva Ecija indicates that the bottom 50 per cent of landowners account for only 9.8 per cent of the land, while the top 10 per cent possess 58.3 per cent. The largest landowner in the sample had 3741 ha. Many people in rural areas, of course, owned no land at all and thus were excluded

Table 2.3

Ownership of Coconut Farms, 54 Landowners in Quezon and Laguna, Southern Tagalog, Philippines

Size (ha.)	Number of farms	Percentage of farms	Area (ha.)	Percentage of farms
5—14.9	12	22.2	104.5	2.9
15—19.9	8	14.8	134.7	3.8
20—29.9	10	18.5	242.0	6.7
30—99.9	13	24.1	665.6	18.5
100—199.9	8	14.8	1122.5	31.2
200—299.9	2	3.7	442.0	12.3
300 and above	1	1.9	884.05	24.6
Total	54	100.0	3595.4	100.0

Source: Compiled from data supplied by Enriqueta A. Bernal, College of Agriculture, Laguna, Philippines.

Table 2.4
Ownership of Rice Farms, 101 Landowners in Bulacan and Nueva Ecija, Central Luzon, Philippines

Percentage of farms	Percentage of total area
0–10	0.7
11–20	1.4
21–30	2.2
31–40	2.5
41–50	3.0
51–60	4.1
61–70	6.1
71–80	8.4
81–90	13.1
91–100	58.3

Source: Compiled from data supplied by Enriqueta A. Bernal, College of Agriculture, Laguna, Philippines.
Note: The top decile includes farms from 227 to 3,741 ha.

from the universe from which the sample was drawn. If one could obtain data on the distribution of landownership among those active in agriculture the extent of inequality would be even more apparent.

Most of the data in the Philippines are presented in such a way that it is virtually impossible to detect the degree of inequality in the distribution of landed wealth. The data are organized according to the size of the operational unit, and since most landowners — particularly in the rice-growing regions — break up their estates into a large number of small tenant farms, a size distribution of farms gives a misleading impression of equality. Farm sizes may be equally distributed; farm ownership is not.[3]

[3] The distribution of farms by size in the Philippines is as follows:

Farm size (ha.)	Percentage of farms	Percentage of area
0–4.9	81.0	43.1
5–19.9	18.0	39.0
20 and over	1.0	17.9

The implicit price of land

There is a spectrum along which landownership or the various sizes of farms will be distributed. Farm sizes are not accurately described by a bi-modal distribution. The rural economy is not, in this sense, dualistic. Nevertheless, it simplifies thought to imagine for the moment that farms are owned either by big landlords or by small peasants. The main difference between the two groups is that the implicit rental rate of land to the landlord tends to be less than the social opportunity cost of land, while the implicit rent paid by peasants tends to exceed the social opportunity cost. In symbols,

$$r_s \geqslant r \geqslant r_b$$

where r is the scarcity value of land and the subscripts s and b refer to small peasants and big landlords, respectively.[4]

Under 'perfect' market conditions the above inequalities would disappear, since those who possess abundant land (and hence value it relatively lowly) would sell or rent to those who possess little or no land (and hence value it highly). In some localities, however, the inequalities may in practice persist indefinitely because the local monopolist may be aware of his market power and knows that if he sells land he will drive the price down against himself. Moreover, as shall be argued below, the control of land gives the landowner ease of access to other resources as well. Thus, in extreme cases, there may be no local market in land at all. Land may simply be unobtainable by small peasants; its price to them may be infinite.

The landlord — tenant relationship

There are many cases, however, such as the Philippines, in which landownership is concentrated, but the land rental market is nevertheless competitive. This seems to occur most

---

[4] If there is a discrepancy between observed rental rates and the opportunity cost of land the inequalities must be of the form indicated in the text, since the opportunity cost could neither exceed all rental rates (unless there are no smallholders) nor be less than all rental rates (unless land becomes a free good to the economy).

frequently in regions such as Central Luzon or Java where labour is unusually abundant relative to land. In these circumstances competitive rental rates will be high and wage rates will be low. The landlord will have little incentive to withhold his land from the eager mass of bidders, since most of the value of production will accrue to him in any case as payment for the use of land.[5]

As long as factor markets are efficient, the allocation of resources in agriculture will be much the same whether the landowner has a share-cropping or leasehold contract with a tenant, farms the land himself or hires labour to do the work.[6] In each case, the landowner will ensure that the workers receive no more than they can earn in alternative employment. The type of contractual arrangement between landlord and peasant will not affect the efficiency with which resources are used, as long as competition prevails, but it will determine how the risks of production are distributed.

The three basic types of tenure arrangements are owner-operation, sharecropping and fixed rental or leasehold systems. An owner-operator hires labour for a fixed wage, organizes production himself, bears all risks and reaps all profits. Under this system the workers essentially become a rural proletariat. Sharecropping is an alternative arrangement, whereby the landlord and tenant share the costs, risks and profits — not necessarily equally, of course. Both parties to the contract typically have a role to play in the decision-making process. Under the leasehold system, in contrast, the landlord usually bears no risk and becomes a pure rentier; the tenant assumes all risks, makes all decisions and reaps the profits, if any. The tenant, in effect, becomes a small entrepreneur.

It is important to note that there is no necessary connection between ownership of land, entrepreneurship and risk taking. He who makes the decisions, bears most of the

---

[5] In parts of Java and Madura, for example, sharecroppers often receive only 30 or 40 per cent of the crop, and they are required to pay for seeds out of their share.
[6] See Steven N. S. Cheung, *The Theory of Share Tenancy*. It is assumed, of course, that under a sharecropping system both costs and output are shared proportionately.

risks,[7] but he who bears the risks need not own the land. Thus the extent to which the peasant is able to make many of the decisions which affect his well-being depends upon the type of contract he is able to negotiate with a landlord. The three basic tenure systems are presented below in schematic form; the arrow points toward those who bear the risks of production.

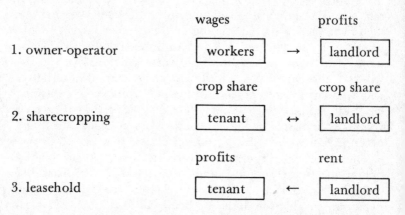

	wages		profits
1. owner-operator	workers	→	landlord
	crop share		crop share
2. sharecropping	tenant	↔	landlord
	profits		rent
3. leasehold	tenant	←	landlord

Even the three basic tenure forms allow landlords and peasants to adopt a variety of roles — agricultural worker, share-tenant, leaseholder, owner-operator, rentier, and crop-sharing landlord. Moreover, most of these roles can be found within any given locality and, indeed, many individuals will combine roles. For example, an individual may be simultaneously, or alternately, a sharecropper, an owner-operator and a wage labourer. Thus even in the simple rural community we have described, social differences are rather blurred; there is no sharp class differentiation.

Reality, in fact, is far more intricate than our naive model suggests. Many landlords, for instance, are absentees and require intermediaries to look after their interests. In some cases these intermediaries are merely supervisors and rent

---

[7] In some cases, however, landlords can both compel peasants to borrow and insist that the loan be used for specific purposes. The risk is borne by the peasant, since he must repay the debt regardless of the outcome of the landlord's 'advice', but the latter makes the decisions.

collectors, but in other cases they adopt an entrepreneurial function and bear all or part of the risks of cultivation. Six of the most common tenure forms involving intermediaries between the peasant and the landlord are presented in outline below.

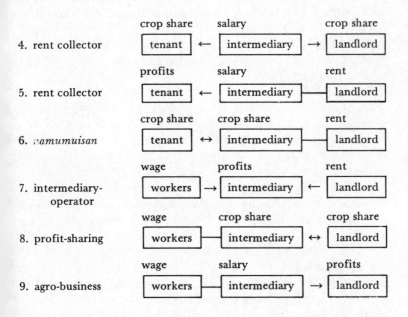

In the first two cases (items 4 and 5 above) the intermediary receives a salary in return for which he merely collects the rent for the landlord, and the tenant has either a cropsharing or fixed rent contract with the landlord. The intermediary may be an outsider to the rural community or he may be a prominent and trustworthy tenant. In the next three cases the intermediary assumes part of the risk of production and becomes an entrepreneur. Under the *namumuisan* system in the Philippines, the intermediary pays a fixed rent to the landowner, thereby eliminating all risk to the latter, and enters into a sharecropping agreement with the tenant.[8] Thus the risk is shared between the tenant and the

---

[8] See Akira Takahashi, *Land and Peasants in Central Luzon.*

intermediary. In other instances the intermediary may pay a fixed rent to the landlord and undertake production with the help of wage labour. In this case, the entire risk is borne by the intermediary. In still other, relatively rare cases, the intermediary cultivates the land with hired labour and divides the crop with the landlord, thereby spreading risks. Lastly, farming may be organized as an agro-business, in which hired labour is directed by salaried management who are responsible to the landlord for obtaining as much profit as possible. Under this system neither the peasants nor the intermediaries bear any risk.

The diversity of tenure and class relationships we have described above seems to be common in many countries of monsoon Asia. We shall argue below, however, that as a result of the technical changes that are presently occurring in several tropical regions the tenure system will tend to become simplified and class relationships will tend to become polarized. Landowners will increasingly become owner-operators or agro-businessmen and the peasantry will tend to be reduced to the status of agricultural workers who no longer perform any entrepreneurial functions.

The rural capital market
So far we have claimed that there are monopolistic elements in many, but not all, of the land markets of underdeveloped countries. Imperfections in the rural capital market, however, are ubiquitous and more pronounced. Landlords are more liquid than small peasants. The former have idle cash balances upon which they can draw to finance purchases of material inputs and make wage payments. Moreover, they can obtain capital easily on the organized credit market. They have ready access to commercial banks outside the farming locality and can obtain loans at preferential interest rates since their wealth, income and status make the risk of lending to them minimal. Furthermore, the larger farmers are able to use their political influence to ensure that government credit programmes cater to their needs, to the neglect of the needs of less powerful and influential cultivators. The small peasant, in contrast, has little working capital and restricted access to credit. Often his land title is disputed or his tenancy

arrangement is insecure, and as a result he may not be eligible to borrow on the organized credit market. Instead he turns to the informal market – the village moneylender, a local shopkeeper or a large landowner. Rates of interest in this market tend to be very high, in part because of monopoly elements, but more important because of the high risk of default, the lack of collateral and the large overhead costs of small loans. The cost of capital to the peasant is so high not just because he is exploited by moneylenders and middlemen but because land tenure institutions are defective and the political system is biased against him.

Thus the capital market is fragmented. The big landlords tend to pay less than the social opportunity cost of capital, while small peasants often pay substantially more. In symbols,

$$i_s > i > i_b$$

where i is the social cost of capital and i_s and i_b are the price of capital to small and large cultivators, respectively.[9]

Empirical evidence to test this hypothesis is difficult to find, primarily because farmers are reluctant to disclose the rate of interest they pay on credit obtained from money-lenders. It is well known, of course, that government credit institutions charge very low rates of interest – indeed, they often run at a loss – and are biased in favour of large farmers. In Pakistan, for example, the Agricultural Development Bank provides tubewell loans only to those who own a minimum of 12.5 to 25 acres. This lending criterion excludes over 80 per cent of the nation's farmers. In the Philippines it appears that farmers supply about 20 per cent of their financial requirements from their own savings. Roughly 32 per cent of the finance is supplied by institutional credit, bearing an

---

[9] Given a particular institutional context, it can be argued that risk and the transaction costs of small loans account for at least part of the difference between i_s and i_b. These transaction costs are true costs and are not a reflection of market imperfections, although transaction costs will vary depending upon the institutional framework that is assumed.

If the price of capital is subsidized to all farmers, $i > i_b$ and i_s, while if all farmers are denied capital the inequality may be reversed. In general, however, the inequality is likely to be as described in the text.

interest charge of 8–15 per cent a year. The remaining 48 per cent comes from the informal credit market, where the rate of interest varies from zero to over 200 per cent. About a third of the informal credit comes from landlords and about half from merchants and moneylenders; the rest comes from friends and relatives.

Table 2.5 contains information collected by Jose Gapud on interest rates paid by 224 rice farmers in Nueva Ecija, Philippines. According to the data in the table, 15 per cent of the borrowers paid an interest rate of over 200 per cent, while one-fifth of the borrowers paid no interest at all. Gapud discovered, however, that the true rate of interest paid by the latter group was actually 16 per cent. The difference between the reported and actual rates arose from the practice of merchants of underpricing harvest repayments and over-pricing goods purchased by debtors.

Table 2.5
Interest Rates Paid by 224 Rice Farmers in Nueva Ecija, Philippines, 1957/58

Interest rate	Percentage of borrowers
0	20.0
1–14	13.0
15–29	9.0
30–100	23.0
100–199	20.0
Over 200	15.0

Source: Jose Gapud, 'Financing Lowland Rice Farming in Selected Barrios in Muñoz, Nueva Ecija,' *Economic Research Journal*, September 1959, p. 79.

A study of 16 farmers in South Sulawesi, Indonesia indicated that five farmers received no credit from any source. Four of the others obtained credit from neighbours and apparently paid no interest. The remaining seven obtained credit from moneylenders, a state bank and a government owned fertilizer company.

Half of the farmers in the sample owned some upland acreage on which a variety of crops was grown using traditional practices. That is, the land was ploughed once, levelled once, and hand weeded two or three times. No fertilizer was used and only one farmer occasionally used insecticides. All of the farmers possessed lowland paddy farms and ten out of the sixteen used cultural practices recommended by extension agents. The credit was required mainly to purchase fertilizers and insecticides for this lowland rice farming.

Table 2.6

Interest Rates in the Rural Capital Market, South Sulawesi, Indonesia

Farmer	Average size of lowland farm area (ha.)	Percentage rate of interest per month
A	0.20	15
B	0.25	25
C	0.50	10
D	1.00	1
E	1.19	1
F	2.00	15
G	5.00	1

Source: Agency for International Development, Djakarta, Indonesia.
Note: Farmer F obtained credit in the form of fertilizer that was repaid in rice.

Those farmers who had half an hectare or less borrowed from a moneylender and paid interest at the rate of 10 to 25 per cent a month. Three out of four of the farmers with one hectare or more, on the other hand, were able to obtain credit from a state bank (BRI) at a montly rate of interest of one per cent. The remaining farmer acquired fertilizer from PN Pertani and repaid in rice; the estimated rate of interest is 15 per cent a month. Although there are very few observations, the data in Table 2.6 illustrate our hypothesis that larger farmers have greater ease of access to capital. As we shall demonstrate below, this has numerous implications for the pace and direction of technical change in rural areas.

Ease of access to credit, however, depends not only on the financial price that must be paid, i.e. the rate of interest, it also depends upon the amount of time required to process a loan. In general, those farmers who are personal friends of bank officials, who tend naturally to be the larger ones, are able to obtain loans with a minimum of delay, while the other farmers are sent to the end of the queue. A study in India concluded as follows: 'Great variations in the time taken for receiving loans (30 to 165 days) were noticed. . . . Personal acquaintance of the farmers with bank officials gained considerable weight over the objectivity, rationality and necessity of the loan concerned in certain cases. At some places bank officials did not go far beyond the personal acquaintance in regard to advancing loans. . . .'[10]

Wage rates

Unequal access to land and capital frequently is accentuated by unequal access to water and technical knowledge.[11] The large landowners, in effect, are able to exercise some control over all the material inputs in their locality, and because of their greater literacy, social status and political influence they are invariably the first to learn about and adopt new methods of production. This inevitably increases inequality. Furthermore, in an agrarian economy, control of land, credit and water enables landowners to influence the local labour market as well. That is, monopoly of material resources gives

[10] Gurbachan Singh and H. S. Sandhu, 'Anatomy of Commercial Banks' Advances to Agriculture', *Indian Journal of Agricultural Economics*, Conference Number, October–December 1971.

[11] 'Under rationed conditions, and unfortunately these often prevail for inputs in Asia, it is the larger farmers who obtain the fertilizer and receive the irrigation water.' (Walter P. Falcon, 'The Green Revolution: Generations of Problems', *American Journal of Agricultural Economics*, December 1970, p. 706.

As governments become more intimately involved in accelerating agricultural growth, the extent of input rationing is likely to increase. Land reform and colonization agencies distribute land on a basis other than price, and the same usually is true of public irrigation authorities, state owned rural banks, the extension service, etc., which distribute water, credit and technical knowledge. The greater is the participation of government in the provision of inputs, the less important are market forces in determining the allocation of resources and the more important becomes access to the bureaucracy. That is, political power replaces market power in determining who gets what.

the landlords monopsony power over labour. In this way, landlords are able to exploit labour by reducing the wage rate below what it would have been in a fully competitive market, i.e. below its social opportunity cost.

In any locality dominated by a large landlord the supply curve of labour facing that landlord has a positive elasticity. That is, the amount of labour hired by a single landlord (or small group of landlords) markedly affects the local wage rate. Landlords often are aware of this and adjust the number of workers hired until the marginal cost of labour equals the marginal revenue product. At this profit maximizing point the number of workers employed and the wage at which they are employed will be lower than would prevail in a competitive market. In other words, an unequal distribution of land ownership, a defective tenure system, and privileged access to the capital market may combine to give landowners monopsony power over labour and where this occurs the result will be lower wages and less employment than would otherwise be the case. 'Surplus labour' — or, strictly speaking, underemployment — in these economies is a product of land tenure and market structure and not, as is often believed, a product of high population densities.

Everything else being equal, the wage rate paid by a large landlord would be similar to the 'shadow wage' of the small peasant. In practice, however, landlords sometimes are required to pay a legally fixed minimum wage or are subject to various 'social' charges. In these instances the cost of labour to the landlord would be greater than the opportunity cost of labour to the peasant. In symbols,

$$w > w_b \geqslant w_s,$$

where w is the wage rate.

This hypothesis is extremely difficult to test, since one observes neither the social opportunity cost of labour nor the implicit wage of small peasants. It is possible to demonstrate, however, that wages are not an institutional constant, as the surplus labour hypothesis would predict, but that in more than one instance real wages of agricultural workers have fallen. In both Sri Lanka (Ceylon) and the Philippines, for example, per capita income has increased about 2 per cent a year since 1955, and yet in both these countries not only has income inequality increased,[12] but in some periods the real wages of agricultural workers have fallen. That is, during a period in which the average productivity of labour rose substantially, a large proportion of the population experienced an absolute decline in their standard of living.

In Sri Lanka there may have been a slight tendency for real wages in agriculture to drift downwards, and if one compares the mid-1950s with the early 1970s they have fallen about four per cent. In the Philippines the decline in rural wages was much sharper, particularly between 1955 and 1964. Moreover, real wages of common labourers in industry also fell in the Philippines: the average real wage in industry in the two years 1967–1968 was 7.3 per cent lower than the average of 1955–1956.[13] One would not normally expect increasing poverty of a large section of the labour force in countries experiencing rising per capita income, and the fact that this is happening in several nations is *prima facie* evidence that factor markets, including the labour market, are highly imperfect.

Control of the labour supply
Monopsony power is present whenever an employer's demand for labour directly affects the price he must pay. Market power of this type is unlikely to arise unless there is a high degree of land concentration within a locality and there are few alternatives for employment outside of agriculture. If these conditions do not prevail the supply curve of labour to an employer is likely to approach infinite elasticity and the landowner will become a 'price taker' rather than a 'price maker'.

Nonetheless, social institutions may be devised which enable landowners as a group to control the supply of labour, even though no single landowner can affect the wage rate. These institutions normally operate by shifting the entire

[12] Income inequality in Sri Lanka increased between 1953 and 1963 as measured by the share in income of the bottom 30 per cent of households; after 1963, however, inequality probably diminished.
[13] See G. L. Hicks and G. McNicoll, *Trade and Growth in the Philippines*, p. 91.

Table 2.7

Real Wages of Agricultural Workers in Sri Lanka and the Philippines

Year	Sri Lanka	Philippines
1953	93.5	109.0
1954	95.3	114.5
1955	99.2	116.0
1956	100.0	100.0
1957	98.7	99.4
1958	98.4	99.5
1959	98.0	99.4
1960	99.6	96.0
1961	98.7	94.6
1962	98.4	91.5
1963	97.4	86.3
1964	96.7	80.0
1965	96.7	90.8
1966	96.7	95.8
1967	98.1	81.6
1968	106.8	85.5
1969	99.4	83.7
1970	94.9	74.0
1971	95.1	n.a.

Sources: Sri Lanka: Central Bank of Ceylon, *Bulletin*, August 1971, Table 37. Figure for 1971 is the average of the first seven months. Philippines: Data prepared by Miss Cristina Crisostomo of the International Rice Research Institute, Los Baños, Philippines. The observations for 1953 to 1955 may not be strictly comparable with those for the following years.

labour supply curve to the right, and thereby reducing the wage rate for any given level of demand. That is, the effect of these institutions is to increase the number of workers seeking employment in low-income occupations. This is done by creating a distinction between those who are entitled to enter certain occupations and those who are not.

The criteria by which distinctions can be drawn are limited only by the wit of man. The most obvious basis for discrimination is racial, and the apartheid system of South Africa is a classic example. In the Andean region of South America, however, linguistic and cultural characteristics provide the basis for discrimination: the 'indio', like virtually everyone else in the region, is of mixed ancestry, but he is distinguished from others — and 'kept in his place' — by his attire, his habits of consumption, etc. In Asia, the caste system of India uses religious sanctions to impose an assignment of hierarchies from which it is impossible to escape — except, perhaps, by changing one's religion. The *harijans* and *chamars* (formerly called untouchables) are denied access to skilled jobs and landed property by virtue of their caste, and this has the effect of increasing the numbers of those who must seek a livelihood by offering their services as labourers and sweepers to those who own land, i.e. to *jats* and *brahmins*.[14] The caste system restricts entry into high-wage occupations, and thereby helps to maintain the high wages, while restricting exit from the low-wage occupations, and thereby helps to maintain the low incomes of those at the bottom of the hierarchy. Thus the system operates in such a way that unskilled labour is exploited, and this can occur even if no single landowner possesses monopsony power.

B. Techniques of Cultivation

One of the features of agricultural production is that the farmer has considerable choice in determining the method of cultivation to be used in producing a given output. A small wheat farmer in the Punjab, for example, may cultivate with a pair of bullocks, a wooden plough, a seed drill or two, and perhaps a few other simple tools. Most of the work will be done with human and animal power. His neighbour, however, may be a somewhat larger farmer and may add a tubewell and chemical fertilizer to the 'traditional' package of inputs used by the subsistence cultivator. Chemicals and capital equipment in this case partially replace human and animal power. A large capitalist landlord, on the other hand, is likely to be highly mechanized. In addition to one or more tubewells, he will have a 45 h.p. tractor and attachments, a power sprayer, a cultivator, a thresher, etc.

[14] A small amount of land has been distributed to a few *harijans*, but this is only a token gesture. In most villages of the Indian Punjab, for example, the *jat* Sikhs own the land and the *harijans* labour on it.

Similarly, a rice farmer may broadcast his seed or plant in straight rows; he may transplant seedlings or not; he may use chemical weedicides, remove weeds by hand or do no weeding at all; he may prepare the soil with a hoe, a water buffalo or with a tractor; he may irrigate or rely on rainfall or flooding; he may harvest with a combine or with a sickle or knife. In other words, there are a variety of methods for producing foodgrains in tropical areas; the techniques of production are not fixed. On the other hand, factor substitutability may not be continuous; there are discontinuities in the production function. One does not, for example, plough with a hoe and reap with a combine, or plant in straight lines yet do no weeding; nor would one normally encounter a farmer who used large quantities of fertilizer but did not irrigate.

A technique consists of a bundle of inputs. Within each bundle a certain amount of substitution is possible, but we assume for the sake of simplicity that this occurs within rather narrow limits, and for practical purposes it can be assumed that for each technique the factors of production are combined in fixed proportions. Farmers, thus, choose among alternative techniques, but once a basic method of cultivation has been selected the possibility of varying factor proportions is severely constrained.

The most profitable technique

The alternative methods of cultivating a particular crop, say, rice, can be represented in terms of a discontinuous isoquant (curve qq) which indicates the various combinations of labour (N) and material inputs (M) which can be used to produce a given quantity of rice. Each farmer will try to maximize his income, or, what is the same thing, minimize the cost of producing any given quantity of foodgrains. Which is the most economical method of cultivation will depend on relative factor prices. Our argument is that the price of material inputs is relatively dear to small peasants and cheap to big landlords. Thus we would expect that the two types of farmers would adopt different techniques of production.

In Figure 2.1 below, the relative factor prices which the peasant faces are represented by the line *Pp*, whereas those faced by the large farmer are represented by the line *Ll*. It can be seen that the peasant adopts technique α, which is relatively labour intensive, while the large farmer adopts technique β, which is relatively intensive in the use of material inputs, that is, in the use of working capital and the services of fixed capital. In comparison with the socially optimal combination of inputs, the small farmer tends to be insufficiently capital intensive and the large farmer tends to be insufficiently labour intensive.

We showed in Section A that the tenure system and market structure in underdeveloped countries are such that landlords and peasants face very different factor prices. The economic power of large landowners ensures in general that they receive most factors of production at less than their social opportunity cost, whereas peasants tend to pay more than the social opportunity cost for land and capital and receive less than the social opportunity cost for their labour. The system, thus, results in great inequality in the distribution of income. We now argue that, in addition, the system results in allocative inefficiency. Because land and capital are

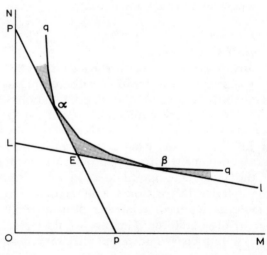

Figure 2.1

cheap relative to labour, the big landlord tends to adopt techniques of production — which from the point of view of the social optimum, but not from that of private profit maximization — are characterized by excessively high land-labour and capital-labour ratios. Conversely, the small peasant will combine less than the socially optimal amount of land and capital with his labour. Total output would increase if factors were redistributed so that landlords used more labour intensive methods of farming and peasants used more land and capital intensive techniques.[15]

These differences in methods of cultivation result in differences in yields and labour productivity. It is widely recognized that, with few exceptions, output per unit of land shows a strong tendency to be higher on smaller farms than on large farms.[16] Similarly, the average productivity of labour tends to rise as average farm size increases. The explanation of these differences should now be obvious: small farms have high yields because they are cultivated very

---

[15] The reader will note that our argument is conducted in terms of average factor productivities rather than in terms of the theoretically more appropriate marginal productivities. Since one never observes a marginal productivity, but can readily calculate averages from field data, our method enables one to test hypotheses directly without having to make arbitrary assumptions about the nature of the production function. Moreover, unless one makes very peculiar assumptions indeed, enterprises with high average output per unit of a particular input also will have a high marginal output per unit, and for many purposes this is all one needs to know.

One must recognize, however, that the statement that small farms produce more per ha. and large farms more per man tells us little about the efficiency of resource allocation on the two types of farms. Which type of farm has a higher total factor productivity depends on relative factor scarcities. That is, the 'best' measure of efficiency is value added divided by the value of all inputs — when these are valued at their social opportunity cost. Thus, the lower the real cost of labour relative to land and capital, the more efficient is the small farm relative to the large. Given that underdeveloped countries are characterized by a relative abundance of labour, it follows that there is a very strong presumption that small farms are in fact the more efficient.

[16] See, for example, R. Dayal and C. Elliott, 'Land Tenure, Land Concentration and Agricultural Output', in UNRISD, *Social and Economic Factors in Economic Development*, Report No. 5, 1966.

intensively and large farms have a high labour productivity because they are cultivated relatively extensively. These differences in the intensity of cultivation, in turn, are due to the differences in relative factor prices that the two types of farmers confront. Thus the basic characteristics of the agricultural sector of an underdeveloped country, at any moment in time, can be explained in terms of imperfections in the factor markets. These characteristics are summarized in the table below.

Table 2.8
Characteristics of an Underdeveloped Agricultural Sector

	Small peasant		Big landlord
Factor prices			
wage rate	w_s	$\lessgtr$	w_b
rental rate of land	r_s	$\lessgtr$	r_b
interest rate	i_s	$>$	i_b
Techniques of production			
labour-land ratio	$[N/L]_s$	$>$	$[N/L]_b$
capital-labour ratio	$[K/N]_s$	$<$	$[K/N]_b$
capital-land ratio	$[K/L]_s$	$\lesseqgtr$	$[K/L]_b$
depending on whether	$[i/r]_s$	$\lesseqgtr$	$[i/r]_b$
Output per factor input			
yield per ha.	$[Q/L]_s$	$>$	$[Q/L]_b$
productivity of labour	$[Q/N]_s$	$<$	$[Q/N]_b$
productivity of capital	$[Q/K]_s$	$\gtreqless$	$[Q/K]_b$

Although we have suggested that in many countries there will be imperfections in all factor markets, i.e. in the markets for land, labour and capital, our conclusions regarding income inequality and allocative inefficiency do not depend on this. It is sufficient for our purposes that there be monopoly elements in one market only. Suppose, for example, that the labour and land markets are perfectly competitive but that the capital market is organised in such a way that peasants pay substantially more than large landowners for credit. This single inequality implies that the price of land and labour *relative* to the price of capital will be higher for the landlord than the peasant, and in consequence the proportions in which factors are combined will differ on the two types of farms, as well as the productivity of the various factors of production.[17] Hence, inequality and inefficiency will arise if any factor market is a local monopoly in the manner we have described. Of course, the more widespread are the monopolistic elements, the greater will be the disparities in income and the lower will be total production.

The evidence from Sri Lanka

In Table 2.9 we have assembled data from a survey of 3000 farms conducted by the Central Bank of Ceylon in 1966–67. Sri Lanka is an interesting case because despite the widespread availability of credit and material inputs, the allocation of resources within the rice sector varies considerably

Table 2.9

Inputs and Output Per Acre of Paddy in Sri Lanka, 1966/67

Farm size (perches)	Labour cost per acre (Rs.)	Quantity of seed per acre (bushels)	Tractor cost per acre (Rs.)	Weedicides, etc. per acre (Rs.)	Fertilizers per acre (lbs.)	Yields per acre (bushels)
0–20	428	2.57	18.5	1.65	107	36.4
21–40	405	2.29	18.7	4.25	118	37.3
41–80	335	2.24	19.3	2.36	129	33.6
81–160	259	2.30	21.1	2.12	112	31.8
161–320	204	2.22	42.4	3.64	77	33.0
Over 320	180	2.56	65.2	5.22	157	33.7
Average	212	2.45	51.3	4.34	136	33.5

Source: Central Bank of Ceylon, *Survey on Cost of Production of Paddy*, 1969.
Note: One acre = 40 perches.

[17] Strictly speaking, this will be true only if both types of farmers are able to earn a profit. In the long run the small farmer would go out of business, possibly becoming an agricultural labourer and contributing to a downward pressure on rural wages. If peasants pay more for capital than landlords and no less for any other factor of production, their total costs must be higher and this will doom them to extinction.

with farm size. As the table indicates, labour input per acre (including imputed value of family labour) is negatively correlated with the size of farm. The larger farms, on the other hand, rely to a much greater extent on tractors. Again, the value of weedicides and pesticides per acre appears to rise with farm size. This probably is due to the fact that, given the opportunity cost of their labour, small farmers prefer to weed by hand. In other words, the larger farmers tend to substitute tractors and agro-chemicals for labour when it is possible to do so. Fertilizers, in contrast, are a substitute for land, not labour, and there appears to be no systematic tendency for fertilizer use to vary with farm size.

In other words, the large farmers are using material inputs to replace labour, not land. One way of illustrating this is to compare the capital-labour ratio on large and small farms. The data in Table 2.9 enable use to calculate a numerical fraction which indicates very accurately the way techniques of cultivation change as the size of farm increases. The numerator of this fraction is the sum of expenditure per acre on tractors and agro-chemicals other than fertilizer, and the denominator is the per acre cost of labour. In Table 2.10 this fraction has been expressed in index number form, using the smallest' farms as the base point. It can be seen from the table that the degree of capital intensity rises systematically, and without exception, as the size of farm increases. The farms in the largest two categories are five to eight times more capital intensive than the farms in the smallest two categories.

Table 2.10
Index of Capital Intensity on Rice Farms in Sri Lanka,
1966/67

Farm size (perches)	Capital intensity
0–20	100
21–40	120
41–80	137
81–160	190
161–320	479
Over 320	833

Despite the much greater use of machinery and chemicals by the large farmers, their output per acre – as we have seen – is less than that of the small farmers. The latter use more labour intensive techniques of production than the larger farmers, and they were the only ones in 1966/67 who managed to obtain an average yield greater than 35 bushels an acre. If the data from this sample of 3000 parcels are trustworthy, it would appear that Sri Lanka could increase both employment and rice output by dividing the larger holdings among several small farmers. Given that unemployment is increasing, that real wages may be falling and that the country continues to import a substantial proportion of its rice, a policy of redistributing land would bring multiple benefits.

The case of Thailand

Thailand is rather different from Sri Lanka in that most of the rice is grown in river basins and is subject to deep flooding. Since the high yielding varieties of rice that have recently been developed are short stemmed plants, it is hardly surprising that the 'green revolution' has made no impact there. In fact, rice yields have remained essentially unchanged since 1966.

Nevertheless, despite the differences in environment and in the trend in yields, Thailand and Sri Lanka have certain features in common. Most holdings are small. In Thailand the modal size of farm is between 10 and 20 rais:[18] 26.1 per cent of the farms fall in this range and they occupy 16.7 per cent of the area.[19] The distribution of land is unequal, particularly at the bottom end of the distribution. Farms smaller than 10 rais account for 32.8 per cent of the holdings but only 6.3 per cent of the land. At the other extreme, the top 14.9 per cent of holdings occupy 43 per cent of the land. In addition, over 40 per cent of the rural labour force are landless.

As in the other countries of monsoon Asia, rice yields vary inversely with farm size. In Central Thailand, the main rice

[18] One acre = 2.5 rais.
[19] See G. A. Marzouk, *Economic Development and Policies: Case Study of Thailand*, Rotterdam University Press, 1972.

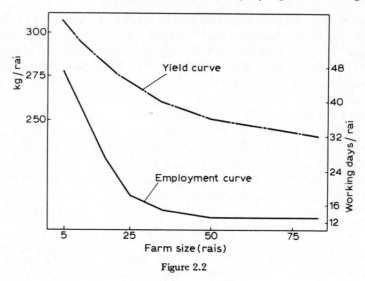

Figure 2.2

producing area, yields decline systematically from 306 kg. per rai on holdings of 2–6ʺ rai to 194 kg. per rai on holdings of 140 rais or more. The yield curve is depicted in Figure 2.2, and it can be seen there that the decline is non-linear.

Also drawn in Figure 2.2 is an employment curve. About half of total employment in rice farming in Central Thailand occurs in three months, viz., from June through August. Again, as in Sri Lanka, employment varies inversely with farm size. Farms up to 10 rais provide nearly 48 working days per rai of rice, but thereafter labour intensity declines very sharply, and on farms larger than 40 rais, little more than 12 working days per rai is required.

The tendency for yields and employment to fall as size of holding increases suggests yet again that output and employment could be increased if the larger farms were broken up and redistributed. The implementation of such a policy also would result in a more equal distribution of rural income, of course. At present the bottom 40 per cent of rural households receive only 14 per cent of rural income, while the richest 5 per cent receive 22 per cent of rural income. This pattern could be radically altered if the land now organized in large farms were cultivated with more labour intensive techniques of production. Indeed, as is evident from the figure, a redistribution of land would have a significantly greater impact on employment than on output. Those who are anxious to create more jobs in the rural areas of underdeveloped countries should be ardent supporters of land reform.

An example from Indonesia

Let us consider one more case, that of the island of Java in Indonesia. Java is interesting because it is a relatively small area with very high population density. Land is extremely scarce – the per capita holding is about 0.1 ha. – and population density is nearly 500 persons per square kilometre, i.e. roughly three times greater than India. One might imagine that under these circumstances the markets for land and labour would approach perfection and thus there would be little difference in methods of cultivation from one farm to another. The reverse, however, is the truth.

The average size of farm in Java is very small, but the distribution around the average is highly skewed. Half the households who own land possess less than half an hectare, yet the top one per cent of landowners account for about one-third of the land. At the other extreme, roughly half the rural households own no land at all. Members of these households work either as labourers or as tenants. About 62 per cent of all land is cultivated by owner-operators; the rest is cultivated by tenants.

Sharecropping is the most common form of tenant system, of which there are two major variants. Under the *mertelu* arrangement the tenant supplies all inputs and bears all costs other than the land tax. In return, he is entitled to one-third of the harvest, the other two-thirds going to the landowner. In the most densely settled parts of Java, however, the *mertelu* contract has been replaced by *mrapat*. This is the typical system of Central Java and it is gradually spreading to the somewhat less populous areas of East and West Java. Under *mrapat* the tenant supplies labour and the landowner is responsible for all other inputs. The harvest is divided into four parts, 25 per cent going to the tenant and 75 per cent to the landowner. The tenant, in effect, is little more than a

Table 2.11

Technology and Yields on Owner Operated Sawah Farms in Subang District, West Java, Wet Season, 1969/70

Farm size (rank)	Number of farms	Family labour per ha, average of 3 seasons (index)	Hired labour per ha. (index)	Fertilizers plus pesticides per ha. (index)	Yield (index)
1	6	100	100	100	100
2	26	43	94	89	104
3	10	25	114	116	105
4	13	30	111	116	85
5	3	17	92	122	78

Source: Agro-Economic Survey, *Analisa Usaha Tani Padi Sawah Dan Tataniaga Beras Ditiga Kabupaten Di Djawa Barat,* 1971, Appendix tables 1c, 1d, 12a, 12b, 12c, 15e.

labourer; his wages are paid in kind and the exact amount depends upon the size of the harvest.

Almost half the area under food crops in Java is used to grow rice, and most of this is irrigated. Rice grown in flooded, irrigated fields is known as *sawah*. The table opposite summarizes information about yields and technology of 58 owner-operated *sawah* farms in the Subang district of West Java. The average size of these farms is 1.33 ha. Notice that all the farms are growing the same crop, in the same season, in the same district, under the same system of tenure. Thus neither pattern of production nor time, place or tenure system can convincingly account for differences in methods of cultivation and output per hectare.

The farms are classified into five groups of increasing size and the indicators which interest us are expressed in index number form, with the smallest size group serving as the base. It is clear from the table that as the size of farm increases the amount of family labour per hectare declines substantially. This, perhaps, is not too surprising, since family size tends to increase less than proportionately with the size of farm. The amount of hired labour per hectare shows no systematic variation with farm size. That is, large farms in West Java apparently do not hire proportionately more labour than small farms. Indeed, the opposite probably is nearer to the truth. The evidence in the table, thus, does not support the commonly voiced proposition that a more equal distribution of land would reduce the employment opportunities of wage labourers. Moreover, when family and hired labour are considered together, it is obvious that the smaller farms are more labour intensive. On the other hand, the larger farms tend to use more fertilizer and pesticides per hectare. The three largest farms, in fact, used about a third more of these chemicals than the modal group. Nevertheless, the yields of the largest farms were significantly lower than those of the small farms. In other words, the general characteristics of large and small farms on Java are similar to those observed in the rest of Asia.

CHAPTER 3

Technical Change and Income Distribution

A. The Nature of Technical Change

Having described in the previous chapter the factor markets and the various methods of cultivation that are available to a farmer, we must now consider what are the effects of these market and technical characteristics upon the propensity to innovate in the agricultural sector. We know from the work of W. E. G. Salter on technical change in industry[1] that when the cost of investment is cheap relative to labour, the spread between the best practice technique and the average will tend to be narrow. By analogy, the lower is the relative cost of material inputs in agriculture, the more widespread will be the adoption of an innovation, i.e. the more readily will farmers invest in capital which embodies an improved technology. Either a fall in interest rates, or a decline in the price of equipment or a rise in wages will tend to induce farmers to abandon old methods of production and introduce new methods which are more intensive in the use of material inputs. On the other hand, when the cost of investment is expensive relative to labour, material inputs will not be widely used and the sector will appear to be 'traditional'.[2]

The introduction of an innovation requires expenditure on fixed and working capital, and this expenditure will not occur unless material inputs are cheap relative to labour. We

---

[1] *Productivity and Technical Change*, 1960, pp. 66–70.
[2] It should be clear from the previous discussion that 'traditional' is not synonymous with 'inefficient'. Indeed it is quite likely that the small, traditional peasant comes closer to using resources in the socially optimal proportions than does the large, capitalist farmer.

have seen, however, that the land tenure institutions and market structures which prevail in underdeveloped countries tend to create 'surplus' labour and make it relatively cheap. Thus the characteristics of the sector are responsible for the fact that both large and small farmers in poor countries sometimes appear to be unprogressive and the speed of innovation often is relatively slow.[3] Only when a 'revolutionary' technical change sharply reduces unit costs will innovation be rapid and widespread.[4] The speed of diffusion of an innovation can be expected to vary positively with the rate of profit associated with a technical change. Thus, for example, if the high yielding varieties of rice are more profitable in irrigated areas than in regions dependent upon rainfed agriculture, the rate of diffusion will be faster in the former than in the latter.

If technical change is biased in a capital-using direction neither big landlords nor small peasants will have a high propensity to innovate because the market structure in rural areas has produced a relatively low wage economy. But the larger farmer can be expected to be more 'progressive' than the peasant because his real cost of innovation is lower. That is, for any given wage, no mater how low, the cost of capital and other material inputs will be lower for the large farmer than the small, and hence the incentive to innovate will be greater.

Thus the land tenure institutions and market structures which are found in most underdeveloped countries imply that small peasants have more restricted access to factor

[3] If most agricultural inventions are intensive in the use of material inputs — because, e.g. they were developed in the wealthy capitalist countries and reflect the relative factor prices prevailing there — they will not be adopted by farmers in countries in which factor endowments result in very low relative wages. In terms of the concepts developed in the next section, many new techniques may be technically efficient but 'economically irrelevant' at the current (different) factor price ratios which both large and small farmers face.

[4] One must be careful to distinguish between innovation and an expansion of output. Production will increase if profits rise, regardless of the reason for the rise. For example, an increase in the world price of a plantation crop would provide an incentive to increase output, but this need not be accompanied by innovation and technical change.

markets than do large landlords. These market 'imperfections' can be represented in terms of the different relative factor prices which the two types of farmers confront. The differences in relative prices have several consequences: they increase the degree of income inequality, they result in a lower level of agricultural production, they create 'surplus' labour and underemployment, they reduce the propensity of the agricultural sector to innovate, and finally, they increase the likelihood that if any innovation does occur, it will be the large landlord who does it. This last conclusion deserves closer scrutiny and it is to this point that we now turn.

Biased innovation
The 'green revolution' is essentially a process innovation. That is, the 'revolution' consists of a new method of producing a particular commodity.[5] The method is embodied in a technology which can be represented in our simple model by the proportions in which labour and material inputs are combined to produce a given output. A new technology is potentially useful if it displaces all or part of the original isoquant toward the origin. It can easily be demonstrated that relative factor prices will determine whether a new technique is adopted and, if so, by whom.

In terms of Figure 2.1 on page 36, there are five zones in which an innovation could occur. First, new techniques in the space to the right of isoquant qq are 'inferior' to the existing technology, in the sense that they require more inputs per unit of output than methods which already exist.

---

[5] The introduction of high yielding varieties of foodgrains, although basically a process innovation, also contained certain features of a product innovation. Several of the new wheat seeds and the first 'miracle' rice (IR-8) possessed some properties (taste, milling and cooking characteristics) which differentiated them, unfavourably, from the local varieties of grain. As a result, the new varieties were sold at a discount. The undesirable characteristics have been largely eliminated, however, and the price discount has virtually disappeared.

Research is now underway to develop a high lysine variety of maize. Similar work has been started to raise the protein content of rice. If these experiments are successful, and new commercial varieties are introduced, product innovation will have become an important part of the 'green revolution'.

Thus these new techniques would be adopted by no one who wished to maximize profits. Innovation in this zone is technologically irrelevant for all relative factor prices. Only new technologies that are located in the space to the left of qq are 'superior', in the sense that they are technologically efficient and would represent a profit maximizing technique for at least one relative factor price ratio. This set of superior techniques can, in turn, be divided into several zones.

Second, new technologies located in the area $OLEp$ are 'ultra-superior' and would be adopted by all producers given the relative factor prices they now face. In an extreme case an 'ultra-superior' technological change would result in the collapse of the isoquant into a single point. Regardless of whether or not this occurs, however, innovation in this zone would be of advantage to all producers and one would expect the new technique to be adopted universally.

Third, a new technique might be developed which falls in one of the shaded spaces of Figure 2.1, i.e. in the area between the price lines and the isoquant. These new techniques are technically efficient but they are 'economically irrelevant' at current factor price ratios. There is some factor price ratio at which these techniques would be adopted, but it does not pay to do so at present given the prices of labour and material inputs which currently prevail.

We now come to the two most interesting zones of innovation. Fourth, any new technology which falls in the space LEP is ultra-superior from the point of view of those currently using technique α, but economically irrelevant from the point of view of those using technique β. That is, the new technique could be adopted with profit only by those farmers who pay low wages relative to the price they must pay for material inputs. Those farmers, in contrast, who enjoy preferential access to the markets for credit and material inputs would not adopt the new technology because it would not be profitable for them to do so. We will call this type of technical change 'peasant-biased' because it is biased in favour of small farmers who use labour-intensive methods of cultivation.

Finally, new techniques which occur within the space pEl are ultra-superior from the point of view of those currently using technique β, but they are economically irrelevant from the point of view of those using technique α. That is, technical change in this zone would be adopted only by those who enjoy a relatively low price of capital and material inputs. We have previously identified this group with the large landowners and, accordingly, technical change in this zone will be called 'landlord-biased'. A landlord-biased innovation is depicted in Figure 3.1 below.

We have assumed in the figure that a new technique of cultivation is developed (β') which partially shifts the isoquant from qq to qq'. It is clear from the diagram that given the relative factor prices which peasants and landlords face, β' will not be adopted by the former but it will be adopted by the latter. The technical change, thus, is landlord-biased. The movement of larger farmers in figure 3.1 from technique β to technique β' is associated with a rise in the proportion of material costs to total costs. It is also associated with greater 'technological dualism' in rural areas. Both of these phenomena have been widely observed in countries undergoing the 'green revolution'.

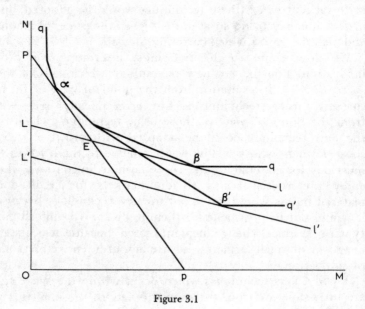

Figure 3.1

The bias of technical change makes a considerable difference to the rate of increase of production and the distribution of income. If one is primarily interested in raising agricultural output, one would welcome landlord-biased technical change. The reason for this is that most of the land is controlled by large landowners, and they use β-type techniques of production. Thus a landlord-biased innovation could be expected to spread over most of the cultivated surface and have a large impact on production. On the other hand, a landlord-biased innovation would strengthen the landlord class and would help perpetuate the status quo. Moreover, it would accentuate income inequality and could easily increase the absolute poverty of the non-innovating peasant producers. This would occur, for example, if the increased supply of foodgrains resulted in a fall in agricultural prices while an increased demand for material inputs resulted in a rise in the cost of production.

In contrast, peasant-biased technical change, although it would contribute relatively less to raising production, would have a greater impact on increasing the welfare of rural inhabitants. The reason for this is that the majority of people tend to be employed with α-type techniques, although they occupy a minority of the land. Thus, if one is more interested in raising rural welfare rather than agricultural production, peasant-biased technical change should be encouraged. This type of innovation would tend to reduce income inequalities in the countryside and, by strengthening the peasantry vis-a-vis the landlords, it would also tend to undermine the status quo.

The bias of the 'green revolution'

The evidence available indicates that the high yielding varieties of wheat and rice that have been developed and recommended by the research institutes tend either to be landlord-biased or ultra-superior. I know of no recent case of a peasant-biased technical change. Some innovations have been ultra-superior, however. In these cases the new technology tends to become universal and may well constitute the sole efficient technique. Indeed, the obvious test to apply in empirical work is to ask whether a single technology is used by all farmers confronting similar climatic and soil conditions. At the moment, it appears that the new varieties of rice developed in Taiwan are one of the few innovations that can pass this test. Technical change in Taiwanese agriculture is widespread and the reason for this, in our opinion, is that landownership is equally distributed in small parcels and that all peasants have approximately equal access to fertilizer, water, technical knowledge and credit.[6] In these circumstances, a technical change that is profitable for one farmer will be equally profitable for all other farmers and innovation, in consequence, will be rapid and universal.

In most of the other countries in which high yielding varieties of foodgrains are being introduced, technical change is heavily biased in favour of some farmers and against others. In part this is a result of the biological characteristics of the new seeds: they require an abundant and controlled water supply and hence are most suitable for regions which already enjoy a good irrigation system. In part, also, technical change has had a discriminatory impact because the new varieties are intensive in their use of material inputs, especially fertilizer,[7] and market imperfections restrict the access of small peasants to many factor markets, particularly credit.

Perhaps the most important reason for the bias of the 'green revolution' is the bias of government policy. For many years research, extension and investment programmes in

[6] The land reform in Taiwan which occurred between 1949 and 1953 virtually abolished both absentee ownership and tenancy. Between 1949 and 1966 owner-operators increased from 34 to 67 per cent of the total number of cultivators while tenants declined from 43 to 12 per cent. Those who combined tenancy with owner-operated land fell marginally from 23 to 21 per cent.

[7] Some economists have argued that the bias in favour of using more fertilizer and less land is to be welcomed. But they neglect to add that the bias in favour of using more material inputs and less labour should be deplored! Hayami and Ruttan, for example, state that '. . . . it appears that the technical changes embodied in the new high-yielding cereal varieties is [sic] biased toward saving the increasingly scarce factor (land) and using the increasingly abundant factor (fertilizer) in the economy. It clearly indicates a rational response of public agencies to economic forces.' (See their *Agricultural Development*, 1971, p. 213.)

agriculture have been devoted to raising output (preferably exportable output); their primary concern has not been to increase the welfare of the rural population and improve the distribution of income and wealth. More interest has been expressed in increasing the marketable surplus than in reducing rural poverty; more money has been spent on irrigating the relatively rich river valleys than on improving conditions in regions which depend on rainfed agriculture. Large farmers have been granted generous incentives to mechanize, while small farmers have been denied the credit necessary to improve their operations.

It has been argued that tractors are complementary with labour in cases where timely ploughing makes double cropping possible.[8] It has also been argued that by reducing the need for animal power, tractors may release land used for fodder crops. In yet other cases it is claimed that tractors enable hard soils to be ploughed which otherwise would not be used, or which otherwise could not be ploughed until after the rains had softened the ground. While this is indeed correct in some instances, it seems that in many cases tractors have been used by large farmers to reduce their need for labour and bullocks. In Taiwan small hand tractors are widely used and one observes very few four-wheel tractors. Thailand, parts of the Philippines, India and Pakistan, in contrast, rely on large four-wheel tractors of 40 horsepower or more. Imports of large tractors have also increased in Sri Lanka.

The government of Pakistan, for example, has encouraged the use of large tractors and wheat combine harvesters through its policies of subsidizing interest rates and the price of foreign exchange for imports of agricultural equipment. Even as early as 1964/65, over a third of all loans granted by the Agricultural Development Bank were for purchases of tractors and other mechanical equipment. Contrary to the expectation, or hope, that mechanization would increase the demand for labour, the widespread introduction of tractors in the Punjab and Sind has led to the eviction of tenants, a

---

[8] See, for example, Martin Billings and Arjan Singh, 'Mechanization and Rural Employment with Some Implications for Rural Income Distribution', *Economic and Political Weekly*, June 27, 1970.

decline in employment on large farms and an attempt by big
landlords to increase further the size of their holdings.[9] In
one study, in fact, it was estimated that increased use of
tractors on large farms led to a reduction in the utilization of
labour by as much as 50 per cent per acre.[10]

Pakistan is not unique in pursuing policies which unduly
favour large farmers, although it may have carried this
tendency further than most countries in South Asia.[11]
Likewise, the growing inequality and heightened social tension which these policies have created are not confined to
Pakistan, although, once again, they may be particularly
acute in that country.[12] The policies and their tragic consequences are common, however. Moreover, these policies
have been supported by foreign aid institutions: both A.I.D.
and the World Bank have given large loans to Pakistan for
farm mechanization, and the Bank has given similar loans to
India, the Philippines and Sri Lanka.[13] Thus nationally and
internationally agricultural policies and programmes have
been landlord-biased.

Innovating landowners
The thrust of our argument has been that land tenure, market
structure and government policy combine in such a way that

[9] Some of these issues are discussed at greater length in Keith Griffin
and A. R. Khan, eds., *Growth and Inequality in Pakistan*.
[10] S. R. Bose and E. H. Clark, 'Some Basic Considerations on Agricultural Mechanization in West Pakistan', *Pakistan Development Review*,
Autumn 1969.
[11] In Malaysia and Thailand, the government has established training
programmes for tractor drivers and mechanics and provides low cost
loans to help farmers purchase tractors. The Department of Agriculture
in some states of Malaysia actually provides tractor services to farmers.
[12] A study in India by A.I.D. reports that 'the majority of farmers —
probably as many as 75 per cent to 80 per cent in the rice belt — have
experienced a relative decline in their economic position; and some
proportion, representing unprotected tenants cultivating under oral
lease, have suffered an absolute deterioration in their living standard.'
(United States A.I.D., *Country Field Submission: India*, September
1969.)
[13] The I.B.R.D. is having second thoughts about this policy and has
initiated research to determine more accurately what are the consequences of mechanization. The Agriculture Projects Department of the
Bank, however, remains firmly pro-tractor.

most of the incentives to innovate are directed toward the large landlord. There is considerable evidence from several parts of the world that it is indeed the large landowner (or his tenant) who is the first to introduce a technical change. In Pakistan the new wheat seeds were first distributed to the larger farmers, because the Department of Agriculture was anxious to accelerate the growth of production as quickly as possible. By 1970, however, over four-fifths of the small farmers were using improved seeds and three-fourths were applying fertilizer to them.[14]

In Central Luzon, Philippines many of the innovators, according to Professor Ishikawa, were cultivating landlords or non-cultivating landlords who converted themselves into commercial farmers.[15] A detailed case study of Gapan, Nueva Ecija, Philippines indicated that in 1966 the first batch of IR-8 rice seed was distributed to landlords who possessed ten hectares of paddy or more. The landlords, most of whom lived in town, offered the seeds to the tenants who cultivated their 'best' land. No seeds were given directly to share-croppers or leaseholders; in each case the landlord acted as an intermediary in distributing the improved variety.[16] A negative correlation of small magnitude, and statistically insignificant, was found between the conversion of sharecroppers to a leasehold system and the spread of high yielding varieties of rice. The authors suggest that 'this pattern may be due to the fact that leasehold operators are seldom able to acquire loans for fertilizer, pesticides and other agricultural inputs from the Rural Banks and are almost never extended credit by their landlords, who because of fixed rental, no longer have anything to gain from improved yields'.[17]

[14] The small farmers applied considerably less fertilizer per acre than the large farmers — probably because the cost of fertilizer to them (including interest charges on borrowed capital) was relatively high.

[15] Shigeru Ishikawa, *Agricultural Development Strategies in Asia: Case Studies of the Philippines and Thailand.*

[16] R. E. Huke and James Duncan, 'Spacial Aspects of HYV Diffusion', in Department of Agricultural Economics, College of Agriculture and the International Rice Research Institute, *Seminar on Economics of Rice Production in the Philippines*, 1969.

[17] R. E. Huke and James Duncan, *op. cit.*, *Seminar on Economics of Rice production in the Philippines*, 1969, p. 30.

A careful study in India discovered 'a strong positive linear association ... between the proportion of farmers adopting HYV seed and the size of farm'.[18] For example, in the wheat growing regions, 45 per cent of the farmers in the lowest size decile used high yielding seeds, whereas 90 per cent of the farmers in the top decile used the improved varieties. A detailed regression analysis demonstrated that these results were equally as true in the rice growing regions as in the wheat areas. For instance, a regression of the proportion of farmers adopting a high yielding variety of rice in Coimbatore, Tamil Nadu on decile farm size groups produced a slope coefficient of 0.1585 and an R^2 of 0.98. A similar regression of wheat farmers in Ahmednagar, Maharashtra produced an identical R^2 and a slope coefficient of 0.1127.[19]

If the large farmers are able to innovate more readily than the small, one would expect income disparities to widen. Indeed this is precisely what is happening. For example, a study of 126 wheat farms in Ludhiana district of the Indian Punjab, in the period 1967—68 to 1969—70, concluded that 'it is clear ... that both relative and absolute increase in disposable income per holding was higher in the case of large sized holdings as compared to small and medium sized holdings'.[20]

Size, however, is not necessarily correlated with the type of land tenure. We have already implied that a sharecropper may behave differently from a leaseholder who cultivates a farm of similar dimensions. Equally, a small owner-operator may not behave in the same way as a tenant. Research in West Bengal has uncovered cases in which small cultivators plant high yielding varieties of rice only on the land obtained from a landlord, and only when the additional expenses are

[18] Brian Lockwood, P. K. Mukherjee and R. T. Shand, *The High Yielding Varieties Programme in India*, Part 1, Programme Evaluation Organization, Planning Commission of India and Department of Economics, Australian National University, 1971, p. 88.
[19] Brian Lockwood, P. K. Mukherjee and R. T. Shand, op. cit., Table 11, p. 169.
[20] Gurbachan Singh and H. S. Sandhu, 'Income Distribution by Farm Size', *Agricultural Situation in India*, July 1971, p. 194.

shared with the landlord; the land which the cultivator personally owns is devoted to the traditional varieties, in which the costs of production and the need for credit are lower.[21]

The pattern of innovation, thus, is very complex.[22] Cultivators in some regions are more likely to introduce high yielding varieties than cultivators of a similar size in other regions — primarily because of a greater availability of irrigation water in the 'progressive' regions. Some cultivators introduce the new varieties on only part of the land they cultivate — primarily because of a lack of credit. Still other cultivators introduce an improved seed and later revert to the traditional practices — primarily because the new technology was unprofitable given the prices they must pay for material inputs. Some of these points can be illustrated with data from the Philippines.

It is well known that to achieve maximum effectiveness the new rice seeds should be used on farms which enjoy an assured supply of water throughout the year. Regions where the water supply is poorly controlled will be slow to adopt the new technology and will benefit little from it. This is demonstrated by a study of 513 farms in Nueva Ecija, Philippines.

It is clear from the table below that those farmers who depend on rainfed agriculture are at a considerable disadvantage, particularly compared to those who are able to double-crop their land using irrigation. Farmers in rainfed regions use high yielding varieties on a minority of their land and obtain yields only two-thirds as high as those in the most favoured situation. Since the irrigated farms were more prosperous than the rainfed farms even prior to the introduction of the improved seeds, the new technology has led to an increase in inequality.

[21] S. Sengupta and M. G. Ghosh, 'HYVP for Rice: Performance in a Bengal District', *Economic and Political Weekly*, October 26, 1968; Gyaneshwar Ojha, 'Small Farmers and HYV Programme', *Economic and Political Weekly*, April 4, 1970.
[22] For additional evidence on this point see Shigeru Ishikawa, 'Technological Change in Agricultural Production and Its Impact on Agrarian Structure — A Study on the So-Called Green Revolution', *Keizai Kenkyu (Economic Research)* Vol. 22, No. 2, April 1971.

Table 3.1

Water Supply and Adoption of High Yielding Varieties of Rice on 513 Farms in Gapan, Nueva Ecija, Philippines, 1970

		Irrigated 2 crops	Partially irrigated	Rainfed
1	Percent of area planted to HYVs	96.5	62.5	31.6
2	Yield per hectare (tons)	2.7	2.1	1.8
3	Nitrogen per hectare (kg.)	49.8	28.9	20.5
4	Percent of farmers using insecticides	90.5	78.2	56.8
5	Percent of farmers using herbicides	52.0	21.8	11.4
6	Percent of farmers using tractors for ploughing	32.0	20.0	22.0

Source: International Rice Research Institute, Los Baños, Philippines.

Furthermore, it would appear that in at least some instances the use of the new seeds on rainfed farms results in a lower net income for the cultivator. On the rainfed farms in Gapan, for instance, between 1965 and 1970 the area under high yielding varieties rose from zero to 31.6 per cent, yet yields rose only from 1.7 to 1.8 tons per hectare. At the same time the amount of fertilizer used more than doubled, rising from 9.2 to 20.5 kg. per hectare, and the proportion of farmers using herbicides, insecticides and tractors increased by well over one hundred per cent. Since output remained roughly the same while material inputs rose substantially, value added must have declined. Innovation almost certainly led to greater poverty on these farms and one could antici- pate that in the future the farmers will revert to the traditional varieties of rice.

The story is quite different, of course, on those farms which are able to harvest two crops of rice a year. The new technology causes yields to increase by 20 to 50 per cent and net profits undoubtedly rise as well. The new technology, however, does not alter some of the basic patterns we have identified earlier. The larger farmers tend to use more mechanized techniques of production, while small tenants

Table 3.2
Yields and Technology Employed on Irrigated 2-Crop Farms in Gapan, Nueva Ecija, Philippines, 1970

	Less than 2 ha.	2–4 ha.	More than 4 ha.
1 Yield per ha. in tons, 1965 (pre-HYV)	2.4	1.7	1.8
2 Yield per ha. in 1970	2.9	2.6	2.2
3 Percent of area planted to HYVs, 1970	97.0	96.9	93.0
4 Per cent of farmers using tractors	20.0	37.0	43.0
5 Per cent of farmers using herbicides	48.2	53.4	52.4
6 Per cent of farmers using insecticides	85.5	91.8	95.2
7 Nitrogen per hectare (kg.)	51.4	45.1	42.5

Source: International Rice Research Institute, Los Baños, Philippines.

use more labour intensive methods of cultivation. Moreover, the smallest farmers frequently obtain higher yields per hectare, both before and after the introduction of high yielding varieties. Once again, this can be illustrated with data from the Gapan sample. (See Table 3.2.)

It is noteworthy that the yields of the smallest farmers were 32 per cent higher than those of the largest farmers[23] and that the former had a larger proportion of the area devoted to high yielding varieties. The large farmers, in fact, obtained lower yields even after introducing the improved

[23] It is quite possible that the difference in yields between small and large farmers is understated. There is evidence that those with very small farms tend to report a larger planted area than the actual area. The bias toward overstating the area planted was inversely correlated with farm size. Since yield is equal to output divided by area, there is a tendency to understate yields, and this tendency is inversely correlated with farm size. Therefore, yield differentials probably are greater in actuality than the reported figures. (See K. A. Gomez and B. T. Oñate, 'Response Bias in the Collection of Rice Statistics', *Philippine Agriculturist*, February–March, 1969.)

seeds than the small farmers obtained before the new varieties were developed. The smaller farmers also used more nitrogen per hectare than the largest farmers — reflecting the fact that fertilizer is largely a substitute for land. The big farmers, in contrast, were twice as likely to use tractors as farmers with less than two hectares, and they were somewhat more inclined to use chemical weedicides and insecticides. In other words, the big farmers tended to substitute machines and chemicals for labour. The large farmers, in short, produced less per hectare, provided less employment, and were relatively more extravagant in their use of scarce capital resources. This is a characteristic of large farmers whether or not they innovate.

The argument summarized

There is evidence that the nature of the water supply system, the size of farm, the type of land tenure and the distribution of land ownership are all important determinants of the pace and direction of technical change in agriculture. It is possible to imagine a situation in which the size distribution of farm units is egalitarian but the distribution of landownership is very unequal. In such a situation we would expect yields and technology to vary less with farm size than with the form of tenure.[24] As we have previous shown,[25] a two hectare farm, for instance, might be managed by (*i*) an owner-operator, or (*ii*) a peasant on a fixed-rent leasehold who receives no services from his landlord, or (*iii*) a sharecropper who is ignored by his landlord, or (*iv*) a tenant — leaseholder or sharecropper — to whom the landlord provides not only land, but also cash credit and loans in kind. Each of these tenure arrangements will be characterized by a different set of incentives and by differences in the ease of access to factor markets. A small sharecropper of a large and enterprising

[24] It is not surprising, therefore, that in a study of 155 farms in the Philippines, Liao and Barker concluded that 'farm size was not significantly related to acceptance of new varieties'. (S. H. Liao and Randolph Barker, 'An Analysis of the Spread of New High Yielding Rice Varieties on Philippine Farms', *Economic Research Journal*, June 1969, p. 19.

[25] See p. 24 above.

landlord, for example is likely to have greater access to factors of production than a small, peasant owner-operator or a leaseholder who is left to fend for himself in an environment in which credit institutions and other markets are poorly developed. In selecting farm size as a crucial determinant, we are using it as a proxy variable and assumed that it was highly correlated with ease of access to factor markets. This assumption may not be valid in regions characterized by several different types of tenure arrangements. Similarly, the assumption may not remain valid over time if the degree of market imperfection diminishes or if tenure arrangements are altered, say, as a result of a land reform. The information that is at present available, however, suggests that technology, public policy and market power combine to ensure that it is the large landowner who benefits most from agricultural innovation.

B. Technical Change, Rural Impoverishment and Class Structure

Agricultural innovation is occurring in a great many countries, but so far its impact on national indicators of economic progress has been relatively slight. Indeed in many nations there has been no perceptible increase in per capita food or agricultural production in the last decade. Consider, for example, the six Asian countries from which we have drawn most of our data. In India and the Philippines agricultural production per head was roughly the same in 1970 as it was in 1960. In Indonesia it was noticeably lower, although the negative trend recently has been reversed. In Pakistan, output

Table 3.3
Per Capita Agricultural Production in Six Asian Nations: Percentage Change 1960–1970

India	0
Indonesia	−4
Pakistan	+14
Philippines	0
Sri Lanka	+10
Taiwan	+15

was 14 per cent higher, but the aggregate figure obscures the fact that in the then East Pakistan — where the majority of the population lived — there was no tendency for food or total agricultural output per head to rise. Production increased 15 per cent in Taiwan, but it is noteworthy that per capita production on the island still was less in 1970 than it had been in the 1930s. In Sri Lanka steady but unspectacular progress has been achieved: during the last decade production per head increased about one per cent a year.

These figures should not be forgotten when striking claims are made on behalf of the so-called green revolution.[26] We have concentrated on countries in which progress has been reported in the last decade; in other nations and regions conditions are even worse, of course. Thus in Burma, per capita food production declined 14 per cent over the period; in South Vietnam and Cambodia the fall was substantially greater. Food production per head in Africa as a whole also was lower in 1970 than 10 years earlier, while in Latin America, agricultural production per head declined and food production remained stagnant.

Agricultural innovation undoubtedly has accelerated in recent years, but the most significant consequence of technical change may have been to alter the distribution of income and class structure in rural areas rather than to eliminate malnutrition and agricultural shortages in urban areas. With few exceptions, aggregate agricultural supplies have not increased spectacularly, but with almost no exception, the relative position of the peasantry seems to have deteriorated. Far too much attention has been devoted to the effects of the 'green revolution' in increasing output of one or two commodities, and not enough attention has been given to the performance of the agricultural sector as a whole. For example, in India between 1964 and 1969, wheat production increased 90 per cent, but rice production in-

[26] The most exaggerated claim is that of Lester Brown: the new seeds 'are likely to be a greater force for change than any technology or ideology ever introduced into the poor countries'. (Lester R. Brown, *The Social Impact of the Green Revolution*, International Conciliation, 1971, p. 44.)

creased only 4 per cent, i.e., less than the population. The output of tea rose 6 per cent, the production of cotton remained unchanged and that of jute declined 7 per cent. In other words, of the major agricultural crops, only wheat output increased faster than the population. Change has occurred in Indian agriculture in a context of essentially stagnant production, and it is the distribution of the benefits and costs of change that merits more study than it has heretofore received.

Risk

Every change involves risk. Farmers who produce entirely for household consumption and who do not purchase material inputs incur only one risk, viz., that the harvest will fail as a result of poor weather. A commercial farmer who produces for the market and purchases material inputs runs two additional risks: first, the price in the product market may decline or the marketing system may become disrupted and, second, the price of purchased inputs may rise or there may be a breakdown in the input supply system. The use of high yielding seeds creates an opportunity for the farmer to make substantial gains but it also implies that losses can be equally substantial. Suppose, for instance, there is a breakdown in the irrigation system or a failure of the monsoon, the progressive, innovating farmer will lose not only his harvest but also the working capital he has expended on fertilizer and other material inputs. Thus the innovator can lose as well as gain more than the traditional farmer, and those who fear a loss of income more than they welcome a rise may be reluctant to introduce an 'improved' technology.

There is relatively little data on the probability distribution of net gains from technical change, but a study from Indonesia of 2500 plots is suggestive. Farmers who used fertilizer were divided into three groups. Group I contains those who obtained rice yields lower than the average of non-fertilized plots. Group II contains farmers who obtained yields between the average of the non-fertilized and fertilized plots, and Group III contains those whose yields were greater than the average obtained on fertilized plots. Rice output and all inputs were valued at local prices. The expected increases (or losses) in West and Central Java, as compared with the unfertilized plots, were as given in the table below.

Nearly two-thirds of the farmers in West Java and over half the farmers in Central Java failed to benefit from the expenditure on fertilizer. Indeed the farmers in Group I suffered a harvest failure (because of inadequate water supply and infestation by pests) and lost their working capital as well. The farmers in Group II managed to increase their yields, but the value of additional output fell short of (in West Java) or only barely exceeded (in Central Java) the cost of the fertilizer. The Group III farmers, on the other hand, benefitted handsomely from using fertilizers, but they were a minority not only of the total farm population but of those who innovated. If subsequent research shows that the results obtained in Indonesia are typical of what is happening elsewhere, one must anticipate that the speed with which fertilizer is introduced will be adversely affected.

It is plausible to argue, although impossible to prove, that small peasants are less able to bear risk than large landowners and, hence, are unwilling to do so. In so far as this is true, it implies that the poor will be more reluctant to innovate than the rich and, therefore, that the long-run benefits of technical change will tend to be reaped by the latter. In other words, it is argued that technical change will lead almost inevitably to

Table 3.4

Probability Distribution of Net Gains From Using Fertilizer in West and Central Java

	Group I	Group II	Group III
West Java			
Frequency (%)	18.5	46	35.5
Benefit-cost ratio	negative	0.79	2.11
Increase in yield (kg./ha.)	−180	+250	+664
Central Java			
Frequency	26.1	28.7	45.2
Benefit-cost ratio	negative	1.06	3.96
Increase in yield	−376	+326	+1213

Source: *National Fertilizer Study Indonesia, Final Report*, July 1971, Tables 14 and 15.

greater inequality in the distribution of income merely because of the risk aversion of the poor. Inequality, it is alleged, is caused not by monopolistic exploitation or government policy but by different attitudes toward chance.

Put in such simple terms, the argument clearly is mistaken. First, small owner-operators and tenants are not, in general, so desperately poor that the loss of a harvest and working capital would markedly increase the likelihood of starvation. In *parts* of India, Indonesia, Bangladesh and Pakistan a harvest failure can lead directly to death, but this is not true in the rest of Asia, nor in most of Africa and Latin America. In my opinion, the poorest people in underdeveloped countries, especially in Asia, often are the *lumpenproletariat* in the cities[27] and the landless, casual workers in agriculture — not small landowners and tenants. Some members of the first two groups may have an absolute aversion to risk, but it is impossible to believe that this is equally characteristic of those who own or have access to land. Thus risk aversion is a relative rather than an absolute concept.

Second, the entire burden of risk does not always fall on the peasant cultivator. Most sharecropping arrangements involve a division of expenses as well as of output, and thus the risk is shared between the landlord and tenant. Moreover, as we demonstrated earlier,[28] numerous other land tenure systems already exist or can be devised which shift the risk to those who are willing and able to support it. In addition, in many countries a peasant in temporary difficulty can count

[27] In India in 1967—68, the nominal per capita annual consumption of the bottom 5 per cent of the urban population was 4.5 per cent greater than the per capita consumption of the bottom 5 per cent of the rural population. It is quite likely, however, that urban prices were more than 4.5 per cent higher than rural prices, and if so, it follows that the poorest people in India are in urban, not rural, areas. (Cf. V. M. Dandekar and N. Rath, *Poverty in India*, p. 31.) Indeed, if one considers food prices alone, it is probable that urban prices are about 25 per cent higher than rural prices (Ibid., p. 7). The general price level in urban areas, however, seems to be about 15 per cent higher than in rural areas. (G. S. Chatterjee and N. Bhattacharya, 'Rural-Urban Differentials in Consumer Prices', *Economic and Political Weekly*, Vol. 4, No. 20, 1969).
[28] See Chapter 2, pp. 22—6.

on assistance from his extended family or his *compadre* or a local political leader. As a last resort, the hardships of disaster can be shared with the landlord and moneylender, merely by postponing or defaulting on rent and loan repayments. In fact, the peasant pays a high 'risk premium' for his credit precisely because it can be foreseen that defaults will sometimes occur.

. Given the variety of ways in which risk can be dispersed, there is little reason why the cultivator should assume the entire burden if he does not wish to do so.[29] Two things follow from this. First, differences in risk aversion should not result in one type of farmer being markedly more prone to innovate than another. High risk will deter investment and innovation in general, but it will not necessarily deter one group more than another. Second, if given the same incentives all farmers are more or less equally eager to innovate, differences in attitude toward risk cannot account for increasing inequality in rural areas. If many peasants fail to benefit from the process of technical change, one should seek for the cause not in their attitudes but in their restricted access to resources.

Economies of scale

The majority of technical changes that are associated with the 'green revolution' are neutral to scale and therefore do not give the large landowner a cost advantage over the small peasant. Seeds and fertilizer, the two most important inputs, are virtually infinitely divisible. Water, of course, also is divisible, although the irrigation systems may not be. Large dams are 'lumpy' investments and their construction cannot be justified unless there is a sizeable area of land to be irrigated. This does not imply, however, that dam and canal irrigation is not feasible unless landownership is concentrated, since the major engineering works invariably are financed by the state. At the other extreme are low lift pumps which are used to lift water from natural rivers onto

[29] The multiplicity of ways in which agricultural risks can be reduced may partially explain why crop insurance schemes have never been very successful in underdeveloped countries.

paddy fields; there are virtually no economies of scale associated with this piece of simple equipment. In between dams and small pumps are tubewells. It is generally agreed in Pakistan and northern India that the efficient use of a tubewell requires 15–20 acres. Farmers who have less land than this are unable to use all the water themselves, but they can, of course, sell the surplus water to small peasants. In fact, this frequently happens.[30] Alternatively, a group of small farmers with adjoining fields can form a tubewell cooperative and jointly finance and manage the tubewell. This, too, happens, particularly in Bangladesh. Thus in those cases where there are economies of scale in irrigation, the problem can be overcome rather easily.

Greater difficulty arises when mechanization becomes profitable. There are indeed economies of scale associated with the use of large four-wheel tractors and combine harvesters. A four-wheel tractor in a wheat region, for example, probably continues to enjoy falling unit costs up to a farm size of 100 acres or more. Combines operate most efficiently over an even larger area. These machines definitely give the large farmers an advantage over the small, although in principle this advantage can be neutralized by forming cooperatives or collectives or by creating a market for custom ploughing, harvesting, etc.

A study of 28 wheat farms in the Indian Punjab indicated that the farms on which tractors were used were over twice as large as holdings on which tractors were not used. (See Table 3.5.) Moreover, investment per acre was twice as large on the former as on the latter. Conversely, farmers who did not own tractors employed 48 per cent more labour to grow wheat than those who did. The evidence from this small sample suggests that an additional investment of Rs. 242.51 per acre

---

[30] One finds, however, that those who have invested in tubewells take advantage of their local monopoly position and charge relatively high rates for the water they supply. As a result, the intensity of use of water is below the economic optimum on farms which must purchase water from their neighbours. This is but another instance of the pervasiveness of market imperfections in rural areas. Contrary to what is often asserted in elementary textbooks, agriculture is not a good example of a perfectly competitive industry.

would enable a farmer to dispense with 52.3 man-hours of employment per acre of wheat.

Given the factor endowments of most underdeveloped countries, it is doubtful that mechanization with tractors and combines is wise. The machines use a scarce factor of production (capital) to economise on an abundant factor of production (labour) and thereby fail to use resources in the most efficient combinations. Furthermore, mechanization of this type will tend to depress the wages of agricultural workers (because they displace labour) and reduce the farm income of small owner-operators (because they reduce costs of production on large farms and this eventually will result in lower grain prices). Thus technical change of this type is likely to increase inequality and poverty. Moreover, it is also likely to lead to a larger average size of farm and even greater concentration of land.

Table 3.5

Mechanization and Employment on 28 Wheat Farms in the Punjab, India

		Tractor Farms	Non-Tractor Farms
1	Number of holdings	6	22
2	Average size of holding (acres)	58.86	21.08
3	Total investment per acre (Rs.)	458.97	216.46
4	Male employment on cultivating wheat (hours per acre)	108.90	161.20

Source: B. Singh, 'Economics of Tractor Utilization — A Case Study', *Indian Journal of Agricultural Economics*, January—March, 1968, pp. 84 and 85.

This scenario is not inevitable, however. Investment in tractors and combines seldom makes economic sense. It is profitable to the large landowner primarily because foreign exchange and capital are supplied to him at a subsidized rate. If the price of foreign exchange and the rate of interest were adjusted so that these prices more accurately reflected social opportunity costs, the incentive to mechanize would greatly diminish.[31] Some machinery, of course, would be purchased, but it would be smaller and less capital intensive and would probably be similar to that currently used in Taiwan and Japan.

In summary, the new technology for producing food is not characterized by important economies of scale and the growth in inequality which has in practice accompanied technical change is not a necessary consequence of attempts to raise yields. The problem arises not from the nature of the most appropriate technology, but from the bias of government policy and the fact that public institutions clearly are not scale-neutral.

Employment

Indeed one could reasonably hope that the new technology would reduce income inequality by increasing employment opportunities. If irrigation permits multiple cropping, this should increase the demand for labour and reduce seasonal unemployment. If the new seeds result in higher yields, the amount of labour required for weeding and harvesting should rise and this should lead to higher real wages. On the other hand, certain types of mechanization will reduce the demand for labour. If this occurs in a context of rapid population growth and stagnant agricultural production, employment and real wages may fall.

A study of 92 farms in Laguna and several provinces of Central Luzon, Philippines gives us an insight into the way employment patterns shift as technical change occurs.[32] Total employment per hectare declined by an average of 4 man-days between the wet season of 1966 and the wet season

[31] W. J. Chancellor has shown that in Malaysia and Thailand the profitability of tractor ownership is very sensitive to interest rates. ('Mechanization of Small Farms in Thailand and Malaysia by Tractor Hire Services', in International Rice Research Institute, *Rice Policy Conference: Current Papers on Rice Technology*, 1971.

Chancellor also has shown that a 4-wheel tractor-year releases 613 man-days in Thailand and 907 man-days in Malaysia, whereas a 2-wheel tractor releases only 60 man-days in Malaysia. (*Ibid.*, p. 18c.)

[32] See the International Rice Research Institute, *Annual Report*, 1970, pp. 174—176.

Table 3.6
Changes in Employment on 92 Rice Farms in Luzon, Philippines, 1966 and 1968
(man-days per ha.)

	Wet season 1966	Wet season 1968
Land preparation		
All farms	18	11
Two-crop irrigated farms	16	9
Transplanting		
All farms	15	16
Two-crop irrigated farms	12	13
Weeding		
All farms	5	8
Two-crop irrigated farms	5	12
Other pre-harvest activities		
All farms	8	9
Two-crop irrigated farms	8	12
Harvesting and threshing		
All farms	18	16
Two-crop irrigated farms	22	22
Total employment		
All farms	64	60
Two-crop irrigated farms	63	68

Source: İnternational Rice Research Institute, *Annual Report*, 1970, Table 2, p. 175.

of 1968. (See Table 3.6.) On the farms which were able to obtain two crops per year under irrigation, however, employment rose by 5 man-days. There was a sharp fall in the amount of labour required for land preparation, due to a greater use of tractors. On the other hand, employment on weeding and 'other pre-harvest' activities increased, despite the much greater use of small mechanical weeders.[33] The most surprising finding, however, is the failure of employment on harvesting and threshing to rise. One explanation for

[33] In 1966 only ten per cent of the farmers who double cropped their land used mechanical weeders; by 1968 the proportion had increased to 41 per cent. Mechanical weeders and labour appear to be complementary, since the most likely alternative is not to weed by hand but not to weed at all. Thus weeders increase output but not unemployment.

this is the greater use of threshers on two-crop irrigated farms, where the proportion of farmers using large threshers rose from zero to 50 per cent in two years. Another explanation, however, is the failure of average yields to rise on rainfed and one-crop irrigated farms. Yields rose 25 per cent on the two-crop irrigated farms, but the average increase for the entire sample of 92 farms was only 5 per cent.

In Luzon as a whole, therefore, the introduction of a new technology in the rice growing areas appears to have had a negligible impact on creating additional demand for labour. Given the rapid growth of the labour force one would expect real wages to fall. This hypothesis can be tested with data collected from 42 farms in Laguna in the period between 1966 (prior to introducing HYVs) and 1969 (after the introduction of HYVs).

Laguna is a good region to study because it is one of the few provinces in the Philippines in which labour intensive methods of cultivation are used. Unlike Central Luzon, where large tractors are common, tenants in Laguna use small hand tractors of 6 to 14 horsepower. Similarly, farmers in Laguna do not use the large mechanical threshers one finds elsewhere on the island. Thus there is a presumption that factor prices in Laguna are less biased in favour of capital intensive techniques of production. The data in Table 3.7 indicate that between 1966 and 1969 the amount of hired labour increased by 85 per cent, thereby confirming our view that under appropriate circumstances the 'green revolution' should increase the demand for labour. Notwithstanding the rise in employment, however, real wages of hired labour declined by over 6 per cent. What may have happened is that the sharp increase in demand for hired labour was confined to a relatively small area, and this was not sufficient to absorb the natural increase of the labour force plus those displaced by mechanization occurring in other sectors and regions. As a result, the incomes of agricultural workers declined, and poverty and inequality increased.[34]

[34] The survey data from Laguna are consistent with the aggregate data presented in Chapter 2, Table 2.7, p. 33. The two sources are independent of each other, and thus one can be fairly confident that real wages in agriculture have fallen.

Table 3.7

Employment and Real Wages on 42 Farms in Laguna,
Philippines

		1966	1969
1	Amount of labour hired (man-days per ha.)	36.3	67.2
2	Wage bill (current pesos)	183	341
3	Wage rate (= 2/1)	5.04	5.07
4	Real wage rate in 1969 prices	5.42	5.07
5	Per cent change in real wages		−6.4
6	Per cent change in amount of labour hired		+85.1

Source: International Rice Research Institute, Los Baños, Philippines.

Even in Laguna, moreover, total labour inputs per hectare, i.e. hired plus family labour, declined. A recent study of 153 farms[35] shows that employment fell from 86 man-days per ha. in 1966 to 80 man-days in 1970. During this period the area under high yielding varieties of rice increased from one to 93 per cent of the total rice area and yields rose from 2.4 to 3.4 metric tons per hectare. At the same time, however, the number of farmers using tractors increased from 37 to 76 per cent, and as a result, labour requirements for land preparation were cut in half (from 20 to 11 man-days per ha.). Part of the labour displaced by tractors was absorbed in weeding and other pre-harvest activities, but even so, there was a net decline in labour utilization and given the rapid increase in population and labour force, this must have exerted a downward pressure on real wages.

In several parts of the world technical change has been associated with falling real incomes. This is true not only in the Philippines but in Pakistan (certainly) and India (possibly) as well. In parts of the Indian Punjab, for example, it appears that landowners are now paying slightly higher real wages to agricultural workers than previously. The additional

[35] Randolph Barker, William H. Meyers, Cristina M. Crisostomo and Bart Duff, 'Employment and Technological Change in Philippine Agriculture', mimeo., I.L.O., Geneva, Switzerland, October 1971; see especially Table 9.

cash outlay, however, may have been more than compensated by terminating payments in kind and abrogating customary rights of landless workers and tenants. Peasants no longer are able to obtain fodder for their animals from the landlord's fields;[36] fuel is no longer provided as part of the wage payment; the landlord no longer feels obliged to grant interest free loans to those who work for him. The cash nexus has replaced tradition, and in the course of doing so the livelihood of the peasantry has become endangered.

From peasantry to proletariat
Technical change in agriculture reduces unit costs of production and raises the average profitability of farming. It also alters the distribution of income. Indeed we have argued at considerable length that the changes which are at present occurring tend to increase relative inequality and in some cases even reduce absolutely the standard of living of large sections of the rural population. There is another dimension of technical change we have yet to explore, however: its social and political implications.

Technical change is closely related to commercial development. The new methods of cultivation require material inputs that must be obtained from agricultural supply industries; the additional output must be sold through established marketing channels, or new outlets must be created. Those farmers who already are producing on a commercial scale, and who have close connections with the money economy, will be able to extend their operations more rapidly than small peasants who rely on family labour for subsistence production. This will tend to increase further the degree of income inequality.

As agriculture becomes more commercialized one can expect greater specialization and division of labour. Occupations will become more specific, social relations will become more distinct and the customary terms on which services are exchanged will tend to give way to formal contracts. As the market penetrates the countryside, the efficiency of labour probably will increase, but this is likely to occur at the

[36] In fact, where combine harvesters are used, there is no fodder to be had.

expense of diversity, and to imply an increase in risk. It will become more difficult for a man to combine, say, share-cropping with driving a pedicab or for a woman both to look after the chickens and manufacture 'Panama' hats. Increas-ingly, the hats will be made in the cities, the hens will be raised in large batteries, the pedicabs will succumb to compe-tition from commercial bus companies and the sharecropper will be transformed into a landless worker. The numerous people who formerly were exercising entrepreneurial func-tions on a small scale will find that they have less control over their own lives. They will cease to be 'penny capitalists' and will become a proletariat.

This change will not occur instantaneously, of course. There is likely to be a prolonged period in which the sharecropping system that is so common in Asia is gradually transformed – the tenant relinquishing part of his responsi-bility for entrepreneurial functions and slowly becoming more dependent on the landowner for investment decisions, the supply of credit, agrochemicals and the services of machines. Eventually the dependence will become complete and the tenant will have been converted into an agricultural labourer. These historical tendencies will encounter resistance and occasionally governments may half-heartedly attempt to reverse the trend, e.g. by enacting legislation to discourage share tenancy and encourage fixed rent leaseholds, as in the Philippines, but the long run outcome in the non-socialist countries seems reasonably clear.

Commercialization will tend to concentrate the function of entrepreneurship into a few hands. In the process, the peasantry will be destroyed. The quantity of goods produced may increase but the quality of life may decrease. As agriculture becomes more commercial and more profitable, the richness and variety of tenure arrangements which we described earlier[37] will tend to disappear and be replaced by two basic types: owner-operators and agro-businesses.[38]

[37] See Chapter 2, pp. 22–6.
[38] Evidence to test this hypothesis is not yet available. One study in the Philippines, however, gives a hint that the changes we anticipate are underway. In Mayantoc, Tarlac – a barrio of Central Luzon, Philip-pines – the proportion of land cultivated by owner-operators rose from

These changes in land tenure probably will lag behind changes in technology[39] and income distribution, but they will be inexorable. Already there are reports from Sri Lanka, India, Pakistan and the Philippines of landowners evicting tenants and taking over the land themselves. Sometimes the tenants are paid a small sum of money in compensation for being evicted, and sometimes they are not. But in either case, a tenant-entrepreneur is converted into a landless labourer and an absentee rentier becomes a capitalist farmer.

This tendency is well illustrated by a case study of a *barrio* in the Philippines conducted by Gelia Castillo and a group of investigators working with her. It was discovered that between 1963 (i.e. prior to the introduction of high yielding varieties of rice) and 1969 (after the advent of the 'green revolution') there was a substantial change in occupational structure: the number of farmers (i.e. tenants) declined from 81 to 74 per cent of the labour force while the number of hired farm workers rose from 13 to 17 per cent of the labour force. One reason, perhaps the major reason, for the decline in tenants and the increase in labourers is that small landowners decided to cultivate the land themselves.[40]

These changes in the division of labour and in land tenure which the Philippines case study illustrates tend to be

----

29 to 35 per cent between 1965 and 1967, while the proportion of land farmed by tenants declined from 20 to 13 per cent. The amount of land farmed by managers also increased, but the proportion of total area farmed in this way was insignificant. (USAID/Philippines, 'The Philippine 'Miracle Rice' Program and Its Aftermath', mimeo, 16 July 1969, Table 4, p. 27.)

[39] Y. Hayami and V. W. Ruttan also argue that changes in institutions such as land tenure are induced by technical change. They suggest, however, that since institutions are changed when it 'pays' to do so, there is little need in most instances for governments to introduce an agrarian reform. Their analysis, although interesting, suffers from the fact that they neglect to ask the question 'pays whom?'. (See their *Agricultural Development*, pp. 59–61.)

[40] Gelia T. Castillo, Alice M. de Guzman, Soledad L. Pahud and Lorna Paje, 'The Green Revolution at the Village Level: A Philippines Case Study (1963–1970)', paper presented at the 28th International Congress of Orientalists, Canberra, 6–12 January, 1971, Table 11, p. 62 and p. 64.

accompanied by a polarization of classes. Two major groups tend to emerge: one which owns and manages property and another which sells labour services for cash wages. The interests of these groups are in fundamental conflict and political alignments are likely to develop which reflect this fact. The politics of language, religion, region and faction should give way to the politics of class conflict. If employment opportunities and income per head are increasing rapidly, the conflict may be mute,[41] but if technical change occurs in an environment in which inequality is rising while employment and output are relatively stagnant, the stage will be set for a violent confrontation.

In many parts of the world technical change has led to open conflict between landowners and workers, and in several nations politicians have begun to respond. In Sri Lanka, Mrs. Bandaranaike made an appeal to the masses. She won the general election but soon lost the allegiance of many of her followers by failing to move quickly enough to create more employment. An insurrection in April 1971 was the consequence. In India, Mrs. Gandhi appealed to the poor, and won. In West Pakistan, Mr. Bhutto based his campaign on an appeal to the class interests of small peasants and urban workers; he too won the election, although he was not allowed to take power until his country disintegrated. Politics in the Philippines, in contrast, is still the politics of factions and regional warlords, and no national leader has emerged as a spokesman for the proletariat. The country, however, is in ferment. Sections of the Catholic Church and the academic community have become alarmed about the plight of the poor; urban labour leaders have become more outspoken; students have lost their lives demonstrating in the streets; a guerilla movement has been revived in Central Luzon under Marxist direction;[42] and political violence in a bewildering variety of forms had become a daily occurrence until martial law was imposed. The Philippines, obviously, is undergoing a transition from the politics of factions to the politics of class.

[41] As, for example, in Taiwan.
[42] An interesting study of agrarian rebellion in the Philippines is the book by Eduardo Lachica, *Huq: Philippine Agrarian Society in Revolt.*

Thus in one Asian country after another, the introduction of high yielding varieties of foodgrains, and the policies and programmes which have accompanied technical change, have had multifarious consequences. Supplies of rice and, especially, wheat have increased, but the impact on aggregate economic performance has been relatively slight. Inequality has become more acute, and in some countries or regions real wages have fallen. Tenant farming has shown some tendency to decline in favour of owner-operators and agro-businesses, and in some cases this is likely to be accompanied by a greater concentration of landownership.[43] Technical change has been intimately associated with greater penetration of the market into rural areas, increased specialization and a new division of labour. This, in turn, is likely eventually to destroy the peasantry and polarize[44] the rural community

[43] A sample survey of 67,800 large farms in 1968/69 in the Punjab, India showed that large landowners were increasing the average size of their holdings.

Size of farm (acres)	Land owned in 1967/68 as per cent of land owned in 1955/56
20–25	104.07
25–30	108.44
30–40	110.11
40–50	107.09
50–75	116.34
75–100	121.13
100–150	138.22
150+	100.00
Total	109.35

Source: Ashok Rudra, 'Big Farmers of Punjab', *Economic and Political Weekly*, 27 December 1969.

[44] Once the process of polarization has begun, economic and political forces are likely to interact in a cumulative, disequilibrating fashion. For example, an increase in poverty and inequality is likely to provoke labour unrest, strikes and confrontations between workers and landowners. This, in turn, will increase the cost to farmers of using labour intensive methods of cultivation as well as the risk of their being unable to complete agricultural operations on time. As costs and risks rise, mechanization will be encouraged, and this will aggravate inequality and unrest further. Cumulative movements such as these can be observed in Kerala, Sri Lanka and, on a gigantic scale, in Bangladesh. Outside of Asia, one can find a cumulative interaction between mechanization, falling real wages and rural violence in certain regions of Colombia.

into two classes whose interest are in conflict. At times the conflict may be violent and at other times it may be pacific, but in either event, the emergence of a new class structure in rural areas will have a profound effect on the methods and objectives of political activity.

C. Policy Strategies

There are two broad strategies that can be adopted in order to reduce the tendency toward polarization and increased inequality which has accompanied the 'green revolution' in monsoon Asia. The first strategy is based on the assumption that relative factor prices are given and efforts are directed toward altering the bias of technical change. The second approach is based on the assumption that the bias of technical change is independent of government policy, and attempts are made instead to alter relative factor prices. The two strategies are not mutually exclusive, however. Indeed, the two can be combined quite easily.

Biological engineering

The new varieties of foodgrains that have been developed require relatively capital intensive methods of cultivation. The new rice seeds, for example, were designed to respond to large doses of fertilizer without 'lodging' and in practice they have performed best on land which can be irrigated throughout the year. The high yielding plants are more susceptible to attacks by pests and disease and should be protected with insecticides and fungicides. Under optimal technical conditions the new varieties grow well, but they are 'landlord-biased' and tend to exclude the peasant from the benefits of technical change.

The bias of technical change need not be inevitable, however. There is no reason why plant research cannot be directed toward developing improved varieties which reflect the factor endowments and ecological conditions which most Asian farmers confront. The desired physical properties of plants can be predetermined by science policy advisors, and the research biologists can then be asked to design such a plant. This process of 'biological engineering', as it is called by the Rockefeller Foundation, could be used to offset systematically the inherent advantage possessed by those who have preferential access to material inputs. In other words, science policy could be used to push technical change in a 'peasant-biased' direction.

For example, most farmers in Asia, certainly many of the poorest ones, are engaged in rainfed agriculture and they have been left behind by the technical changes which have occurred in the irrigated regions. Research could compensate for this, at least in part, by concentrating effort on increasing the yields of upland rice, even if the yields do not approach those of the 'traditional' varieties under irrigation. Similarly, research could be directed toward developing foodgrains which have a genetic resistance to disease and do not require a protective application of chemicals. Even if disease-resistant varieties produced lower yields than the high yielding seeds now available, they would be a great boon to small peasants who have restricted access to credit and agro-chemicals.

The strategy outlined in the previous paragraph rests on the belief that if sufficient time, talent and money are devoted to research, new varieties can be created and new methods of cultivation can be discovered which are 'peasant-biased', i.e. which raise output per unit of land and labour but which lower the ratio of capital to labour. Ultimately, of course, such a strategy is based on faith in the ability of scientists to find solutions to problems posed by those who formulate policy. Given the success of scientists in the past in meeting the demands of government, it would not appear that such a faith is without foundation.

Institutional transformation

Even if science is able to design a 'peasant-biased' technology, however, there is no reason why attempts should not also be made to correct factor prices and improve the markets which supply credit and material inputs. Our analysis indicates that the major cause of polarization in rural areas is inequality in the distribution of land and unequal access to other factors of production. If governments wish to increase welfare, efficiency and output in the countryside, then a substantial effort must be made to reduce monopolistic elements in factor markets and eliminate the political power of large landlords. Neither of these tasks will be simple because those who possess economic power often possess political influence as well. Indeed, the power of the purse seldom counts for much unless the power of the throne supports it.

Unequal access to factors of production is due in part to lack of mobility and information, and some progress could be achieved merely by improving transportation facilities, increasing the size and quality of the agricultural extension service, and broadcasting market information by radio. It is doubtful, however, that these changes would make a major difference. Something more radical is required.

In most poor countries of Asia, with the exception of Taiwan, government policy discriminates in favour of the large landlord. Exchange rates are overvalued and this reduces the local currency cost of imported equipment. In addition, foreign exchange licensing schemes often are designed specifically to encourage the 'modernization', i.e. mechanization, of agriculture. Government assisted or managed rural banks provide inexpensive credit to those who own large pieces of land. Training centres for tractor drivers and mechanics are financed by government. Fertilizers, weedicides and insecticides are subsidized, and diesel fuel and electricity often are as well. Irrigation facilities, dams and tubewells, are financed from general tax revenues and the water is distributed free of charge or at negligible cost to large landowners. Finally, the price of foodgrains often is supported; in fact, in several countries local prices of rice and wheat have been approximately 50 per cent above world prices.[45]

All these policies are landlord-biased. They encourage capital intensive methods of production by a minority of cultivators, by subsidizing inputs, and they give an additional bonus to those who sell a large proportion of their output, by subsidizing final prices. If governments wish to reverse the

[45] The introduction of high yielding varieties of foodgrains should result in a fall in local prices. If governments try to maintain the historical price, this is, in effect, a subsidy. In other words, if costs of production are declining, a subsidy may be introduced, not by raising commodity prices, but by not allowing them to fall.

trend toward greater inequality, they must reverse the policies which promote it.

This is easier said than done. Policy discriminates in favour of some groups and against others, not because governments are ignorant, but because in practice, with the exception of Sri Lanka, political leaders have given low priority to reducing inequality. Governments may claim to rule in the 'national interest', but in reality they act in behalf of their supporters. Prominent among the supporters on most Asian countries are large landowners and other men of property. Exchange rate policy, or credit policy or the pricing policy for agro-chemicals are not just technical matters to be resolved by referring to the rules for efficient resource allocation. They are the instruments by which those who hold political power channel scarce resources to themselves, and it is precisely because of this that one cannot change price policies without first reducing the political influence of those who benefit from these policies.

Where political influence is based on the concentration of property in a few hands, the expropriation of land is almost certain to be a *sine qua non*. The economic and political power of landowners must be reduced if one wishes to increase rapidly the well-being of the rural poor, and the only way this can be done is through a land reform.[46] The purpose of a land reform is not only to remove the most important source of market power, but also to create political conditions in which rural institutions can be totally

---

[46] This, of course, will not be easy, especially for 'reformist' and vaguely 'liberal' governments. Landowners can be expected to try to evade land reform measures, and at times their manoeuvres may become comical — as the attempts to escape the legislation on land ceilings in India demonstrates. 'In Punjab, for instance, the transfer of land in 1971 and early 1972 actually reached such proportions that the Chief Minister is reported to have complained that cases had come to his notice that some landowners had transferred land in the name of their dogs to avoid the ceiling. Apocryphal though it may seem, it was not apocryphal in West Bengal when some horses served the purpose.' (Wolf Ladejinsky, 'New Ceiling Round and Implementation Prospects', *Economic and Political Weekly*, 30 September 1972, p. A-128.)

transformed and factor markets reorganized. Once all cultivators are given equal access to the means of production,
inequality will diminish and output probably will increase,
the trend toward the destruction of the peasantry and the
polarization of the community into two social classes will be
retarded, and a foundation will have been laid on which a
participatory democracy can be built.

APPENDIX: SHARECROPPING AND TECHNICAL CHANGE[1]

Economists have long been interested in the effects of land
tenure on agricultural innovation. There in a strong tradition,
at least within the Anglo-Saxon literature, in favour of the
owner-operated farm and opposed to tenant farming, particularly sharecropping. Two hundred years ago Adam Smith
condemned sharecropping, or the continental European
metayer system, in the following words: 'It could *never* . . .
be the interest [of metayers] . . . to lay out, in the further
improvement of the land, any part of the little stock which
they might save from their own share of the produce, because
the lord, who laid out nothing, was to get one-half of
whatever it produced.'[2]

Smith's view that the share tenancy system was absolutely
unprogressive was modified by subsequent analysis which
attempted to show that incentives to innovate under a
sharecropping system are defective but not totally absent.
The opinion which today is perhaps most widely accepted is
well expressed by Alfred Marshall who claimed that a tenant
would not innovate unless the gross revenue on his outlay
was a multiple of his marginal expenditure. 'For, when the
cultivator has to give to his landlord half of the returns to
each dose of capital and labour that he applies to the land, i
will not be to his interest to apply any doses the total return
of which is less than twice enough to reward him.'[3]

A distinguishing feature of the Smith-Marshall model o

---

[1] This appendix was written jointly with Robert Mabro.
[2] Adam Smith, *The Wealth of Nations*, Modern Library edition, p. 36?
(Emphasis added.)
[3] Alfred Marshall, *Principles of Economics*, 8th ed., Macmillan, 1948
p. 644.

sharecropping is that the decision as to whether or not to invest and innovate is taken by the tenant, not by the landowner. In this model the landlord is passive, a sleeping partner, a pure *rentier*, while the tenant exercises the role of decision maker. Recently, an alternative model has been presented by Amit Bhaduri[4] in which the roles played by the sharecropper (or *kishan* in Bhaduri's terminology) and landlord (or *jotedar*) are reversed: the *jotedar* is the active agent, in the sense that it is he who decides whether or not to innovate, while the *kishan* remains passive, becoming little more than an agricultural labourer paid in kind. Despite the reversal of roles, Bhaduri argues that the sharecropping system, at least as he observed it in West Bengal, is an obstacle to technical change. This conclusion is sufficiently novel and important to merit discussion.

Bhaduri describes the agrarian system of West Bengal as 'semi-feudal' and in this respect he differs from us, since we believe the agricultural systems in most parts of the Third World are essentially capitalist. On the basis of a formal, mathematical model Bhaduri concludes that 'semi-feudal production relations operate as a barrier to the introduction of improved technology'.[5] That is, 'the level of technological improvement ... is constrained in order to ensure the persistence of semi-feudal production relations'.[6] This occurs because 'it is quite probable that they [i.e. semi-feudal landowners] will try to restrict the level of technological improvement'.[7]

Bhaduri's model is based on three key assumptions. First, the *jotedar's* income is derived from a combination of land rent and interest on consumption loans to his *kishans*. Next, the *jotedar* obtains a usurious return on his loans to tenants, yet the income from an alternative use of his capital 'is probably quantitatively insignificant'[8] and can be disregarded. Lastly, the share of the harvest received by the *kishan* is constant and is fixed by law.

---

[4] 'A Study in Agricultural Backwardness under Semi-Feudalism', *Economic Journal*, March 1973.
[5] Ibid., p. 136.
[6] Ibid., p. 130.
[7] Ibid.
[8] Ibid., p. 131n.

It follows from the third assumption that any technical innovation that raises net output must also raise the income of the *kishan* and reduce his dependence on the landowner for consumption loans. It is possible, therefore, given the first two assumptions, that the gain to the landowner from a higher output would be more than offset by diminished income from usury. In such cases no innovation would occur.

The third assumption, viz., that the shares received by the tenant and landowners are constant, is similar to that of Smith and Marshall and is the linchpin of Bhaduri's model of sharecropping. Apparently this share is determined independently of economic forces 'on some legally stipulated basis'.[9] As soon as one examines this assumption carefully, however, his thesis begins to crumble.

Tenurial or contractual arrangements are likely to adjust whenever profitable investment opportunities emerge. To ignore this possibility merely by assuming the law dictates constant shares is unconvincing. In the first place, such laws exist in relatively few countries. Moreover, in countries where they do exist, they are of relatively recent origin and thus cannot account for 'the prevailing backwardness'[10] of Asian agriculture. Third, as Bhaduri knows, 'the tenancy system is usually an enormously complicated one'.[11] The distribution of net output between landlord and tenant can be altered in a variety of ways and laws generally fail to impose restrictions on all of them. It is very difficult to draft comprehensive legislation that is enforceable. Lastly, many if not most governments make little attempt to enforce such legislation.

There are several ways in which landlord-tenant relations can adjust to permit the introduction of a more productive technology, some of which are noted by Bhaduri in his final paragraph. For instance, the landowner could dismiss his tenants and cultivate the land with hired labour, paying a market determined wage rate in cash or kind. This would constitute a change in the tenurial system. Alternatively, the landlord could alter the terms of his tenant's contract while

[9] Ibid., p. 121.
[10] Ibid., p. 120.
[11] Ibid.

keeping the sharecropping system intact. One way of doing this would be by requiring the *kishan* to supply a larger proportion of non-land inputs; another way would be to reduce the size of the plot given free to the *kishan* for his own cultivation, in regions where this system prevails. The landlord could effectively reduce the tenant's share in the net harvest by asking for gifts in kind or key money when contracts come up for renewal. These latter methods were practised in Egypt and parts of India and are open to the landlord when the laws are not well enforced and when they do not stipulate perpetual tenure.

If Bhaduri had incorporated into his model the existence of a pool of wage labourers he would have had to relax the rigidity of his assumptions on the share received by tenants. He neglected wage labourers despite the fact that in some of the villages he studied they constitute up to 20 per cent of the peasantry. The wage earnings of these labourers presumably are determined by the usual forces of supply and demand, taking into account population density and any monopsonistic power the larger landowners may possess. The existence of this pool, given that the *jotedars* have the option of cultivating their land either directly or with tenants, exerts pressures which tend to push, in one way or another, the earnings of the *kishans* towards rough equality with those of wage labourers. In other words, even if the share of the harvest due to tenants appears to be an exogenous constant determined by law or tradition, the actual distribution of net output tends to behave as an endogenous variable determined by the wage rate, the price of paddy and output per *kishan* under different techniques.

The scope of evading a legally fixed share of the harvest to be received by the tenant is virtually unlimited. This share (call it α) is, after all, a percentage. But of what is it a percentage? Is it a percentage of the gross harvest or the net? If the latter, what input costs are deducted – interest, the cost of fertilizer, the cost of other material inputs? Are some or all of these costs deducted before or after the division of the harvest? If there is more than one harvest in a year, does α apply to the second and subsequent crops, including livestock grazing on cereal stubble? The list of such questions is practically endless and the answer to each affects the tenant's income. To a casual observer α may have appeared constant since the beginning of time, but the base to which the percentage is applied varies readily.

Moreover, as we have indicated, the landowner has the option of abandoning sharecropping entirely if he thinks it in his interest to do so. It is impossible to believe (a) that sharecropping is imposed on the landowner against his will, and (b) that α is fixed and enforceable by law and that (c) the base to which α applies is immutable. Yet unless one accepts all three of these assumptions it cannot be shown that existing agrarian systems in Asia prevent the introduction of technical change.

The variability of a tenant's income is enormous. Consider a very simple arithmetic model. Assume there are only two non-labour variable inputs (fertilizer and tractor time) and that the tenant borrows nothing from the landowner. Assume also that α is legally fixed equal to 0.5. Output and variable costs are as follows:

gross harvest   = Rs. 100
fertilizer cost =   10
tractor charges =   5
net harvest   =   85

Even with this simple model the income of the tenant may vary from Rs. 35 to Rs. 50, i.e. by 30 per cent, depending on who pays for fertilizer and the services of machines and whether costs are deducted before or after the division of the harvest. The five possibilities are set out below.

	Tenant's income
α (gross harvest)	= Rs. 50
α (gross harvest − fertilizer − tractor)	= 42.5
α (gross harvest − fertilizer) − tractor	= 40
α (gross harvest − tractor) − fertilizer	= 37.5
α (gross harvest) − fertilizer − tractor	= 35

In other words, even under sharecropping with a constant α, the landowner has considerable flexibility so long as he is able to vary the base to which α applies. Once it is accepted that harvest shares can adjust, either by changing α or the base, it becomes evident that the *jotedar* will encounter no obstacle to introducing technical changes.

The other assumptions of Bhaduri's model call for some qualifications too. First, as the author himself recognizes, the fusing together of the roles of moneylender and landowner 'appears to be a rather special feature'[12] of the area he studied. In most parts of Asia agricultural credit is supplied from a variety of sources, not just one. Even if one ignores the commercial, cooperative and state-owned rural banks which have expanded considerably in the last twenty years, the credit market would still remain wider than Bhaduri suggests. The informal credit market often consists of relatives and friends, merchants and shopkeepers, specialist moneylenders and, of course, landowners. Moreover, evidence is accumulating which indicates that the degree of monopoly in the informal credit market is not as great as is commonly assumed.[13] To the extent that the landowner is not the *sole* supplier of credit, his control over his tenants is reduced. More important in the present context, if the *jotedar* supplies *no* credit to his tenants, the potential conflict between his role of moneylender and landowner disappears, and the analysis of innovation under sharecropping reverts essentially to that of Marshall.

Second, it seems a bit odd to assume that the opportunity cost of the *jotedar's* capital is zero while at the same time claiming that he often obtains 'a fantastically high rate of interest'[14] on loans to *kishans*. It may be true that interest on consumption loans is high, but experience in other parts of Asia suggests that loans for, say, rice processing, transport and storage can be very attractive.

Ironically, Bhaduri's example on page 123 of his article tends to weaken his case. He cites a *jotedar* who lends his

[12] Ibid., p. 122, n. 3.
[13] See, for example, M. Long, 'Interest Rates and the Structure of Agricultural Credit Markets', *Oxford Economic Papers*, July 1968; A. Bottomley, 'The Costs of Administering Private Loans in Underdeveloped Rural Areas', *Oxford Economic Papers*, July 1963; A. Bottomley, 'Monopoly Profit as a Determinant of Interest Rates in Underdeveloped Rural Areas', *Oxford Economic Papers*, October 1964.
[14] A. Bhaduri, op. cit., p. 123.

kishan one mound of rice with a market value of Rs. 60 and approximately four months later is repaid three mounds with a market value of Rs. 20 each. From the point of view of the *kishan*, who is assumed to live by rice alone, the own rate of interest is indeed 200% per harvest period. The *jotedar*, however, is not concerned with the own rate of interest but with the Rs. rate of interest — which in Bhaduri's example is zero per cent. It would appear that the landowner could have obtained Rs. 60 in cash, at no risk and without sacrificing liquidity, by selling one mound at the initial peak price; he gained nothing by lending to his *kishan*, yet incurred a risk of default. This hardly sounds like monopolistic exploitation or usury.

Bhaduri's conclusion about the innovativeness of *jotedars* is highly dependent upon his assumptions about the credit market. In so far as landlords do not receive a usurious return on loans to tenants or are able to find alternative uses for their funds which yield high returns, agricultural innovation will not be inhibited by the lending activities of *jotedars*.

At one point Bhaduri seems to suggest that profitability may not be very relevant to the landlord's decision after all. He argues that even if a technical innovation is clearly profitable to the *jotedar* he may refrain from introducing it because 'it makes the *kishan* free from perpetual debt and destroys the political and economic control of the landowner over his *kishan*'.[15]

Given the primitive agricultural technology employed, the resulting low surplus above starvation per tenant household, and the fact that the *jotedar* 'usually has only a few *kishans* working for him',[16] it is likely that many landowners are far from wealthy. This being so, the price of political dominance is rather high, viz. continued stagnation at a low level of material wellbeing of the landowning class. Perhaps the 'psychic income' from dominance and political control is sufficient to compensate the *jotedars* for the failure of their standard of living to increase, but Bhaduri provides no

[15] A. Bhaduri, op. cit., p. 136.
[16] Ibid., p. 131n.

explanation why this should be true in West Bengal or, for that matter, anywhere else.

It is unclear why landowners should be willing to forgo economic benefits for 'economic control' over their *kishans* in places like West Bengal where labour is not in short supply. Because of population pressures, there tends to be more competition between landless labourers for the tenancy of land than between landlords for the services of labour. The *jotedar* would have no difficulty replacing a *kishan* who chose to leave. Tying labour to the land carries little economic advantage in these circumstances. Indeed, most economists would hold that tenants have a strong interest in security of tenure, not landlords — a fact which land reform laws in many countries seem to recognize in their regulations of the length of tenancy contracts. Perhaps Bhaduri misinterpreted his observations of the Indian villages for it is possible that his *jotedars* are not seeking to tie their tenants to the land for 'economic control' but are themselves tied to the *kishan* because of his historical indebtedness.

Our view is that by introducing technical innovations the landowning class may increase their dominance, not diminish it. If Bhaduri's assumptions are relaxed, a large share of the rise in output per man-day will accrue to the landlord where labour is in abundant supply. Income inequality is likely to increase. Landlords would grow richer both in absolute terms and vis-à-vis the landless population. They need not forgo opportunities for improvements in order to retain either economic or political control, which their increased wealth will in any case enhance.

Our remarks have focused on Bhaduri's theory, not on facts. Before concluding this appendix, however, it is worth recalling that there in considerable empirical evidence from all over Asia which is difficult to reconcile with Bhaduri's model yet is quite consistent with the alternative view we have put forward. This evidence does not suggest that the existing agrarian systems are incapable of change or that landowners lack an incentive to change; the evidence does suggest, however, that if technical changes are introduced they may have far reaching effects on the system of land tenure and income distribution. Some of the data from the large number of Asian case studies and sample surveys concerned with agricultural innovation have been cited in previous chapters. All that need be done here is to refer briefly to research conducted in India.

Most observers of recent technical innovations in India have concluded that the benefits of the green revolution have been captured by the 'kulaks'.[17] There is no evidence that the larger farmers as a class have encountered obstacles to introducing new technology. On the contrary, the larger farmers — because of preferential access to the means of production — have been quicker to innovate than the smaller. A statistical analysis by Lockwood, Mukherjee and Shand of data from many districts in India discovered a strong association between the proportion of farmers adopting high yielding varieties of wheat and rice and the size of farm.[18] This finding has been supported by numerous locality and regional studies. In some cases the large farmers have ejected their tenants and begun farming with wage labour.[19] In other cases the landowners have retained the sharecropping system and have simply reduced the share received by the tenant.[20] Evidently, either contracts have been revised or the tenure system has been changed whenever landowners found it in their interest to do so. Finally, technological change in Indian agriculture has strengthened the political dominance of land-owners[21] and accentuated income inequality;[22] in some

[17] See John P. Lewis, 'Wanted in India: A Relevant Radicalism', *Economic and Political Weekly*, Special Number, July 1970, pp. 1219–1220.
[18] Brian Lockwood, P. K. Mukherjee and R. T. Shand, *The High Yielding Varieties Programme in India*, Part 1, Programme Evaluation Organization, Planning Commission of India and Department of Economics, Australian National University, 1971, p. 88.
[19] See Ashok Rudra, 'The Green and Greedy Revolution', *South Asian Review*, July 1971; Wolf Ladejinsky, 'Green Revolution in Bihar — The Kosi Area: A Field Trip', *Economic and Political Weekly*, 27 September 1969.
[20] Wolf Ladejinsky, 'The Green Revolution in Punjab: A Field Trip', *Economic and Political Weekly*, 28 June 1969; S. Sengupta and M. G. Ghosh, 'H.Y.V.P. for Rice: Performance in a Bengal District', *Economic and Political Weekly*, 26 October 1968; Ashok Rudra, *op. cit.*

areas a combination of rapid demographic increase, slow growth of non-agricultural employment opportunities and agricultural innovation biased against labour may have resulted in a deterioration of the standard of living of the mass of the rural population.[23]

Let us recall that Bhaduri's *jotedars* appear to be rather small landowners and that the credit market in the villages he observed was poorly developed. Is it not possible, given the evidence mentioned above from other parts of India, that the access of his *jotedars* to an improved and more profitable technology was itself limited or restricted? The stagnation of agriculture and the persistence of a 'semi-feudal' system in West Bengal may be due not to the landowner's reluctance but to their inability to innovate. Bhaduri, in other words, may have provided a wrong explanation of a phenomenon whose causes lie elsewhere.

In our view the problem in India and in other agrarian economies is not that some types of tenure systems are inflexible and inhibit innovation but that as long as the ownership of land is unequally distributed, and access to investment opportunities restricted, the benefits of whatever innovation does occur will be captured largely by the more prosperous classes.

---

[21] F. R. Frankel, *India's Green Revolution: Economic Gains and Political Costs.*
[22] T. J. Byres, 'The Dialectic of India's Green Revolution', *South Asian Review*, January 1972.
[23] See, for example, T. Scarlett Epstein, *South India: Yesterday, Today and Tomorrow*, London: Macmillan, 1973.

CHAPTER 4

Resource Allocation and Size of Farm in Mexico and Colombia

The analysis of the previous two chapters was illustrated largely with data obtained from the rice growing regions of monsoon Asia. The analysis itself, however, is quite general and in no way is limited to any particular crop or region. In fact, the analysis may be even more applicable in Latin America, where the concentration of economic and political power is greater than in Asia and the disequilibrium in factor markets is substantially more acute.

There is no need to repeat our argument in detail, but it may be helpful to provide some empirical evidence from two non-Asian nations in order to demonstrate the relevance of our approach in a different context. Fortunately, there is available considerable literature on Mexico as well as a comprehensive study of agricultural mechanization in Colombia which contain a great deal of quantitative material upon which we can draw. The author of the Colombia study, Wayne Thirsk, explores an hypothesis that is identical to our own, namely, that 'dualism is a species of distortion ... arising from the unequal terms on which resources such as foreign exchange, labour, capital and public services are made available to large and small scale production units in the agricultural sector'.[1]

[1] Wayne Thirsk, *The Economics of Farm Mechanization in Colombian Development*, Draft Ph.D. thesis for Yale University, Chapter III, p. 4. I am very grateful to Mr. Thirsk for allowing me to cite material from the draft of his thesis.

Table 4.1

Percentage Distribution of the Rural Population in Mexico

	Landless Peasants	Private Landowners	Ejidatarios
1930	68	17	15
1940	36	32	32
1950	43	28	29
1960	53	22	25

Source: R. Stavenhagen, 'Aspectos Sociales de la Estructura Agraria en Mexico', in *Neolatifundismo y Explotacion*, Nuestro Tiempo, Mexico, 1968, p. 13.

The experience of post-revolutionary Mexico

Mexico is of considerable interest both because it has succeeded in achieving a fairly rapid growth of agricultural output over quite a long period and because several decades ago it introduced radical land reform measures. The land reform had three major effects. First, it enabled a majority of the rural labour force in Mexico to have access to land and to improve the material basis of their livelihood. Between 1930 and 1940 the proportion of the rural population represented by landless peasants declined from 68 to 36 per cent. Second, in creating the *ejido*, the land reform destroyed the hegemony of private property and transferred a significant proportion of the agricultural terrain from private to collective (village) ownership.[2] By 1940 nearly a third of the rural population consisted of *ejidatarios*. Third, the land reform abolished the latifundia system, in which the profitability of farming depended upon monoply of land and exploitation of labour, and created instead a large commercial sector in which the profitability of farming depends upon access to capital — especially irrigation facilities, tractors and combine harvesters.

In the post-reform period it is the commercial sector which has achieved ascendancy. The proportion of landlessness has sharply increased since its low point around 1940; the *ejidos*

[2] Although the land was collectively owned by the village, it was farmed collectively only in a minority of cases.

provide a livelihood for a diminishing fraction of the population; and the concentration of land in private hands has increased, as the fall in the proportionate number of private landowners suggest. These trends were not inevitable; they are a product of policy, not fate. Moreover, the policies which channeled capital to the large commercial farms, and which have been so widely applauded for having accelerated the growth of output, are responsible for creating agricultural dualism, increased income inequality and allocative inefficiency.

The data in Table 4.2 describe the distribution of land, labour and capital among the *ejidos*, small private farms (mostly minifundia) and the large private farms (which because of data limitations have had to be defined as farms

Table 4.2
Factor Productivity and the Distribution of Resources in Mexican Agriculture, 1960

	Large Private farms	Small Private farms	Ejidos
Percentage distribution of primary resources			
land	63	3	34
labour	28	27	45
capital	69	5	26
Percentage distribution of output	57	8	35
Relative average factor productivity			
land	.88	2.60	1.00
labour	2.60	.38	1.00
capital	.61	1.19	1.00

Sources: Distribution of land and output: Salomon Eckstein, *El Marco Macroeconomico del Problema Agrario Mexicano*, CIDA, January 1969, Table B-26; distribution of population: *Population Census 1960*; distribution of capital courtesy of Miss Sofia Mendez.
Note: Large farms are defined as those with more than 5 ha., while small farms have less than 5 ha.

larger than 5 hectares). The bottom half of the table contains
calculations of relative average factor productivities on the
three types of farms. It is clear from the table that the large
farms are characterized by relatively high productivity of
labour and low productivity of land and, especially, capital.
A remarkable feature of the contemporary Mexican agricultural system is that despite the fact that capital and new
technology, particularly the high yielding varieties of wheat,
have been concentrated on the large commercial farms, yields
on these farms are 12 per cent lower than yields on the *ejidos*
and only a third as high as yields on the minifundia. Thus
neither in terms of equity nor efficiency can the agricultural
development strategy of the country be deemed a success.[3]

Inequality and technology in Colombia
Recent research on the distribution of income in Colombia
indicates that inequality in both the rural and urban areas is

Table 4.3
The Distribution of Personal Income in Colombia

Percent of persons	Agricultural income, 1960 (percentage)	Urban income, 1964 (percentage)
0–60	21	17
60–70	6	9
70–80	8	11
80–90	13	16
90–100	52	47

Source: R. A. Berry, 'Land Distribution, Income Distribution and the
Productive Efficiency of Colombian Agriculture', Economic Growth
Center, Yale University, Discussion Paper No. 108, 20 March 1971,
p. 6; M. Urrutia and C. Villalba, 'La Distribucion del Ingreso Urbano
para Colombia en 1964', *Revista del Banco de la Republica*, September
1969.

[3] For additional material on Mexico see Clark Reynolds, *The Mexican
Economy*, Yale University Press, 1970; Folke Dovring, 'Land Reform
and Productivity in Mexico', *Land Economics*, August 1970; Donald
Freebairn, 'The Dichotomy of Prosperity and Poverty in Mexican
Agriculture', *Land Economics*, February 1968.

unusually great even by the standards of underdeveloped countries. In contrast to most of Asia, however, the rich in rural areas of Colombia have a larger share of income than their urban counterparts: the top ten per cent of persons in agriculture receive 52 per cent of the sector's income whereas the top 10 per cent in urban centres receive 47 per cent of the income. The reason for this is that the middle class in agriculture is relatively small compared to the urban middle class: those between the sixth and ninth deciles receive only 27 per cent of the income in agriculture and 36 per cent of the income in urban areas.

As one would expect, the unequal distribution of income in agriculture is associated with an unequal distribution of the ownership of land. The data in Table 4.4 indicate that nearly thirteen per cent of those engaged in agriculture own no land. Roughly another 56 per cent own farms which the Inter-American Committee for Agricultural Development (CIDA) considers to be too small to enable a family to satisfy its minimum needs and productively employ the labour of the household throughout the year. This bottom 69 per cent of the rural population owns less than six per cent of the land. Family sized farms account for a bit more than a quarter of the population and a bit less than a quarter of the land. Owners of these properties correspond to the rural middle class, i.e. those who fall approximately within the sixth to ninth deciles of the income distribution presented in Table 4.3. Next come the medium and large multi-family

Table 4.4

The Distribution of Land Among the Agricultural Population of Colombia, 1960

Tenure category	Percent of rural households	Percent of area owned
Landless workers	12.8	0.0
Sub-family farms	55.8	5.5
Family farms	26.3	24.5
Medium Multi-family farms	4.0	25.1
Large Multi-family farms	1.1	44.9

Source: CIDA, *Tenencia de la Tierra y Desarrollo Socio-Economico del Sector Agricola en Colombia*, pp. 72 and 133.

sized farms[4] which between them account for five per cent of the rural households and seventy per cent of the land. It is the owners of these farms who receive a very large share of all the income generated in the agricultural sector.[5]

In countries like Colombia where the concentration of land in a few hands is very great, we should anticipate considerable disequilibrium in factor markets. In particular, the implicit price of land relative to labour should be low for large landowners and high for small cultivators, with family sized farms falling somewhere in between the extremes. These differences in relative factor prices, in turn, should lead to differences in methods of cultivation. Specifically, we would expect that the man-land ratio would fall as the size of farm increases, and indeed this is exactly what the data do show.

If one considers Colombia as a whole, ignoring regional variations and any differences that may exist in the quality of land among different sizes of farms,[6] it is quite clear that the minifundia are much more labour intensive than the latifundia. The smallest farms, i.e. those less than half an hectare, require only 0.34 hectares to provide employment

[4] Both types of farms require more labour than can be provided from within the family. The latter, however, requires an elaborate organization of the labour force, with work-gangs, foremen, supervisors, etc., whereas the former does not. The large multi-family farms provide employment for more than 12 man-years, whereas the medium multi-family farms generate 4—12 man-years of employment.

[5] Roger E. Soles has estimated the extent of land concentration in various 'departments' of Colombia and is reported to have discovered 'a relationship between the degree of concentration of land ownership and the number of rural land invasions. . . .' In seven 'Non-invasion Departments' Gini's coefficient of concentration was 0.79, whereas in seven 'Invasion Departments' the coefficient was 0.86. (Land Tenure Center, University of Wisconsin, *LTC Newsletter* No. 33, February—July 1971, p. 17 and the table on p. 20).

[6] Observation suggests that large farmers have the best land (the river valleys) as well as the worst (the barren terrain at the tops of mountains), while small farmers occupy the intermediate slopes. At present sufficient data are not available to construct an accurate index of land quality, although scholars like R. A. Berry have made valuable attempts to do so. Moreover, even if data were available, it is far from clear how one would distinguish between the 'original and indestructible quality of the soil' and the effects of subsequent investments and husbandry practices which improve the quality of the soil.

Table 4.5
Man-Land Ratios and Size of Farm in Colombia

Farm size (hectares)	Man-years per ha.
less than 0.5	2.71
0.5—1	1.01
1—2	.78
2—3	.54
3—4	.46
4—5	.37
5—10	.27
10—20	.17
20—30	.12
30—40	.098
40—50	.084
50—100	.059
100—200	.037
200—500	.024
500—1000	.017
1000—2500	.011
more than 2500	.0025

Source: R. A. Berry, *op. cit.*, Table A-2, p. 65. The original data were obtained from the 1960 agricultural census. No adjustments have been made in the Table for differences in relative land quality among different farm size classes.

for one man, while the farms larger than 2500 hectares require 400 ha. In other words, the man-land ratio is 1084 times larger on the smallest than on the largest properties! Moreover, the ratio varies inversely, and systematically, with farm size, as is evident from Table 4.5.

Factor prices and techniques of production
So far, we have presented the evidence on inequality and implied that inequality is responsible for the observed differences in agricultural technology. The link between inequality and technology is factor prices, and it is to this that we now turn.

Wayne Thirsk has studied a small sample of large crop and cattle farms in Valle and Meta, and small farms in Valle, Boyaca, Caldas and Meta. In Table 4.6 we reproduce some

Table 4.6

Characteristics of Small and Large Farms in Valle, Colombia

		Small farms	Large crop farms	Large cattle farms
1	Number of farms	30	28	20
2	Average size of farm (ha.)	3.1	377	848
3	Land rental per ha. (pesos)	1753	1460	1224.5
4	Daily wage rate paid to hired labour (pesos)	14	22	20
5	Man-days per ha.	261	55.2	19.3
6	Value of farm machinery per man-day (pesos)	2.36	41.7	20.1
7	Value of farm machinery per ha. (pesos)	617	2377.6	374
8	Value added per ha. (pesos)	7160	5017.4	1551.5
9	Value added per man-day (pesos)	27.42	90.0	80.2

Source: Wayne Thirsk, *op. cit.*, Chapter IV.

of his data from farms located in the province of Valle. The average size of his thirty small farms was 3.1 ha., while the large crop farms were 377 ha., and the cattle ranches were 848 ha. (line 2). The price of land and labour, as our hypotheses would predict, varies with the type of farm. The small farms pay 300 pesos more per ha. than the large crop farms and over 500 pesos more than the cattle farms (line 3).[7] Similarly, the wage rate for hired labour is 14 pesos per day on small farms and 20—22 pesos on large farms, a difference of about 50 per cent (line 4).[8] Thus relative factor

[7] It is possible that cattle ranches occupy land of lower quality than farms devoted to crop production and that this — rather than farm size — accounts for the difference in the price of land on large crop and cattle farms. On the other hand, a great deal of good crop land in the savanna of Bogotá has reverted from wheat to pasture in the last three years, in response to lower wheat prices resulting from large imports of P.L.480 wheat from the United States.

[8] Real wages in agriculture at the end of the 1960s were about the same as they were in the mid 1930s, when data were first collected. The peak was reached in 1962, and since then real wages have tended to drift downwards. (See R. A. Berry, *op. cit.*, p. 23).

prices encourage labour intensive techniques of production on small farms and land (and capital) intensive techniques on large farms.

Farmers do respond to differences in relative factor prices. The man-land ratio is nearly five times higher on the small farms than on the large crop farms and more than 13 times higher than on the cattle ranches (line 5). Conversely, the capital-labour ratio is substantially higher on the large farms (line 6), while the capital-land ratio is indeterminate, being smallest on the ranches and largest on the large crop farms (line 7). These are precisely the relative factor proportions that our theory led us to predict.[9] Given these differences in techniques of production, it follows almost automatically that net output per hectare will be lower on the large farms (line 8) and the productivity of labour will be lowest on the small farms (line 9). The data from Colombia, thus, are totally consistent with the hypotheses developed in the previous chapter and illustrated with information acquired in the rice growing regions of Asia.

[9] See Table 2.8 on p. 38.

PART TWO

The Disposal of Production

CHAPTER 5

The Marketable Surplus:
Origin and Destination

A. Introduction

The marketable surplus of agricultural commodities has been a topic of considerable interest to many economists and policymakers in underdeveloped countries. In several instances, in fact, it appears that agricultural policy has been more concerned with increasing the amount of food sold in the market than with augmenting the volume of food production. Why has this occurred? Why has the focus of attention, at least until recently, been on sales rather than output?

Part of this explanation is that in many economies, notably in Africa, it is easier to obtain accurate information on the quantity sold than on the quantity produced, and sales are used merely as a proxy — often a poor one — for output. In other countries the government may be anxious to alleviate balance of payments difficulties and may attempt to do this, as in Burma, by inducing or forcing the peasantry to sell a larger proportion of a stagnant output. In most countries, however, governments have been preoccupied with increasing the marketable surplus because this is an integral part of the mechanism by which resources are transferred from rural to urban industrial areas.

In many poor regions of the world the organization of the agricultural sector and the thrust of development policy have combined to favour the urban population in general and the growth of industry in particular. That is, institutions and policy have been biased against agriculture. An effect of this bias has been to compel the peasantry to supply wage goods, specifically foodgrains, at a low price and thereby help to

103

keep urban money wages low and profits high. In other words, there has been an unequal exchange of food for industrial goods and inhabitants of rural areas have been squeezed in order to promote manufacturing. One aspect of this squeeze is the low price of foodgrains relative to industrial goods. Another aspect is the relatively high real wage and rate of profit in manufacturing compared to the low rate of return to the efforts of the peasantry. The marketing system is the channel through which resources released by the squeeze flow to urban areas, but the marketing system is not primarily responsible for the squeeze. This is not to say that the marketing system does not suffer from serious deficiencies — clearly, it frequently does, but the defects of the marketing system are not the fundamental cause of the relative poverty and inequality of rural areas. Too often the penury of the peasantry has been attributed to exploitative and monopolistic middlemen and moneylenders, with whom the peasants are in immediate contact, when the responsibility really lies elsewhere.

B. Transfer Mechanisms

It is well known that sustained growth of output requires a continuous process of capital accumulation, and in the absence of gifts from abroad this is impossible unless the population as a whole refrains from the immediate consumption of all that the economy produces. That is, growth requires net savings. Of course the consumption of some individuals may be restrained more than that of others, and investment in some sectors may be greater than that in others. Historically, in fact, it has usually been the rural population which has had to restrain its consumption and bear the burden of savings, while it has been the industrial sector which has enjoyed most of the benefits of capital accumulation. In other words, particularly in the early stages, growth has been associated historically with a shift of investible resources from agriculture to industry. This shift of resources cannot occur unless the rural areas produce a surplus and either voluntarily or by compulsion dispose of it in either urban or foreign markets. The size and destination of the marketable agricultural surplus are major determinants of the pace and pattern of development.

There are three basic methods by which resources can be transferred from agriculture to the other sectors of the economy, notably to industry and the government. The first relies on voluntary transfers through the market system, that is, on unforced monetary savings by landowners and culti- vators. Rural savings are invested in urban industry presum- ably because the rate of return on capital is higher in urban areas than in the countryside. The second method supple- ments voluntary savings with indirect government controls which alter free market relationships essentially by turning the terms of trade against agriculture. The third involves direct intervention by the government through the use of quotas, taxation in kind, compulsory delivery schemes and other direct controls. In East Java, for instance, as much as 30 per cent of the land is required by government edict to be devoted to sugarcane — which the government purchases at fixed, low prices. The three methods are not mutually exclusive, and one encounters different combinations of voluntary savings, indirect and direct controls in different countries.

Free market transfers
The most important source of a marketable surplus in capitalist economies is voluntary sales of agricultural com- modities by producers and landowners in a market free of government intervention. When agricultural sales are greater than the purchases by the agricultural sector of consumption and investment goods, the marketable surplus is accompanied by a net transfer of resources out of agriculture. In other words, a net transfer will occur via a free market when three conditions are satisfied. First, the agricultural sector must sell part of its production to other sectors, i.e. there must be a marketable surplus. Second, the agricultural sector must consume less than its total income, i.e. there must be net savings by the sector. Finally, investment in agriculture must be less than savings by agriculture. If these three conditions are satisfied, agriculture will have a 'balance of payments' surplus with the rest of the economy and will accumulate real and financial urban assets (including money).

If the agricultural areas of underdeveloped countries were populated by stereotyped subsistence farmers producing exclusively for household consumption, there would be neither a marketable surplus nor a resource transfer. The conventional model of subsistence agriculture, however, fails to capture an essential feature of the rural economy of many countries — its domination by powerful landowners. In the tenant farming communities of Asia as well as on the latifundia of Latin America, the landlord is the key figure in the marketing and resource transfer systems. Through his control of the land he is able to appropriate the agricultural surplus and sell it to the towns. Furthermore, his landed wealth enables him to amass a large income and save substantial amounts (even if these savings are only a small proportion of total income). Equally important, his connections with the city enable him to transfer his savings to urban investments easily and relatively efficiently. Thus a single individual — the landlord — by virtue of the fact that he controls the major source of income, is able to generate a marketable surplus and enforce a net resource transfer from agriculture.

Recent research in India, for example, has shown that the proportion of agricultural output disposed of via the market rises steadily with increasing size of holding. At one extreme, farms of 2.5 acres or less sell, on average, 24.5 per cent of their production. These holdings account for 48.2 per cent of the rural population but only 9.6 per cent of the output and 6 per cent of the marketable surplus. At the other extreme, holdings of 50 acres or more sell 65.4 per cent of their output. These large holdings are responsible for 15.9 per cent of the marketable surplus yet account for only 1.2 per cent of the rural population and 9.5 per cent of the agricultural output. More generally, 7 per cent of the rural population, with holdings of 20 acres or more, is responsible for over 45 per cent of the marketable surplus.[1] Evidently, the concen-

[1] The data in this paragraph were obtained from Utsa Patnaik, *The Organisational Basis of Indian Agriculture with Special Reference to the Development of Capitalist Farming (i.e. Based on Wage Labour and Following Economic Criteria for Investment) in Selected Regions in Recent Years*, Oxford D. Phil. thesis, 1972, Tables 4.1 and 4.9, pp. 140 and 147 respectively.

tration of land in India plays an important role in transferring agricultural commodities from rural areas.

In some countries, however, e.g. Indonesia and Taiwan, landlords no longer occupy a dominant position in agriculture. When this occurs, one of two things usually follows: either the peasants consume most of what they produce and the marketable surplus declines or the bureaucracy (i.e. the government) replaces the landlord and appropriates the surplus by substituting taxes for rents. Indonesia, for instance, is a large net importer of rice. The rice sector has a small marketable surplus and the main source of the resource transfer from agriculture is not rice farmers on Java but the state owned plantations on Sumatra. Taiwan, in contrast, is self-sufficient in rice and even exports small quantities. Government controls, described below, ensure that paddy is cultivated and that a large proportion is available for urban consumption.

The marketable surplus and the associated resource transfer pass through a rather complicated marketing system, at each stage of which an intermediary makes a profit. We shall argue below, however, that particularly in a landlord dominated system, the profits of intermediaries usually are rather low;[2] the real squeeze on the peasantry occurs when the harvest is divided between the landowners and his tenant-labourers. This can be illustrated by considering the marketing system for rice.

In a typical rice producing region of Asia the tenant farmer and landless labourers will receive roughly half of the gross output of paddy. A large fraction of the peasants' share, however, may be turned over immediately to the landlord in repayment of debt. In regions where landowners do not supply credit (in cash or in kind) to their tenants, the peasants may have to deliver part of their share of the harvest to local merchants and moneylenders as repayment of loans. Of the remainder, some of the paddy will be transformed in a small, local mill into rice for household consumption and

[2] This does not imply, of course, that intermediaries are poor. Some may have a small profit margin on a large turnover and earn a substantial income.

108

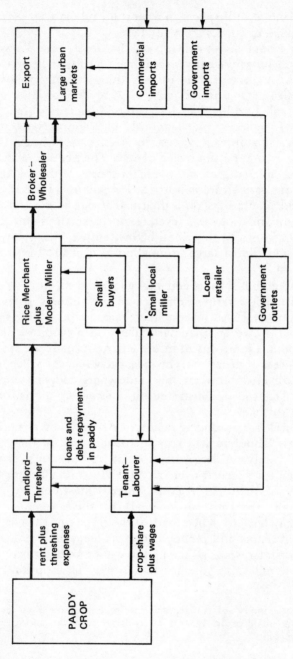

Figure 5.1. The Rice Marketing System

some will be sold to small buyers for cash. In many instances the amount of rice obtained by the tenant will be insufficient for the needs of his household and he will be compelled to obtain foodgrains either from local retail outlets or, in Sri Lanka and the Philippines, from the government under a rationing scheme. In India, Pakistan and Indonesia, for example, about a third of all farmers are net purchasers of foodgrains, and they finance these purchases by supplementing their income from farming with off-farm work.

The paddy obtained by the landlord and the owner of the threshing machine, who is often the same person in nations where large threshers are common, is sold to a rice merchant or miller. The mills may be in either the private or the public sector. The paddy is then transformed into rice and sold either to a local retailer or to a rice broker-wholesaler who supplies rice to large urban centres and for export. In some countries the government levies taxes in kind and part of the paddy (or rice) accumulated by the landlord would be paid directly to the government. The various flows of paddy and rice are presented in schematic form in the figure opposite.

The rice marketing system described in Figure 5.1 is rather abstract. It does not correspond to the system that prevails in any one country, but it does contain most of the features which characterize rice marketing in all of the countries where landlords are still dominant. In other countries, e.g. Taiwan, the absentee landlord class has been abolished and a new marketing system has been developed. In still other countries, e.g. Indonesia, part of the marketing system is nationalized. Despite the differences that exist between one country and another, however, there are certain basic features in common. First, a large proportion of the agricultural produce that ultimately reaches the urban and foreign markets originates with absentee landlords and the larger owner-operators. Second, most of the paddy that remains with the tenant after he has paid his debts and rent to the landlord is consumed by his household after being processed in a small, primitive mill. Third, a portion of the paddy which is sold by the tenant for cash is later re-purchased in the form of rice after it has passed through the hands of several small buyers, a miller and a retailer. The price of this rice frequently is a multiple of the price at which the paddy originally was sold.

In the table below we present the price of paddy and rice in different markets and in four different countries. In no country are the data complete, but one can obtain a composite picture of price relatives by studying the table as a whole. The Burmese data suggest that, at least in countries where rice is exported and taxed heavily, the export price of rice may be as much as 300 per cent higher than the price of paddy received by the producer. The data from Thailand give the same impression: the export price of high quality rice is about 240 per cent higher than the wholesale price of paddy. Part of this huge differential obviously is due to export taxes, but the data from South Vietnam and Thailand also indicate that the gross markup for milling is large, viz. about 50 per cent. Even this estimate, however, probably is too low, as we shall show below.

A more systematic presentation of the relative prices of paddy and rice in different markets is included in Table 5.2. Like the marketing system described in Figure 5.1, this is an

Table 5.1
The Price of Paddy and Rice in Various Markets in Various Countries (U.S. cents per kg.)

		Thailand	Burma	South Vietnam	U.A.R.
1	Producer price of paddy	n.a.	3.1	n.a.	7.3
2	Wholesale price of paddy	6.0	n.a.	19.0	n.a.
3	Wholesale price of milled rice	9.0	n.a.	26.6	12.9
4	Export price of milled rice	20.3	10.4—12.7	n.a.	n.a.

Source: FAO, *Production Yearbook 1970*, 1971.
Notes: *Thailand:* Wholesale price of milled rice refers to 15 per cent brokens while that of exports refers to 5—7 per cent brokens. The reference year is 1968.
Burma: The producer price is at the port. The lower export price is for the Sri Lanka market while the upper is for the Japanese market (15 per cent brokens). The reference year is 1965.
South Vietnam and U.A.R.: Data refer to 1969.

Table 5.2
Relative Prices of Paddy and Rice in Different Markets

Market	Price relative	Per cent markup
Paddy at farm gate	100	
Mill dry paddy at the mill	119	19
Milled rice ex-mill	214	80
Rice at the warehouse	229	7
Rice at a retail store in a major urban centre	261	14
Rice f.o.b. at the port for export	300	15

abstract scheme, and the figures correspond to no country in particular. They are not too dissimilar, however, to data published for Indonesia although Indonesia is not, of course, an exporter of rice.[3] Data from Senegal also suggest that the retail price of whole rice is about 120 per cent higher than the price of paddy received by the farmer. Thus the numbers in the table, although illustrative, are broadly consistent with what little we know about actual market prices.

In practice, of course, the margin between the different processing stages will vary, depending upon the distance of the farm from the mill and of the mill from the final market, the cost of transport, the mechanical efficiency of the transformation industry, the extent of competition and the level of taxation. In all countries, however, the markups for threshing, drying, transporting and retailing are relatively low. There is considerable ease of entry and exit into these activities and consequently the degree of monopoly is low. Threshing, for example, can be done by hand, and thus the cost of hired labour sets a ceiling on what the owner of a threshing machine can charge. Similarly, the main wet season crop usually can be dried out-of-doors, in the village square or on the public highway if necessary, and hence commercial driers can reap few monopoly rents. Again, paddy can be

[3] See Leon A. Mears and Saleh Afiff, 'An Operational Rice Price Policy for Indonesia', *Ekonomi dan Keuangan Indonesia*, XVII, 1969. Also see D. Usher, *The Price Mechanism and the Meaning of National Income Statistics*, Ch. 14 for a discussion of the chain of rice prices in Thailand.

transported by carrying-pole, water buffalo or bicycle, and this limits the price truck owners can obtain for their services. A perusal of the appendix, in which the machanics of rice processing are described, may help to dispel some of the myths about exploitative middlemen.[4]

It is often asserted that middlemen reap monopoly profits at the expense of the peasantry by purchasing the harvest at low prices and selling later at much higher prices. There is no empirical evidence, however, which supports this assertion. Indeed, on the contrary, what little evidence there is tends to support the opposite hypothesis. The cost of holding foodgrains is not cheap, and depends upon the amount of storage losses (from spoilage, theft and infestation by rats), the cost of insurance, the rate of interest and the cost of warehouse space. Research by Leon Mears in the Philippines suggests that seasonal variations in rice prices do not result in large profits for traders. Moreover, it does not pay the farmer to store grain himself. If he were to do so he probably would lose money. 'It is only when the farmer considers his own funds as having zero opportunity cost or can obtain an interest-free loan that his probability of loss would reach levels that might possibly be tolerable.'[5] Similarly, research by Uma Lele into the efficiency of jowar marketing in India indicates that the seasonal rise in prices was sufficient only to cover storage costs and risks; no monopoly profits were discovered.[6]

An examination of the data in Table 5.2 may lead many readers to suspect that monopoly profits are likely to arise at the milling stage. Large commercial rice mills, it could be argued, represent a substantial sum of capital and this in itself is likely to reduce entry into the industry. Moreover, the 80

[4] Also see Vernon W. Ruttan, 'Agricultural Product and Factor Markets in South east Asia', *Economic Development and Cultural Change*, July 1969.

[5] Leon A. Mears and Teresa L. Anden, 'Who benefits from the Post-Harvest Rice Price Rise?', Institute of Economic Development and Research, School of Economics, University of the Philippines, Discussion Paper No. 71–18, 6 September 1971, p. 19.

[6] See the contribution by Uma Lele to J. Mellor *et al.*, *Developing Rural India*.

per cent markup in the table may appear to be enormous and to include a large monopoly element. Such reasoning, however, probably is erroneous. In the first place, only a relatively small proportion of the rice crop is processed by commercial mills. In Indonesia, for example, it was estimated that in the period 1952—1967 about 85 per cent of the crop was hulled and milled by hand pounding; only 15 per cent of the crop was processed in commercial plants.[7] Thus it would appear unlikely that the six or seven hundred commercial plants could obtain monopoly profits while competing with the thousands of small household mortars and pestles. Secondly, the markup of 80 per cent is misleading. The conversion rate at the mill for transforming paddy into rice is about 66 per cent; the rest consists of husks (about 20 per cent), bran and polish, germ and foreign material. In other words, the price of paddy is low relative to the price of rice in part because much of the paddy consists of waste materials. The gross markup on the rice equivalent of paddy is less than 19 per cent.[8]

Thus even in the rice economies of monsoon Asia, where the price difference between paddy at the farm gate and rice at the retail store or port can be several hundred per cent, it does not appear that the major problem of the peasant is exploitation by monopolistic middlemen. This does not imply that moneylenders and merchants never have mono- poly power, but once the landlord has taken his share of the output there is relatively little left for the mass of inter- mediaries to exploit. The middlemen must be content with the crumbs left over from the landlord's bite. In other words, the peasantry is squeezed not by middlemen but by landowners — or, where they are absent, by government. It is the lack of access to land and other resources on the part of the peasantry, and the control of the major factors of

[7] Report to the Government of Indonesia, *The Rice Processing Industry*, FAO, No. TA 2617, 1969, p. 4.
[8] Using the data in Table 5.2, this is calculated as follows:

$$\frac{214 \times 0\cdot66}{119} - 1 = 0\cdot186$$

production by landowners, which enables the latter to appropriate the surplus and transfer it to urban areas.

This can be demonstrated in yet another way. So far we have looked at the problem from the point of view of the middlemen — and speculated about costs of processing and marketing, the ease of entry and degree of competition, etc. Let us now look at the problem from the point of view of the cultivator.

Consider an Indian tenant with 2 hectares of paddy land. Assume that his yield is 1610 kg. per ha. (the average for India in 1969) and that he shares the output equally with his landowner. The size of the tenant's household is, say, the equivalent of four adults, each of which consumes an average of 2000 calories per day. Thus the annual caloric needs of the household are 2.92 million calories (= 4 x 2000 x 365). A kilogram of milled rice has 3600 calories, and thus the household needs 811 kg. of rice to satisfy its basic subsistence needs. Assuming a rate of conversion at the mill of 65 per cent, this is equivalent to 1249 kg. of paddy.

In other words, once the tenant has paid his landlord and satisfied his physiological subsistence needs, there is only 361 kg. of paddy which is surplus to the tenant and which in principle could be extracted from him by exploitative middlemen. This exploitable surplus is equal to 11.2 per cent of the harvest. Thus even if the intermediaries succeeded in appropriating the entire marketable surplus of the tenant, which is most unlikely, they would collect little more than one-fifth as much paddy as the landlord. It is for this reason that we claim that the peasantry is squeezed not by middlemen but by landowners — or, where they are absent, by government tax collectors and other authorities who are anxious to maintain a transfer of resources from rural to urban areas.

The Latin American Case

The institutional arrangement by which this occurs varies from one country or region to another. In those parts of Asia where landlords are dominant they tend to break up their properties into small tenant farms. A similar pattern also has developed in parts of Latin America, a region where the concentration of land is particularly acute. An example which is typical of parts of Chile and much of western South America is presented in Table 5.3 below.

Table 5.3
Disposal of Production by a Typical Sharecropper, Coquimbo, Chile, 1955—56
(percentages)

	Payment to landowner	Household consumption	Market sales
Wheat	50	50	0
Maize	50	50	0
Alfalfa	50	50	0
Beans	50	50	0
Chickens	0	100	0
Goat meat	0	100	0
Hides	0	0	100
Goat's cheese	0	12	88
Total output	21	36	43

Source: Compiled from data in Andres Pascal, *Relaciones de Poder en una Localidad Rural*, 1968, Table 14, p. 103.

The sharecropper and landowner divide the crops equally. The landlord's share would be entirely marketed (presumably) while the share of the peasant is entirely consumed on the farm. Wheat, maize and beans are largely consumed by the peasant and his family, and the alfalfa is used to feed his donkey. The cash income of the peasant is derived exclusively from small scale production of livestock, notably goats. Twelve goats, i.e. an average of one a month, were slaughtered and their meat was consumed by the household; the skins were sold for cash. The main source of cash, however, was from the sale of goat's cheese, the product of a small cottage industry. Thirty-six chickens also were killed and consumed within the household.

The marketed surplus was equivalent to 64 per cent of the value of production. Two-thirds of this surplus originated from the sale of cheese and goat skins by the peasants. Half the value of crop production was placed on the market and over 74 per cent of livestock production was sold.

The question arises as to how much of the marketable surplus can be attributed to the institution of sharecropping. The answer depends upon the peasant's income elasticity of demand for home produced goods. If rents were suddenly abolished the peasant's income would rise by nearly 27 per cent. If his demand elasticity were zero, the marketed surplus would remain unchanged and sharecropping as such would have no effect on the quantity of production that is sold. Depending on the propensity to save of the peasant compared to that of the landlord, and of their relative preference for investing in urban and rural activities, the abolition of rents would alter the resource transfer from agriculture to industry but it would not reduce the marketable surplus. On the other hand, if the peasant's demand elasticity were positive, as is likely, the elimination of the landlord would certainly reduce the marketable surplus and almost certainly reduce the resource transfer as well. Suppose, for example, that the demand elasticity is equal to one. In this case the peasant would sell 54.4 per cent of the output belonging to his ex-landlord, i.e. the same proportion he sold of the output previously accruing to himself. The marketable surplus would then fall from 64 to 54.4 per cent, i.e. by 15 per cent. Moreover, ignoring taxation and assuming the peasant does not invest in urban assets, the net resource transfer would fall to zero — regardless of the propensity to save of the peasant. This is the real significance of the sharecropping system.

Results similar to those of a tenant system can be achieved through other institutional arrangements, however. In several parts of Latin America large properties are maintained intact and farmed as latifundia or large ranches. The landowners organize production themselves and directly appropriate the surplus. Part of the surplus is used to finance consumption and part is saved. Of the latter, a portion — perhaps a large portion — will be channeled into industrial activities, and this will be facilitated by the fact that many large landowners in Latin America also are large industrialists and financiers. The wealthy have diversified their assets and are able to reap a profit wherever attractive opportunities occur.

In parts of Latin America the latifundia are gradually being replaced by large, mechanized commercial farms. This process is especially noticeable in Mexico. In the northern part of the country commercial farms using hired labour occupy the rich irrigated land, while the majority of the rural population is confined to minifundia and ejidos. As a consequence, in Mexico 70.7 per cent of the farmers account for only 6.6 per cent of the marketable surplus, while at the other extreme, 55.4 per cent of the total value of marketed agricultural commodities is supplied by commercial farmers who represent only 1.9 per cent of the cultivators.[9]

In a study of 154 small maize farms in Puebla, Mexico it was discovered that the average annual cash income of each household was only $504. Moreover, 52.8 per cent of the farmers' cash income was obtained from off-farm work and from other non-farm income, such as cottage industry. Over 61 per cent of the maize farmers studied sold no maize at all and another 16 per cent of the farmers sold 25 per cent or less of their production. In other words, the marketable surplus of the bottom three-quarters of the farmers was negligible.

Regardless of whether the system of production in Latin America is based on sharecropping, extensive ranching or commercial farming, the implications are similar. In each of these three cases it is the control of the land by a minority which gives them control of the produce of the land. The concentration of output and income, in turn, results inevitably in a marketable surplus and creates the potential for a substantial transfer of resources from rural to urban areas. This resource transfer from agriculture occurs at the expense of the peasantry and for the benefit of landlords, industrialists and those urban workers who are employed in large enterprises. The conflict of interest between landlords and peasants is so acute that in many instances policies and economic changes which appear to benefit agriculture as a whole actually lead to a deterioration of the relative and even absolute position of those who own no land. For example, the introduction of food price supports would affect ad-

[9] Michel Gutelman, *Reforme et Mystification Agraires en Amérique Latine: Le Cas du Mexique*, p. 199.

versely the standard of living of the many peasants who are net buyers of food. Similarly, if the demand for food rises in the cities, this will lead to an increase in food prices which will be followed by a rise in land rents. The counterpart to a rise in rents will be an increase in the marketable surplus and a decline in the share of the crop received by the peasantry. This will occur whether rents are in cash or in kind and whether they are expressed as shares or fixed payments. Competition among tenants and would-be-tenants will ensure that the rise in the value of land will be to the sole benefit of the landowner. The standard of living of the peasantry will not decline — under assumptions of perfect competition it will remain unchanged — but the distribution of income will become worse, i.e. the relative position of the peasantry will decline. Conversely, if the landlord class is abolished and their property is distributed to the peasantry, the short-run consequences are likely to be a decline in the marketable surplus, a curtailment of the resource transfer from agriculture, a rise in urban food prices and a decline in the standard of living of the industrial proletariat.[10] It is no accident that peasant political movements seldom receive the support of the urban working class.

Controlled market transfers

The combination of a free market and concentration of land is sufficient to generate a marketable surplus in a capitalist economy, but this combination is not sufficient to ensure that there will be a net transfer of resources to urban areas. The landlords may save relatively little and invest little of their savings in urban activities. In order to make sure that not only the peasantry but also agriculture is squeezed, virtually all governments have intervened in the market mechanism and intentionally turned the terms of trade against agriculture.

This intervention has taken a variety of forms. In some countries agricultural exports are taxed, e.g. jute exports

[10] In the longer run, as we have argued elsewhere, a land reform is likely to lead to a more efficient allocation of resources in agriculture and an increase in production. During the transition period, however, output may actually fall.

from Bangladesh and rice exports from Thailand. In other countries, e.g. Burma, state export marketing boards have been used to tax agriculture. Similarly, tariffs and other trade restrictions have been used to protect domestic industry and raise the price of manufactured goods relative to the prices of agricultural commodities. Exchange rates frequently have been overvalued and therefore exports, which are usually agricultural products, have been penalized. Whatever the means, the terms of trade have been turned against agriculture to the benefit of the non-agricultural sectors, including government. Resources have been transferred from rural areas in the form of higher profits in industry and larger tax revenues for the government.

Massive evidence has accumulated that the resources thus transferred have not been used productively. First, a large proportion of the resource transfer has supplemented consumption rather than investment; the peasantry has been squeezed in order to raise the standard of living in urban areas rather than to accelerate the rate of investment. A study of Pakistan, for instance, suggested that the net resource transfer from agriculture was equivalent to 15 per cent or more of the value of the sector's output, and perhaps as much as 80 per cent of this transfer was channeled into urban consumption.[11] The government has used its increased resources to increase the number of civil servants and their salaries, to improve their living and working conditions (e.g. the construction of new administrative and housing centres in Islamabad, Pakistan, Quezon City, Philippines and in Brasilia), and to expand the armed forces. Industrialists have used part of their higher profits to build luxury houses, import air-conditioners, travel abroad and accumulate bank deposits in foreign havens. A minority of the urban labour force, particularly those employed in industries replacing imported manufactured goods, has also gained from the resource transfer in the form of higher wages, subsidized medical facilities and social security and retirement benefits.

Secondly, intervention through the market often has resulted in a set of relative factor and intermediate com-

[11] See Keith Griffin and Azizur Rahman Khan, eds., *Growth and Inequality in Pakistan*, Part One.

modity prices which has encouraged industrial inefficiency. The policies pursued have discouraged exporting and earning foreign exchange, they have discouraged the use of locally available raw materials and they have discouraged the adoption of labour intensive methods of production. Conversely, they have provided strong incentives to investors to rely on imported capital equipment and intermediate inputs.[12] In several extreme cases, it was discovered that when all inputs and outputs are valued at world prices manufacturing activities actually had a negative value added: the value of material inputs exceeding that of the output. That is, real national income would rise if these enterprises stopped production.[13]

Although negative value added is rather unusual, inefficiency in industry is widespread. As a result, many manufacturing establishments in underdeveloped countries can remain commercially viable only if they receive a continuing subsidy from the other sectors of the economy, notably agriculture. This subsidy, however, is an additional claim on the resource transfer from agriculture and reduces still further the amount of the transfer that can be directed into socially productive investment. Moreover, as the size of the industrial sector increases, the size of the subsidy also will have to increase — unless, of course, a miracle occurs and industrial costs begin to fall.[14] Barring a miracle, the continued growth of the manufacturing sector requires that agriculture be squeezed further[15] and unless the agricultural sector is able to increase output and factor productivity, the squeeze on agriculture is

[12] This argument is carefully developed in I. M. D. Little, T. Scitovsky and M. Scott, *Industry and Trade in Some Developing Countries.*
[13] Several countries are discussed in B. Balassa *et al., The Structure of Protection in Developing Countries.* For a detailed analysis of industrial inefficiency in Pakistan see Keith Griffin and Azizur Rahman Khan, *op. cit.*, Part Three.
[14] Until quite recently it was widely believed that with the passage of time and the acquisition of experience 'infant industries' would be miraculously transformed into competitive enterprises. Nowadays, even the most ardent advocates of industrial protection are not so confident.
[15] See Stephen R. Lewis, Jr., 'Agricultural Taxation and Intersectoral Resource Transfers', Institute for Development Studies, University of Nairobi, Working Paper No. 4, November, 1971, pp. 13—14.

certain to result in greater poverty for the peasantry. If agriculture is incapable of transferring additional resources to industry, the rate of growth of the manufacturing sector will decline and the entire development strategy based on indirect intervention through the market mechanism will collapse.

Walking on two legs: Taiwan
The strategy of manipulating tariffs, export taxes and exchange rates in order to encourage industry at the expense of agriculture reaches a limit when it is no longer possible, politically or economically, to increase the marketable surplus and transfer additional resources from rural areas. Once this limit is reached either the economy will become stagnant or measures will have to be introduced to stimulate the growth of agricultural output.

As long as the agricultural sector is very large and industry is insignificant, it is possible to obtain impressive rates of growth of manufacturing output by squeezing the peasantry and transferring resources out of rural areas. If such a policy continues for very long, however, per capita agricultural output will begin to fall and eventually this will result in a decline in the industrial growth rate as well. When this point is reached, further growth of both sectors will necessitate an increase in per capita agricultural production. In other words, there comes a time when the economy must walk on two legs or it will not walk at all. A strategy based on 'primitive capital accumulation' must be transformed into one based on 'balanced growth'.[16]

A balanced growth strategy does not imply, of course, that agriculture and industry must grow at the same rate, but it does imply that agriculture must grow fast enough to permit a rise in the marketable surplus and a continuation — although perhaps at a declining rate[17] — of a real resource

[16]We assume that foreign aid is not available in large quantities and that there is no large mineral exporting sector from which resources can be transferred.
[17]Once the industrial sector becomes dominant, balance growth no longer is essential and a resource transfer from rural areas becomes unnecessary, since industry can finance its expansion from its own surplus.

122   *The Political Economy of Agrarian Change*

transfer to urban areas. These conditions are unlikely to be satisfied unless agricultural production increases faster than the population. Indeed, one would expect to find a close association between the ratio of agricultural sales to agricultural output and the level of agricultural output per head.

Taiwan is of interest in this regard because it is one of the few non-socialist countries of Asia which has enjoyed sustained agricultural and industrial growth over a long period of time. Agricultural growth was interrupted only during the decade of the 1940s when the economy was seriously disrupted by the second world war. Between 1910 and 1935 agricultural output per head rose over 40 per cent, and agricultural sales increased from 56.3 per cent of total agricultural production in 1911–1915 to 71.7 per cent in 1931–1935.[18] Thereafter, per capita production declined for fifteen years, as did the sales ratio. However, a slow recovery in agricultural output per head began in the 1950s and this was accompanied by a rise in the sales ratio from 58 per cent in 1950–1955 to 61.9 per cent in 1966–1969.

This rise in the sales ratio occurred despite the fact that a series of land reform measures were introduced between 1949 and 1953. One reason why the marketable surplus continued to increase is that the peasantry gradually was becoming less poor as a result of higher yields and greater output per agricultural labourer. A second reason is that the peasants were not allowed to reap the full benefits from the reduction of rents and the later abolition of absentee landownership. Resources continued to flow from agriculture. In the period up to 1940 most of the resources transferred from agriculture were in the form of rents and interest payments extracted from the peasantry by landlords. Since 1950, however, rents have declined sharply in importance. In the 1950s, taxes and fees charged by the State accounted for most of the gross outflow of resources, while in the following decade most of the resources from agriculture were transferred through financial institutions. These

[18] Data on the marketable surplus were obtained from T. H. Lee, 'Strategies for Transferring Agricultural Surplus Under Different Agricultural Situations in Taiwan', Table 1, pp. 26–27, mimeo., 19 July 1971.

latter resources do not represent voluntary savings of the peasantry that were channeled into urban investment; on the contrary, they consist largely of payments by the peasantry to the government for the land they acquired as a result of the land reform policies. Taxes and land payments replaced interest and rent payments; in effect, the State replaced the landlord.[19] This emerges quite clearly from the data in Table 5.4.

Table 5.4

The Flow of Resources from Agriculture, Taiwan, 1911–1969 (per cent of gross outflow)

	Land rent and interest	Taxes and fees	Transfers through financial institutions
1911–1920	80.1	18.4	1.4
1921–1930	77.2	21.6	1.2
1931–1940	73.1	22.4	4.5
1950–1955	39.8	53.2	7.0
1956–1960	28.2	55.5	16.2
1961–1965	9.4	30.2	60.3
1966–1969	9.8	22.2	68.0

Source: T. H. Lee, 'Strategies for Transferring Agricultural Surplus Under Different Agricultural Situations in Taiwan', mimeo., 19 July 1971.

As we have seen, the government in Taiwan was successful in maintaining a high ratio of sales to agricultural output. Moreover, through its tax and financial policies it was able to extract a large gross outflow of resources from agriculture and thereby virtually compel the sector to have a high rate of

[19] A prominent feature of many land reforms has been the substitution of the landlord by the State. This has happened not only in Taiwan but also, e.g., in Mexico, where the purpose of the Banco Nacional de Credito Ejidal has been not just to serve the ejidatarios but to maintain control over them. In Africa, where the concentration of land has yet to become a widespread problem, the State has assumed the role of the landlord and has extracted a surplus from the peasantry through tax policy and the operation of numerous agricultural marketing boards.

savings. In the early postwar years the gross outflow of capital from agriculture was considerably lower than in the Japanese colonial period, but by the end of the 1960s the gross outflow had very nearly reached the proportions obtained thirty years previously. This can be seen in the first column of Table 5.5. The big difference between the 1930s and 1960s is that in the earlier period there was a net capital outflow from agriculture equivalent to about 20 per cent of the sector's total output, whereas today agriculture contributes almost nothing to capital formation in other sectors. The large outflow of funds is offset by a large inflow in the form of public investment and subsidies plus private income transfers from relatives employed in urban activities. Agriculture continues to provide a marketable surplus but it no longer is required to transfer resources to industry.

Government direct intervention in the rice market in Taiwan is considerable. In fact, in the last twenty years the government has collected between 44 per cent (in 1969) and 74 per cent (in 1955) of all the rice delivered to the market.[20] The State, evidently, has a commanding position in the market; the amount of rice delivered by farmers has little to do with the free play of supply and demand.

The government acquires rice in a variety of ways. In 1969, for example, over five thousand tons were obtained in payment for paddy land sold to tenants under the Land-to-the-Tiller Act. Nearly twentyone thousand tons were obtained in repayment in kind of loans made to rice farms. Both of these sources were of minor importance, however.[21] Land taxes and local government surtaxes on paddy lands are collected in kind. Moreover, landowners are compelled to sell a fixed quantity of paddy to the government at prices which are 20—30 per cent below free market prices. The government also collects rent in kind from the use of public lands. In 1969, land taxes, rents and compulsory sales amounted to 152,210 tons of rice, or nearly 30 per cent of the total amount collected by the government.

[20] About half of all the rice that is produced is sold.
[21] The maximum obtained under these two categories was 50,780 tons for land repayment in 1959 and 114,618 tons for loan repayments in 1954.

Table 5.5
Gross and Net Capital Outflow from Agriculture, Taiwan,
1911–1969
(per cent of total agricultural production)

	Gross outflow	Net outflow
1911–1920	28.8	39.2
1921–1930	26.8	22.0
1931–1940	26.3	22.4
1950–1955	18.5	1.6
1956–1960	16.3	0.6
1961–1965	20.4	0.3
1966–1969	25.1	0.3

Source: T. H. Lee, op. cit.

The largest quantity of rice received by the government, however, is obtained through the rice-fertilizer barter exchange programme. The Provincial Food Bureau, through its agent, the Farmers' Associations, exchanges fertilizer for rice on either a spot or loan basis. Since the government has a monopoly of fertilizer production and distribution, it is able to affect the terms of trade which rice farmers confront by altering the rate of exchange between fertilizer and rice. The

Table 5.6
Production and Disposal of Rice in Taiwan, 1969
(metric tons of brown rice)

Production	2,321,633
On-farm consumption	1,171,446
Total sales	1,150,187
Commercial sales	643,292
Government collection, of which	506,895
Land tax and compulsory purchase	152,210
Barter exchange	328,472
Repayments of loans	20,952
Payment for land	5,261

Source: T. H. Lee, 'Government Interference in the Rice Market in Taiwan', mimeo., n.d. (1971?).

government has used its monopoly power to impose a high price for fertilizer in Taiwan and this has enabled it to acquire very large quantities of rice.

In 1969 almost 65 per cent of the rice collected by the government was obtained through the barter programme. There are three reasons why this programme has been so successful. First, the demand for fertilizer is very great and apparently inelastic over the relevant range with respect to price. As early as 1938 fertilizer consumption per hectare was 623 kg. in Taiwan. Second, supply fell virtually to zero by 1945 and in 1948, when the barter exchange programme was introduced, fertilizer consumption per ha. still was only 121 kg. The pre-war peak was not exceeded until 1956, by which time the man-land ratio had risen considerably and there was a pressing need to increase agricultural yields. Thus the government was able to take advantage of a situation of acute scarcity. Thirdly, paddy farmers could not shift easily to other crops, and thereby avoid the unfavourable barter exchange rate, because taxes and land price repayments on terrain technically suitable for cultivating rice were levied in kind. Thus farmers were forced by the tax system to grow rice,[22] and they were forced by the barter system to deliver a large part of their production to the government. The size of the marketable surplus was not left to chance.

Part of the rice obtained by the government was used to stabilize prices in the domestic market and another part was exported. Approximately half the rice collected by the government, however, was distributed as rations to civil servants (including teachers), the police, armed forces and their dependents. In 1952 there were 1,780,000 persons who were entitled to receive rice rations. This corresponds almost exactly to the number of Chinese Nationalists who moved to Taiwan after retreating from the mainland. It seems, thus, that the major purpose of the elaborate procurement system was to extract rice from Taiwanese peasants in behalf of the Chinese Nationalists in urban areas.[23]

[22] In 1961—1965 about 47 per cent of the crop area was devoted to growing paddy.
[23] The barter system was abolished in late 1972. This was one of several changes in policy designed to give the Taiwanese a new deal.

C. Conclusions

Underdeveloped capitalist economies wishing to industrialize encounter two major problems: first, how to obtain a marketable surplus of exportable commodities and wage goods from the agricultural sector and, second, how to obtain a net transfer of resources from agriculture which can be used to increase investment in manufacturing. The free market mechanism, i.e. *laissez faire*, usually will succeed in producing a marketable surplus, particularly if the ownership of land, and hence income, is highly concentrated.[24] But *laissez faire* does not guarantee that landowners will save a large proportion of their income or that these savings will be channeled into manufacturing. To ensure that the marketable surplus is accompanied by a resource transfer many governments intervene indirectly, via the market, through their tax, tariff and exchange rate policies.

Indirect government controls have several disadvantages. First, by turning the terms of trade against the sector where the largest number of poor people obtain a livelihood, indirect controls almost inevitably accentuate income inequality. Next, they often lead to an increase in consumption in urban areas rather than to an increase in industrial capital formation. In addition, they create a set of incentives based upon relative factor prices which fail to reflect the real scarcity of capital, labour and foreign exchange. As a result, industries are established and techniques of production are adopted in which the country does not have, and can never hope to acquire, a comparative advantage. The control system tends to produce an industrial sector whose existence depends upon a continuing subsidy from agriculture. Lastly, as the size of the industrial sector increases, the required subsidy from agriculture also increases, and eventually this leads to stagnation in rural areas and the collapse of the entire growth strategy.

[24] In regions where output per man-year is low and the ownership of land is not highly concentrated, the marketable surplus of foodgrains will be small, as in Java and Bangladesh. The growth of manufacturing in these regions will depend upon the possibility of extracting resources from other primary activities, e.g., jute in Bangladesh and the plantation and oil sectors in Indonesia.

The collapse can be postponed, of course, if it is possible to accelerate the rate of growth of agricultural production without having to reduce the net flow of resources going to urban areas. This has been one of the most important effects of the 'green revolution'. The introduction of high yielding varieties of foodgrains in regions which already are relatively well endowed with irrigation facilities has enabled the marketable surplus to be increased, and the resource transfer to continue, at a negligible cost in terms of investment in rural areas. The significance of the 'green revolution' is not so much that it has resulted in an improved livelihood in rural areas (although certain groups clearly have prospered) as that it has allowed governments to persist with industrial policies which had taken many nations to the brink of catastrophe.[25]

We argued in the previous chapters that there was a marked tendency for the increase in output of foodgrains to be concentrated on farms belonging to large landowners. A major reason for this was the bias of public policy which systematically channeled scarce resources to the larger and more prosperous farmers. Although policy aggravated inequality in the countryside, it had the virtue, from the point of view of the government, of encouraging commercial agriculture and thereby augmenting the marketable surplus. Given the needs of urban areas for cheap and abundant wage goods and for a continuation of the subsidy to industry from agriculture, the best thing that could have happened, did happen: the 'green revolution' strengthened those in the countryside who were natural allies of the urban ruling groups and it enabled these ruling groups to perpetuate the status quo essentially unchanged.

In some countries, however, the government was unwilling or unable to rely on a combination of rural income

[25] India, after several years of declining agricultural production per head, was on the verge of famine in the mid-1960s. In the Philippines the industrial growth rate had declined considerably. In Sri Lanka, massive imports of rice and the resulting balance of payments difficulties were seriously disrupting the development effort. In Pakistan the 'green revolution' arrived too late: the political strains created by a pitiless squeeze on rural East Bengal resulted in the disintegration of the country.

inequality, indirect controls and improved seeds to provide an adequate marketable surplus. In several instances where food supplies were very scarce the government intervened directly. The most common form of intervention has been rationing of basic foodgrains. In Sri Lanka, everyone is entitled to a weekly rice ration. This ensures that calories are distributed in an equitable manner, although it leaves the distribution of wealth and income essentially unaltered. In Indonesia, food rations are supplied free of charge as part of the wage to members of the armed forces and to government civil servants. A similar policy is followed in Taiwan, where about 20 per cent of the population, mostly Nationalist Chinese, receive food rations from government sources.

The government of Taiwan not only distributes food to a large proportion of the urban population, it also intervenes directly on the supply side to ensure that a large marketable surplus is forthcoming. Apparently, having established a relatively egalitarian system of small family farms, the government believed the peasantry could not be relied upon voluntarily to deliver sufficient quantities of rice to urban areas. Rather than use a free market mechanism, a complex and sophisticated set of controls was created which allowed the government to determine the quantity of rice to be delivered. This system has two essential components. First, taxes are collected in the form of paddy, and thus the peasants are compelled to grow rice. Next, fertilizer production and distribution are nationalized and fertilizer is exchanged for rice on a barter basis at terms fixed by the government. Thus by a suitable combination of the level of taxation and the barter exchange rate the authorities are able to collect whatever quantity of rice they deem necessary.

Direct controls, for example of the type employed in Taiwan, although far from ideal, are superior to both *laissez faire* and indirect intervention via the market. They are superior to *laissez faire* in that they are consistent both with an equitable distribution of the ownership of land (as in Taiwan) and with an equitable distribution of food supplies (as in Sri Lanka). They are superior to most indirect controls in that they need not result in stagnation in agriculture and inefficiency in industry. Direct controls suffer from several disadvantages, however. They tend to be blunt and rather clumsy instruments; they are slow to change in response to changing circumstances and hence tend to become out of date, giving a conservative bias to government policy; they are difficult to operate effectively and make extraordinary demands upon the time and talent of the civil service; and they provide numerous opportunities for corruption.

A redistribution of income and nationalization of agricultural land are alternatives to the measures which governments may employ. First, a more equitable distribution of income would in itself ensure a more equitable distribution of food.[26] Under such a policy there would be no need for rationing, for the collection of taxes in kind or for direct intervention in the processing and marketing of food by the bureaucracy.[27] Second, nationalization of the land would abolish the landlord class and private rents. As owner of the land, the state would be entitled to collect rents and by manipulating the level and disposal of rents the state could affect the volume of the marketable surplus and the extent to which resources are transferred from rural to urban areas. Thus, in two strokes, the government would be in a position to determine the distribution of consumption goods, including food, as well as the rate and pattern of capital accumulation. The marketable surplus, as such, would cease to be a constraint on growth.

[26] It is assumed that those who need more food are not ignorant of their needs and would purchase additional foodstuffs if given the financial opportunity to do so. In some cases this assumption may be wrong and measures which supplement the market may be necessary, e.g. programmes for feeding children at school and special dietary supplements for young mothers and infants.

[27] Direct intervention may be necessary for other reasons, however, e.g. to control private monopolies which may exist at certain stages of food processing.

APPENDIX: THE MECHANICS OF PROCESSING AND MARKETING RICE

In the main body of the text we called attention to the considerable differential that exists between the price of paddy at the farm gate and the retail price in major urban centres. We suggested that this differential can be attributed in large part to the cost of processing and marketing and that monopoly profits usually are rather low. We do not have the detailed cost and sales data that are necessary to fully test this hypothesis, but an examination of the sheer mechanics of rice processing may be enough to convince the reader that our hypothesis is at least plausible. Given the widespread belief that those who come between the cultivator and the consumer somehow manage to exploit both, and that therefore governments should assume a major role in processing and marketing, it is worth our while to consider briefly what is actually involved in converting a rice plant in the fields into an item suitable for human consumption.

There are six basic stages through which paddy passes before it becomes rice: harvesting, threshing, parboiling, drying, hulling and polishing. Between several stages transport and storage facilities are required, so that the final price paid by the consumer reflects the cost of cultivation, the cost of processing, the costs of transport, storage and selling, plus the profits of each intermediary. Costs, in turn, depend upon factor prices, the scale of operation, the efficiency of production, and the quality of the final product desired. Evidently, costs and prices can be expected to vary from one country to another.

The first stage in processing is *harvesting* and the key decision here is the timing of the harvest. If the rice plants are harvested too early the physical returns from milling will be low due to the presence of chalky and immature grains. On the other hand, if the rice plants are allowed to stand in the fields too long, many kernels will become sun-checked, i.e. broken, before harvest as a result of alternately wetting and drying the mature kernels. In addition, a delay in harvesting will lead to shattering of the grain during milling.

Except in arid regions like the Punjab of Pakistan, many cultivators leave their rice plants in the fields too long and harvest when their plants begin to dry out and the optimum moisture content (21—24 per cent) has been passed. The reason for this is that farmers usually are unwilling to sell wet stalk paddy at a price discount and are reluctant to run the risk that they will be unable to sun-dry their paddy properly when harvested at a high moisture content. Unless adequate mechanical drying facilities exist, or a dry, sunny period can confidently be predicted, it 'pays' the farmer to allow part of the drying process to occur in the fields even though this lowers the quality of rice and reduces the quantity of rice obtained from a given volume of paddy. Thus in most parts of Asia the peasants prefer to harvest during dry weather and when the plants have a low moisture content, say, 15 per cent. The paddy is then dried and stored out-of-doors, with little protection from rain, rats or birds. During the cutting and sun-drying process some of the over-mature paddy will fall off the stalks. Indeed as much as 20 per cent of the field yield may be lost during these early stages of processing.

The next step is *threshing*. There are various methods of separating the grain from the stalk. For example, in the Philippines and Java much threshing is done by foot or hand, e.g. by beating the heads of the plant against a wooden rack or even against the ground. In Sri Lanka, in contrast, threshing usually is done by driving a team of water buffaloes or a four-wheel tractor over the paddy on a dirt threshing floor. Naturally, this results in some damage to the grains, particularly if the moisture content is low. A number of threshing machines exist which require less labour than the Indonesian method and inflict less damage than the Ceylonese methods, but the machines are expensive and it is not obvious that their purchase can be justified.

Once the paddy has been threshed it is ready to be *sold* for further processing. If the paddy is sold to a government agency the peasant will almost certainly have to deliver it himself to a collection point. The method of conveyance may be by carrying-pole, ox-drawn cart, bicycle or truck, but in any event in most Asian countries it is likely to be laborious and expensive. Moreover, when the paddy reaches the collection point it will have to meet the minimum standards of cleanliness and dryness established by the government. In

Sri Lanka, for instance, the Multi-Purpose Cooperative Societies purchase paddy at a guaranteed price on behalf of the government; this paddy must contain no more than 12 per cent by volume of chaff and dead grains and have a moisture content no higher than 17 per cent. Paddy which fails to meet these standards is purchased at a discount. Instead of selling to the government, the peasant may choose to sell to a private buyer. In this case the buyer usually will collect the paddy at the farm. The paddy need not be clean or dry, but its condition will be taken into account in determining the price.

By this time it is likely that several varieties of rice and grain types will have become thoroughly mixed. In part this is due to the fact that a farmer may grow more than one variety of rice in his fields. In part, too, it is due to the fact that cultivators-cum-harvest workers often are paid in paddy, and this paddy may be mixed with the paddy grown on their own fields before it is sold. In addition, shop-keepers and moneylenders frequently are repaid in paddy and it is difficult to keep the various types of paddy separate before it is sold to a rice merchant or miller. Thus, for all these reasons, the miller is likely to receive a mixture of several types of paddy of different moisture content which is combined with variable amounts of chaff, dirt and stones. Some of the kernels will be soft and chalky; some of the grains will be empty; some of the grains will be coloured, spotted and mildewed as a result of lodging, insect attacks and moulding; and some will be cracked as a result of late harvesting or incorrect drying.

This mixture then is either *parboiled* or immediately hulled and polished. In Indonesia virtually none of the paddy is parboiled, whereas in India 40 per cent is treated in this way and in Sri Lanka about 85 per cent. Although parboiling increases the cost of processing, it does have certain advantages. First, parboiled rice contains more vitamins and is more nutritious than raw rice. Second, parboiling causes the broken portions of kernels to fuse together and thereby improves the milled quality of rice which has been damaged by 'sun-checking'. Third, parboiled rice is easier to store. Whether these advantages justify the extra expense depends upon several factors: consumer preferences, the nutritive quality of the average diet, the proportion of kernels damaged by 'sun-checking' and the cost of alternative methods of eliminating or compensating for this, and the cost of improved storage facilities.

There are several methods of parboiling. The technique used in the Sind has been described by James Wimberly as follows:

> The paddy is parboiled in 'chatties', which are clay pots, holding ½ maund of paddy. The paddy is placed in chatties, then the chatties are filled with water. Husk is spread around the chatties, and then burned slowly, to increase the water temperature during soaking. This reduces ... soaking time from 24—36 hours to 12 hours, and eliminates most of the disagreeable odour caused with cold water soaking. After the paddy is soaked, it is drained, and steamed in an open pan. This is a large dish shaped metal pan, usually 5' in diameter, where a husk fire is built under it, and with the soaked paddy, a steaming process occurs. The boiled paddy is then spread on the open drying floor, where sun drying is seldom interrupted, and the paddy dries quickly to 14% moisture.[1]

In Sri Lanka most paddy is soaked in cold water before being steamed.[2] Concrete tanks with a capacity of 30—100 bushels of 46 lbs. each are filled with paddy which is then covered with unheated water. The mixture of paddy and debris which we described earlier is allowed to soak for two or three days, or until there is enough sunshine for drying the paddy after soaking and steaming. In the process of soaking gases are emitted, the edible content of the grain is reduced, 'foul odours are generated and the rice grain absorbs and

[1] James E. Wimberly, 'Development of the Rice Drying and Processing Industry in India and Pakistan', in IRRI, *Rice Policy Conference: Current Papers on Rice Technology*, 1971, p. 30.
[2] The description which follows is taken from W. G. Golden, Jr., 'Rice Production, Processing, Purchasing and Marketing in Ceylon', in IRRI, *Rice Policy Conference: Current Papers on Rice Technology*, 1971, pp. 12—13.

retains these objectionable odours and flavours, even through the cooking process'.[3]

Most of these disadvantages can be overcome by using modern parboiling methods. Cleaned paddy is placed in metal tanks with a capacity of 1—6 tons. The paddy is soaked for only 3—6 hours in water which has been heated to 60—75°C. After soaking, the water is drained from the tanks and steam is applied to the paddy for 15—30 minutes. This process prevents loss of weight and discolouration of the grain; it also prevents the grain from absorbing unpleasant odours. The disadvantage of the hot water treatment, however, is that it requires an additional investment in a steam boiler, metal tanks and mechanical drying equipment.

The moisture content of parboiled paddy varies from 25 to 36 per cent and this must be reduced to 14 per cent before milling. In most parts of Asia the paddy is *dried* by exposing it to the sun — on cement platforms, in village squares or, particularly when there is an unusually good harvest, on paved highways. The introduction of high yielding varieties of rice, however, is leading to a gradual displacement of sun drying by mechanical methods of drying. In part this is because existing facilities for sun drying are insufficient to cope with the increased output which the HYVs produce. More important, the HYVs permit multiple cropping and the second harvest frequently occurs during a rainy period when it is impossible to dry large quantities of paddy in the customary way.

One method of mechanically drying parboiled paddy is to move it downward on a metal mesh belt at a 30° slope through air heated to a temperature of about 93°C. The paddy is exposed to this hot air for a relatively short period and then tempered for approximately six hours, after which it is passed through the heated air again. This process is continued until the moisture content is reduced to 14 per cent. Alternatively, a hot air columnar drier may be used. This consists of four separate columns through which the parboiled paddy flows continuously for about 2½ hours through air heated to 60°C.

[3] Ibid.

Continuous flow driers are used also for rice which has not been parboiled. In this case, typically, the paddy is passed through the drier for 30 minutes at about 65°C. After each '30 minute pass' the paddy is tempered and then run through the drier again. The moisture content is reduced by roughly 2 per cent on each pass, and the process is continued until the moisture content is reduced to a level at which the paddy is ready for milling, viz., 14 per cent.

Modern rice *mills* in India consist of rubber roll shellers (which remove the hull from the grain and convert paddy into brown rice), husk separators, paddy separators, polishing equipment (which converts brown rice into white rice), bran separation equipment and rice graders. Under ideal conditions 100 kg. of paddy should yield 70 kg. or more of whole and broken edible rice, 20 kg. of husks, 8 kg. of bran and polish, and 2 kg. of germ.[4] In fact, however, because of the mixture of heterogeneous grains and foreign material which is delivered to the miller, the rice recovery rate usually is much lower, say, 55—66 per cent.

Complete modern plants — including facilities for storage, drying, parboiling and milling — are characterized by economies of scale. A plant with a capacity to process ten tons per hour is likely to entail a capital cost of four times that of a plant with a capacity to process only two tons per hour, but the operating cost of the former should be about 35 per cent less than the operating costs of the smaller plant.[5] In many cases, however, it is not possible to take advantage of the technical economies of scale because of the non-availability of paddy locally and the high cost of transport. Moreover, rice milled in modern plants — even large ones — is more costly than rice milled with more primitive methods. Of course, the quality of the final product is higher too, but the majority of consumers in a poor country may not be willing to pay for this.

In Indonesia, for example, 5 per cent of the paddy is commercially milled, 10 per cent undergoes a single process of machine hulling, while 85 per cent is hand pounded with a

[4] FAO, *The Rice Processing Industry in Indonesia*, TA 2617, 1969, p. 4.
[5] James E. Wimberly, op. cit., p. 26.

mortar and pestle.[6] Evidently, the commercial establishments are unable to compete with extremely rudimentary processing equipment. In Pakistan rice is milled with hullers (in the Sind) or, increasingly, with disk shellers (especially in the Punjab). Only one modern mill exists and this is used to re-process Basmati rice intended for export. In the Philippines, in 1968, there were 9395 rice mills, of which 7389 were simple *kiskisan* mills.[7] The *kiskisan* mills are used primarily in rural areas to process paddy for direct home consumption. Despite the fact that they are mechanically inefficient — the milling recovery rate is as low as 45 per cent — these primitive mills account for about 55 per cent of the capacity of the industry and evidently are preferred by the peasants to the large commercial mills.

In Sri Lanka, almost all the rice mills — of which there are about 1000 — are privately owned, but a substantial proportion of the paddy that is processed belongs to the government. This is paddy which is acquired under the Guaranteed Price Scheme and later distributed to the population as part of the rice ration.[8] Each private miller registered with the government is assigned a weekly quota of paddy to be milled. The miller is paid a fee for processing and is expected to return to the government for every 100 kg. of paddy 51.5 kg. of parboiled rice or 50.5 kg. of raw rice, i.e. rice which has not been parboiled. The government has established quality standards for milled rice, but these are poorly enforced. As a consequence, corruption and profiteering flourish, to the advantage of the miller and at the expense of the consumer. The way this occurs is clearly explained by William Golden.

On the average, a miller obtains a higher percentage of processed rice than is specified [i.e., 51.5 or 50.5 per cent], but he invariably surrenders to government the

[6] FAO, op. cit.
[7] J. D. Drilon, Jr., 'Modernization of Storage, Drying and Milling', in IRRI conference papers published as *Seminar on Consumption and Marketing of Rice in the Philippines*, 1970.
[8] Domestic production is supplemented by imports of rice, which the government controls and distributes by rationing.

minimum quantity stipulated, disposing of the balance surreptitiously and making quite a margin of undue profit. In order to maintain a high percentage of recovery, he gives the minimum polish to satisfy the Food Commissioner's Supply Stores and generally is able to get away with giving rice of a very poor quality. As a result, the raw milled rice contains a great deal of broken and unpolished rice. In the case of parboiled rice, there is generally an offensive smell as a result of parboiling procedures used. A large amount of black and otherwise damaged grains are also to be found.[9]

In fact, the quality of the government's rice is so poor that consumers 'have to polish and purify it in private hulling plants at the loss of at least 2% in the second polishing process.'[10]

This deplorable situation is a consequence of government policy. Either the government should maintain the present quota system for millers but raise the milling percentage and enforce quality standards, or it should allow the approximately 1000 millers to compete for government custom by offering higher quality rice at a lower price, or the government should nationalize the industry and run it in the public interest. The remarkable thing about the situation in Sri Lanka is that the government has managed both to prevent competition and to avoid effective direct controls or state ownership of the industry. Any one of these three policies would almost certainly result in a better quality rice for the consumer at a lower cost to the government. Government intervention, in the form it has taken, has made matters worse rather than better in Sri Lanka. Ironically, Sri Lanka is the one clear case of exploitation by middlemen that we have found, and this is a result not of a few millers controlling the output of the processing industry but of poorly conceived and implemented policy.

[9] W. G. Golden, Jr., op. cit., pp. 7–8.
[10] FAO, *The Rice Processing Industry in Ceylon*, TA 2380, 1967.

CHAPTER 6

International Implications
of the Green Revolution

A. Introduction

Almost half the grain produced in the world consists of either wheat or rice, and the quantities of each are now approximately equal. In 1970, for example, wheat output was 311.6 million metric tons while paddy production was 306.8 million tons. The two grains are not of equal importance in international markets, however. Wheat is the most widely traded grain and about 20–25 per cent of total output is exported. The world market for rice, in contrast, is extremely thin and only about 3–5 per cent of output is traded internationally. The volume of wheat exports is about seven times larger than that of rice.

The structure of the world wheat market, moreover, is quite different from the international rice market. The wheat market is an oligopoly; the rice market is not. The United States and Canada account for over 60 per cent of all exports and these two countries, plus on occasion Australia, have coordinated their production and trade policies in order to maintain relatively high and stable prices. Over 85 per cent of all wheat exports originate in the developed countries, while about 40 per cent of all imports are acquired by the less developed countries.

The U.S.A. as well as Australia and New Zealand export about 35 per cent of their wheat production, whereas Canada and Argentina export 45–50 per cent of their output. Exports from the USSR fluctuate erratically, but on average about 5 per cent of total production is sold abroad. Imports in most nations usually represent a small supplement to domestic production, but in the case of Japan imports are four times larger than local output, and in the U.K. they are 1.3 times as large.

The broad pattern of trade emerges quite clearly from the data in the table below. The quantities sold by the main exporting nations are given for three years — the first preceding the introduction of high yielding varieties of wheat and two others following it. Similarly, the net quantities purchased in the major importing regions also are indicated. Latin America contains two important exporters (Argentina and Mexico) and one large importer (Brazil). Rather than group the Latin American countries together and present a net figure for the entire region, it was decided to present separate data for the three most important countries so that the substantial intra-regional flows of wheat would be apparent.

During the first two decades following the end of the second world war the international rice market was dominated by Thailand and Burma. In 1951, for example, these two countries accounted for 58 per cent of world exports, and even as late as 1965 their share still was as high as 45 per cent. Since then, however, the market has become much more competitive. One reason for this change in market structure was the policies pursued by the two largest exporters. Both Thailand and Burma imposed heavy export taxes and these had the effect of restricting supply and maintaining world prices. Between 1963 and 1970 the growth of paddy production in Burma was about 0.6 per cent per annum and the volume of exports declined by nearly two-thirds. In Thailand, production increased 2.6 per cent a year and exports fell by nearly a half.

Falling exports from the two largest suppliers were reinforced in the mid-1960s by the conversion of South Vietnam from an exporter to a large importer of rice. As a result, rice prices rose very sharply in 1966 and 1967. This provided strong incentives to potential exporters to enter the market and encouraged some countries which had been large importers, e.g. Sri Lanka, Indonesia and the Philippines, to accelerate their programmes of import substitution. By 1967 the United States had replaced Thailand as the largest exporter and the People's Republic of China had moved into

Table 6.1
Net Trade in Wheat, 1964, 1969 and 1970
(100 metric tons)

	1964	1969	1970
U.S.A.	+231,803	+137,191	+190,531
Canada	+150,097	+73,334	+114,875
Australia	+78,078	+53,426	+73,099
U.S.S.R.	-61,558	+63,846	+35,672
Argentina	+37,296	+20,704	+24,121
Mexico	+5,193	+2,528	+417
Brazil	-26,218	-23,731	-19,936
Africa	-35,591	-38,428	-43,372
Asia	-199,493	-183,711	-233,169
Europe	-117,275	-59,665	-78,230

Source: FAO, *Trade Yearbook 1971*, 1972.
Note: + signifies net exports
    − signifies net imports

Table 6.2
Net Trade in Milled Rice, 1964, 1969 and 1970
(100 metric tons)

	1964	1969	1970
Europe	-6195	-6323	-3484
U.S.S.R.	-3587	-3217	-3152
U.S.A.	+13283	+19175	+17203
Mexico, Central America and the Caribbean	-4520	-3258	-3895
South America	+709	+2765	+3742
Africa	-1084	+1551	-988
Oceania	+73	+410	+554
Asia	+1801	-6611	-11352

Source: FAO, *Trade Yearbook 1971*, 1972.
Note: + signifies net exports
    − signifies net imports

third place, thereby relegating Burma to the fourth position. But in 1971 Thailand regained first place (thanks to a reduction of rice acreage in the U.S. of 25 per cent in 1969–70) while Burma was relegated by Japan (probably temporarily) to fifth place.

The data in Table 6.2 above provide a brief summary of the world rice market in the period before and immediately after the 'green revolution'. In the period between 1964 and 1970, Europe, Russia, Mexico, Central America and the Caribbean remained important net importers; the United States and South America increased their exports considerably; and Africa oscillated between being a net importer and a net exporter, depending largely on the rice harvest in Egypt, where output has increased substantially. The most dramatic change, however, was the conversion of Asia, i.e. the region extending from the Near East to the Far East, from a net exporter to a large net importer. In 1964 Asia exported 180,100 metric tons of rice to the rest of the world, while in 1969 the region imported 661,100 tons from the rest of the world. The 'green revolution' in Asia, at least initially, appears to be associated not with increased production and greater exports of rice but with greater imports! This apparent paradox deserves careful investigation.

An examination of the fourteen most important rice producing countries in Asia suggests that these should be divided into five groups. First, there are those countries which are actively promoting rice exports. In fact, there is only one country in this group, viz., Pakistan before its division into two separate nations. The irrigated regions of the former West Pakistan were particularly suitable for cultivating both high yielding varieties of rice and a high quality local variety called Basmati, and the country took advantage of this opportunity to expand production and exports. Next, there are three countries which during the period adopted policies to discourage exports of rice — Burma, Thailand and South Korea. The first two did so partly in order to exploit an oligopoly position which has now practically vanished; the third has done so as a by-product of policies which were designed to encourage exports of manufactured products. The following group contains countries whose exports of rice were disrupted because of the war in Indo-China, viz. Cambodia and South Vietnam. Fourthly, there is a large group of countries which has adopted policies to replace imported rice, partially or entirely, with domestic production. India has succeeded in reducing imports substantially; Western Malaysia and Sri Lanka by perhaps 25 per cent, and the Philippines has greatly reduced the need to import rice on a regular basis.[1] Japan carried her policy of import substitution to such an extreme that by 1969 the country had a massive exportable surplus and in 1969, 1970 and 1971 she dumped rice on the world market. These probably were exceptional years, however, and it is reasonable to hope that in future Japan will reduce if not desist entirely from dumping. The final group contains two countries, China and Taiwan, one a major exporter and the other an exporter of diminishing volume and significance. The two countries are alike, however, in that, as far as one can tell, they are neither encouraging nor discouraging rice exports but are relying on their comparative advantage to determine their pattern of trade.[2]

We saw from the data in Table 6.2 that between 1964 and 1969 Asia became a net importer of rice and there was a reversal of trade equivalent to 841,200 tons. This net change was essentially the outcome of two opposing tendencies. On the one hand, the countries in Groups Two and Three experienced a reduction in exports of about 3.15 million tons, while on the other hand, the countries in Group Four were able to reduce their imports by approximately 2.18 million tons. That is, the fall in rice exports was greater than the reduction in imports and as a result the region as a whole became a net importer of rice. This occurred despite the 'green revolution', not because of it.

The deterioration of the rice export market in Asia was due either to government policy — or perhaps lack of

---

[1] The Philippines currently is going through a 'rice crisis', however. In 1970/71 the country had to import 450,000 tons of rice and in 1972 imports will have been even larger — probably between 500,000 and 650,000 tons. As a result of the severe floods in 1972, the need to import rice almost certainly will continue in 1973 and perhaps longer.
[2] It may sound odd to claim that mainland China, a centrally planned economy partly cut off from trade with the capitalist nations, should adhere to the comparative cost principle. But for many years China has exported rice in order to import wheat, and this probably corresponds to what a rational government following the comparative cost principle would do. China's behaviour also can be interpreted, however, in terms of 'caloric arbitrage', as we shall demonstrate below.

government policy in the face of declining world prices — (the Group Two countries) or to war (the Group Three countries), and in neither group of countries, with the partial exception of South Vietnam, were high yielding varieties of rice introduced on a wide scale. The new seeds were widely used, however, in West Pakistan (which increased exports) and in several of the Group Four countries which sharply reduced imports (notably the Philippines and Sri Lanka). It is reasonable to assume, therefore, that the trade deficit in rice in Asia would have been much greater than it actually was had the high yielding varieties not been developed and introduced.[3]

Table 6.3

Net Trade in Milled Rice in Several Asian Countries, 1964, 1969 and 1970

(100 metric tons)

	1964	1969	1970
1 Countries promoting exports of rice			
Pakistan	+492	+1,193	−866
2 Countries discouraging exports of rice			
Burma	+14,130	+5,408	+6,401
South Korea	+133	−6,312	−7,695
Thailand	+18,936	+10,221	+10,844
3 Countries disrupted by war			
Cambodia	+4,917	+1,028	+2,220
South Vietnam	+487	−3,257	−5,529
4 Countries reducing imports of rice			
Sri Lanka	−6,580	−2,736	−4,796
India	−6,416	−4,716	−3,040
Indonesia	−10,255	−6,046	−9,561
Japan	−4,150	+3,075	+6,114
Philippines	−2,988	+6	+12
West Malaysia	−4,083	−2,239	−2,677
5 Others			
China	+7,845	+7,125	n.a.
Taiwan	+993	+295	+44

Source: FAO, *Trade Yearbook 1971*, 1972.
Note: + signifies net exports
    − signifies net imports

[3] Between 1964 and 1969 rice exports from Asia declined from 5.14 million tons to 3.19 million tons. At the same time, imports of rice fell from 4.96 million tons to 3.85 million tons.

The price of wheat and rice

So far the discussion has been conducted largely in physical terms and the time has now come to consider the evolution of prices. There is, of course, no such thing as 'the' world price of rice or wheat. The price of any foodgrain depends on its quality, the place where the transaction occurs and the time of year in which it is sold. In the case of rice and wheat, moreover, non-commercial sales also affect world prices. The United States is the world's largest producer and exporter of grains; it is also the largest donor of food aid, and hence U.S. policies have an enormous influence on world prices — particularly on wheat prices. The rice market appears to be less oligopolistic but barter deals are not uncommon (e.g., the arrangement whereby Sri Lanka swaps rubber for Chinese rice) and at least one major supplier, viz. Burma, in the past disposed of large quantities of rice under long-term contracts which insulate the country from some of the effects of variations in the spot rice price.

Despite the fact that no single series is a perfect indicator of world market prices, the various series are highly inter-correlated. The level of prices may differ among series but the trends in prices are very similar. Therefore a single series has been selected for each grain. We have selected the export price of Canadian wheat to describe the evolution of wheat prices since 1955. The price of Canadian wheat is established by the Canadian Wheat Board, which exercises price leadership in the United States, and thus this series reflects the price at which most commercial wheat sales are transacted.

It can be seen in Figure 6.1 that wheat prices were remarkably stable between 1955 and 1970. The lowest prices were experienced in 1957, 1960 and 1969 when the export cost was 6.2 U.S. cents per kg.; the peak was reached in 1966, during the period of harvest failures in South Asia, when the price rose to 7.1 cents. Thus the variation from the lowest to the highest price was only 14.5 per cent. The large exporters were able to secure relative price stability by varying their domestic wheat stocks in response to changes in international demand. That is, shifts in demand were reflected not in price changes but in changes in production and inventories. The United States and Canada, in effect,

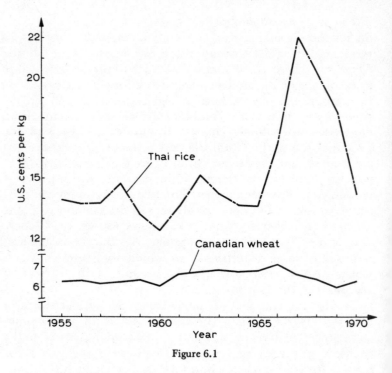

Figure 6.1

operated a commodity stabilisation scheme and the supply curve of wheat in the international market became almost infinitely elastic.

Conditions in the world rice market were rather different. In the early postwar years, when Thailand and Burma still dominated the market, these two countries used export taxes to raise revenue and reap short term monopoly gains rather than to stabilize prices at a level which would inhibit competition. Low domestic prices in the two major exporting nations retarded the growth of world supplies and shortages began to appear in the 1960s: in the period 1961–63 to 1968 world output of paddy increased only 2.4 per cent a year, i.e., less than the increase in population. Since there were few stocks of rice which could be drawn upon, the increase in demand led to a sharp rise in prices — as can be seen in the figure.

The price series in the figure is the export price of Thai milled rice (white, 5—7 per cent brokens). This is a medium-high quality rice supplied by the largest Asian exporter. This quality commands a price premium over the lower quality rice produced in most Asian countries and is therefore more expensive than most other rice exports, but the movements of the Thai rice series are fairly similar to those of other nations. The lowest price of rice in the period 1955 to 1970 was 12.5 U.S. cents per kg. in 1960; the highest was 22.2 cents in 1967. The difference between these extremes is 77.5 per cent. Price fluctuations in the rice market clearly are much greater than in the wheat market.

It also is evident from the figure that the price of a kg. of rice is two or three times greater than the price of wheat. The caloric content of the two grains in virtually identical, however, at 3600 calories per kg. and the protein content of wheat is about twice that of rice. The government of a country which is capable of producing both grains, and which is more concerned about nutrition than maximizing income, could take advantage of these facts and engage in 'caloric arbitrage'. Indeed, it is possible to interpret China's export policy in this way. Let us take 1969 as an example. In that year the price of rice was about 2.88 times the price of wheat and China exported 712,500 metric tons of milled rice. At the prevailing exchange ratio this would enable her to import 2,052,000 metric tons of wheat.[4] Converting the difference in tonnage into a gain in calories, it appears that by engaging in grain arbitrage China increased the domestic availability of food by the equivalent of $48,222 \times 10^8$ calories. Assuming the average Chinese consumes 2200 calories per day, which is more than is consumed in the majority of Asian nations, rice-wheat arbitrage enabled the government to feed over 6 million people for a year.

If food is temporarily in short supply 'caloric arbitrage' may make sense in terms of nutrition. In the long run, however, this may make little sense in terms of economics. Whether it is to a country's advantage to produce rice and exchange it for wheat depends, first, upon the cost of

---

[4] In fact, China imported 3.2 million tons of wheat in that year.

growing rice relative to wheat and, second, upon the price
ratio at which wheat is exchanged for rice. If either the costs
of production or the commodity exchange ratio move against
rice it may not pay to engage in arbitrage. Given the present
state of knowledge it would be hazardous to predict the
direction in which the relative costs of grain production will
move, but something can be said about future prospects for
commodity prices.

B. Surplus Production and Falling Prices
In principle it should be rather easy to predict the rate of
growth of demand for cereals. A simple model relating
changes in demand to demographic increase and the rate of
expansion of per capita income should suffice. These demand
estimates then could be compared with projections of supply
in order to determine the direction in which prices are likely
to move, or the extent to which supply exceeds (or falls short
of) demand at constant prices. This procedure is rather crude,
and more elaborate econometric methods may be preferred,
but it should be accurate enough to indicate the broad trends
in the grain market over a relatively short period, say, ten
years. The margin for error increases substantially, however,
when one begins to disaggregate among countries and,
especially, among different types of grain. For example, the
demand for wheat depends in part upon the price of rice, and
hence in predicting future wheat demand one must consider
not only income elasticities but cross-price elasticities as well.
Similarly, many grains, notably maize, are in part consumed
directly and in part used as animal feed, and thus the demand
for maize depends in part upon the demand for meat.

A further problem arises in projecting exports and imports
of a commodity. The reason for this is that estimates of
international trade are obtained as residuals, i.e. as the
difference between a country's production and its demand.
Small errors in estimating either supply or demand can lead
to very large errors in estimating trade flows. This is
particularly true where the world market is 'thin', i.e. where
only a small proportion of total output is exchanged in the
world market. We already have noted that the world rice
market is very thin, and thus projections of foreign trade in

rice are subject to a high degree of error. The same is true, although to a lesser extent, of the other grain markets, and this should not be forgotten while reading the discussion which follows.

Demand elasticities

Cereals as a group are a slightly inferior good in the world as a whole. That is, as per capita income rises, the level of consumption of cereals tends to fall. This is particularly true in the developed capitalist countries, where a ten per cent increase in per capita income is likely to be associated with a 2.4 per cent decline in cereal consumption per head. In the underdeveloped countries the income elasticity of demand for cereals still is positive, but its value is very low, viz. 0.13. The implication of these figures, assuming they are correct, is that the overall growth of demand for cereals depends largely upon the growth of population rather than upon improvements in the standard of living.

The demand for wheat, the most important grain in world markets, has a surprisingly high negative elasticity. In most rich countries the demand for wheat, which is essentially a demand for bread, declines as per capita incomes rise. There are exceptions, however. For example, the income elasticity of demand for wheat in Japan is positive, viz., 0.10. Moreover, in most underdeveloped countries the demand

Table 6.4
Income Elasticities of Demand for Cereals

	All cereals	Wheat	Rice
World	−.02	−.24	.23
Developed capitalist countries	−.24	−.26	−.21
Underdeveloped countries	.13	.23	.20
Socialist countries	−.10	−.27	.14

Source: FAO, *Agricultural Commodity Projections, 1970–1980*, Vol. II.
Unless otherwise indicated, all estimates of demand elasticities were obtained from this publication. Note that FAO's estimate of the world elasticity of demand for rice appears to be inconsistent with the estimates for the three groups of countries.

elasticity for wheat still is positive, but once again, one can find exceptions: in Argentina the elasticity is minus 0.10.

Rice is a superior good in both the socialist and underdeveloped countries, but it is an inferior good in the developed capitalist countries. In the world as a whole the income elasticity is about 0.23. Thus the per capita demand for rice should continue to expand for quite some time and this demand will be superimposed upon the demand arising from population growth.

It is noteworthy that in the underdeveloped countries the income elasticity of demand for wheat is greater than that for rice, although the reverse is true in the other two groups of countries and in the world as a whole. This probably is due to the fact that in several Asian countries consumer tastes have changed in favour of wheat. A large number of poor countries have been recipients of surplus American wheat supplied under the P.L. 480 programme on concessional terms, and it is likely that once the initial resistance to this strange food has been overcome, consumers will acquire a preference for it and incorporate wheat into their ordinary diet. At least this seems to have occurred in India, Bangladesh and Taiwan. Moreover, a similar phenomenon has been observed in Japan, where wheat is gradually replacing rice.[5] If this hypothesis is correct, it implies not only that the income elasticity of demand for wheat should exceed that for rice, but also that there should be a significant cross-price elasticity. Unfortunately, there is very little evidence to test this hypothesis, but one study by the U.S. Department of Agriculture estimates that the elasticity of demand for rice with respect to a change in the price of wheat is 0.52.[6] If this

---

[5] The income elasticities of wheat and rice in three of the four countries mentioned, and in the former united Pakistan, are as follows:

	Wheat	*Rice*
India	.50	.40
Pakistan	.40	.30
Taiwan	.50	.30
Japan	.10	−.10

[6] USDA, *World Demand Prospects for Wheat in 1980*, Foreign Agricultural Economic Report No. 62, July 1970, p. 48.

figure is accurate it implies that an aggressive price policy by, say, rice producers may enable them to expand sales at the expense of wheat producers, even though the demand for grains as a whole may be growing relatively slowly.

According to FAO the world demand for cereals is projected to increase about 2.2 per cent a year between 1970 and 1980. In other words, the entire expansion in demand is attributed to demographic increase and it is assumed there is no increase in consumption per capita. Demand for some types of cereals will grow faster than 2.2 per cent a year, of course, and some countries may be able to increase their share of the market at the expense of others, but given the low or negative income elasticities which characterize food-grains, it is most unlikely that the overall demand for cereals will grow faster than the population. If the introduction of high yielding varieties of wheat and rice leads to a sharp increase in supply, either prices will fall dramatically or stocks of surplus grain will accumulate rapidly.

Supply projections
The Food and Agriculture Organization of the United Nations recently has completed a comprehensive study of agricultural commodities.[7] This study contains not only estimates of demand, to which we have referred already, but also detailed projections of supply to 1980. The supply projections are based on the assumption of unchanged policies. The projections, therefore, clearly are not predictions or forecasts.

FAO projections indicate that the world supply of all cereals will increase 2.8 per cent a year between 1970 and 1980. This contrasts with the 2.2 per cent rate of growth of demand which we previously mentioned and strongly implies that if present policies are continued, supply will exceed demand by a substantial margin at the prices prevailing in 1970. A major imbalance is expected in the wheat market, where supply is projected to increase 2.6 per cent a year, versus an increase in demand of only 1.8 per cent a year. That is, supply may increase nearly half again as fast as

[7] FAO, *Agricultural Commodity Projections, 1970–1980*, Volumes I and II, 1971.

demand. The projected position in the rice market is less alarming, supply and demand being projected to grow at about the same rate — 2.7 per cent per annum — and the level of the former only slightly exceeding the latter.

On the surface these projections seem to imply that the prospects for wheat are less good than those for rice: output of wheat may increase more slowly than output of rice yet the gap between supply and demand may be greater. Before these projections are accepted as a prediction, however, several points need to be made. First, because the world market in rice is exceptionally thin, a small discrepancy between aggregate supply and demand will have a large proportionate impact on international trade and therefore on prices. In Table 6.5 we reproduce the FAO projections of quantities produced and traded and it is readily apparent therein that a tiny surplus of rice of 2.5 million tons corresponds to more than a quarter of total projected imports. If such a surplus materializes this obviously will exert a strong downward pressure on the world price of rice.

On the other hand, the projected surplus in wheat is an even larger proportion of projected imports, and therefore the price decline may be correspondingly greater. A surplus of the ˙ magnitude projected is unlikely to materialize, however, because the developed capitalist countries — particularly the United States and Canada — are likely to alter their policies and restrain production with the intention of maintaining an 'orderly' market and relative price stability. In other words, it is doubtful that FAO's projection of an annual growth rate of wheat of 2.1 per cent in the developed capitalist economies can be used as a basis of prediction. Surely, supply will increase less rapidly than this.[8]

The supply of rice, in contrast, may increase more rapidly than is projected. FAO assumes that the acreage allotment for rice in the United States will remain unchanged during the decade and that, therefore, production will

[8] Already wheat stocks have risen from 33.6 million tons in 1966 to 65.3 million in 1970 and 50.8 million tons estimated for 1971. Production controls have recently been applied in Canada and the U.S.A.

Table 6.5

FAO Projection of Supply, Demand and Trade in Wheat and Rice, 1980

(million tons)

	Wheat	Rice
1 Production	354.6	255.5
2 Demand	330.1	253.0
3 Surplus (= 1 − 2)	24.5	2.5
4 Export availabilities	55.6	11.7
5 Import requirements	31.1	9.2
6 Surplus production as a percentage of import requirements	78	27

Source: FAO, *Agricultural Commodity Projections, 1970–1980*, Vol. I, p. 42.
Note: The projections exclude the centrally planned economies of Asia.

increase only 0.9 per cent a year, entirely as a result of higher yields. Yet the U.S. government announced on 17 December 1971 that the planned reduction in rice acreage for 1972 had been rescinded and that rice farmers would be allowed to cultivate 183,865 more acres than was previously contemplated. If this represents a reversal of policy by the largest exporting nation, the implications for international rice prices would be important.[9]

Rice output in Japan is projected by FAO to decline by 0.75 per cent a year between 1970 and 1980, the rise in yields being more than offset by a fall in the area cultivated. It is possible, of course, that Japan may succeed in reducing production by 8 per cent in a decade, and that therefore she will need neither to accumulate surplus stocks nor to dump rice abroad, but there is no certainty that this will occur. My suspicion, and it is no more than this, is that Japan will find it difficult to reduce the high domestic price supports for rice and reallocate resources to other crops. Furthermore, even if Japan manages to reduce rice output as projected, it is

[9] One must not forget, however, that rice acreage *was* reduced in the U.S. in 1969 (by 10 per cent) and in 1970 (by 15 per cent). Moreover, rice prices were somewhat higher in 1972 than in 1971 and this may explain the more generous acreage allotment.

improbable that an equality of domestic supply and demand will be achieved, as FAO postulates. The reason for this is that FAO appears to have underestimated the extent to which domestic consumption of rice will decline. FAO has calculated the Japanese income elasticity of demand for rice to be minus 0.10, while the elasticity for the developed capitalist countries as a group is minus 0.21. It is difficult to believe that the switch from rice to meat and wheat will be as slow in Japan as FAO's demand functions suggest.

Thus, production of rice in the high income countries easily could increase more rapidly than the 0.1 per cent projected and demand in the rich countries may increase less rapidly than the 0.5 per cent projected. If either of these events should occur, either the price of rice would fall or undesired inventories would accumulate. This tendency could be offset were China to decide not to export rice at low prices or were South Vietnam to continue to remain a large net importer, but the balance of probabilities suggests to me that the export prospects for rice are somewhat less encouraging than the prospects for wheat.[10] FAO's projections indicate the opposite, but the authors were careful to point out that a projection is not a prediction. They were wise to do so.

C. Foodgrain Autarchy

Most observers agree that one important aspect of the 'green revolution' will be to reduce the relative importance of international trade in foodgrains. As a result of introducing high yielding varieties, more and more countries are approaching self-sufficiency in wheat and rice. For example, India and Pakistan already are virtually self-sufficient in wheat and the Philippines probably is near self-sufficiency in rice, at least in a good year. This trend toward autarchy in foodgrains in almost certain to continue throughout the present decade. The tendency should be particularly strong in wheat, in part because world trade in wheat is much larger than trade in rice and in part because output of wheat in the

[10] For an encouraging view of the long-run prospects for rice prices see J. Norman Efferson, 'Outlook for World Rice Production and Trade', in *Rice, Science and Man*, IRRI, 1972.

underdeveloped countries is expected to increase more rapidly than that of rice.

FAO's projections indicate that wheat output in the underdeveloped countries may increase 4.2 per cent a year between 1970 and 1980. The range of growth rates is 3.4 per cent in the Near East and 5.0 per cent in Latin America. In other words, production is expected to increase substantially faster than the population in all underdeveloped regions of the world. Rice output is projected to increase 3.1 per cent per annum in the underdeveloped countries, growth being slowest in Asia and the Far East (3.0 per cent) and fastest in Africa (4.1 per cent). In rice, too, therefore, output per head should rise in every underdeveloped region.

Table 6.6
Projected Growth of Wheat and Rice, 1970—1980
(percentage per annum)

	Wheat	Paddy rice
All underdeveloped countries	4.2	3.1
Africa	3.5	4.1
Latin America	5.0	3.1
Near East	3.4	3.5
Asia and the Far East	4.6	3.0

Source: FAO, op. cit., Vol. I, p. 17.

Although it may seem a little unlikely to many readers, it is possible to argue that the volume of wheat imports will decline absolutely by 1980.[11] There is no doubt that there will be a relative decline. The FAO, in fact, suggests that international trade in wheat may fall from 21 per cent of total wheat production in 1964—66 to only 12.2 per cent in 1980.[12] This represents a decline of more than 40 per cent in the proportion of output traded internationally.

Despite the acceleration in production and decline in trade, there are unlikely to be dramatic changes in the

[11] FAO projects a decline in wheat imports from 50.7 million tons in 1964—66 to 48.6 million in 1980 (Op. cit., Vol. I, p. 99).
[12] Ibid., p. 67.

Table 6.7
Net Trade in Wheat, 1964–66 Average and Projection to 1980 (million metric tons)

	1964–66	1980
Developed capitalist countries	33.0	21.8
Underdeveloped countries	−18.2	−18.4
importers	(−23.3)	(−24.6)
exporters	(5.1)	(6.2)
Socialist countries	−13.8	−3.4

Source: USDA, Foreign Agricultural Economic Report No. 60, *World Demand Prospects for Agricultural Exports of Less Developed Countries in 1980,* June 1970, Table 8, p. 21.
Note: (−) signifies net imports.

pattern of trade. The United States Department of Agriculture has made several projections of the world market under various assumptions. One set of projections – which the USDA calls set II – is based on the (clearly optimistic) assumption of fairly rapid growth in agricultural output and national income in the underdeveloped countries, i.e., on the continuation of the 'green revolution'. Under these assumptions the USDA projects a decline of about a third in the net exports of wheat from the developed capitalist countries, an approach to self-sufficiency in the socialist countries and a continuation of imports at about the 1964–66 level in the

Table 6.8
Net Trade in Rice, 1964–66 Average and Projection to 1980 (Million metric tons)

	1964–66	1980
Developed capitalist countries	0.7	−0.8
Underdeveloped countries	−1.1	0.9
importers	(−4.3)	(−3.0)
exporters	(3.2)	(3.9)
Socialist countries	0.4	−0.1

Source: USDA op. cit., Table 9, p. 23.
Note: (−) signifies net imports.

underdeveloped countries. The projection is summarized in Table 6.7.

Prospects in the world rice market are rather different. FAO's projections suggest that international sales of rice will decline from 5.4 per cent of total production in 1964–66 to 4.1 per cent in 1980.[13] This relatively small decline in the importance of trade is likely to be accompanied by a radical change in the composition of trade. The USDA's optimistic set II projections indicate that the rich countries may become net importers of rice by the 1980s, the socialist countries as a group may switch from a net export position to self-sufficiency or to a marginal import position, whereas the underdeveloped countries will shift from being a rice deficit group to a rice surplus group. The latter will occur primarily as a result of import substitution in the importing countries rather than expansion in the rice exporting countries. Indeed, import substitution is expected to be twice as important as export promotion in determining the rice trade of under-developed countries. These projections are summarized in Table 6.8.

The movement toward autarchy in foodgrains which has been identified has implications for those countries which continue to rely on world markets either to dispose of surplus production or to satisfy part of domestic demand. If our assumption is correct that the developed wheat exporting nations will restrict supply in order to maintain stable prices,[14] it follows that wheat exporters from under-developed countries should be able to increase their earnings of foreign exchange; importers, on the other hand, should anticipate larger outlays because of an increase in the quantity purchased. As far as the underdeveloped countries are concerned, however, these changes will be marginal. The developed capitalist countries may lose markets and their earnings from wheat exports may decline. The socialist countries, in contrast, may save foreign exchange by import

---

[13] Ibid.

[14] It is perhaps significant that the USDA makes the same assumption. See *World Demand Prospects for Wheat in 1980*, Foreign Agricultural Economic Report No. 62, July 1970.

Table 6.9

*Domestic Prices of Wheat and Rice in Various Countries, 1968
(U.S. dollars per metric ton)*

	Wheat[f]	Paddy[b]	Milled rice[c]
Argentina	48.90[a]		
Burma		36	127[e]
Canada	61.60		
E.E.C. (weighted average)	93.70		
India	71.30[b]	56	159
Japan	151.70	294	383[d]
Mexico	73.10		
Pakistan	95.50[b]		227
Philippines		93	163
Senegal		85	
Thailand			203[e]
Turkey	88.90		
U.K.	64.70		
U.S.A.	65.00	100	

Sources: USDA, Foreign Agricultural Report No. 62, *World Demand Prospects for Wheat in 1980*, Table 8, pp. 31–32; Lyle P. Schertz, 'The Green Revolution: Production and World Trade', *Columbia Journal of World Business*, March–April 1970, p. 57; *FAO, Production Yearbook 1970*, 1971.

Notes: a = 1966/67
           b = government support prices
           c = wholesale price
           d = husked (brown) rice
           e = export price
           f = producer prices

substitution and one of them, the Soviet Union, could once again become an important exporter.

If there is a genuine breakthrough in production, rice could become a buyer's market. The USDA states that 'world trade prices for rice in 1980 are expected to drop close to 15 per cent below the relatively high prices in the base period',[15] i.e. 1964–66. If this expectation is correct, and prices could fall more than 15 per cent, it implies that rice importers,

[15] *World Demand Prospects for Agricultural Exports of Less Developed Countries in 1980*, p. 43.

notably Europe and the USSR, will be able to purchase a larger quantity at a lower total cost in terms of foreign exchange. Exporters as a group, on the other hand, are likely to earn less foreign exchange from the sale of rice in 1980 than they did in the mid-1960s — even if there is an increase in sales volume. Indeed, projection set II of the USDA — which assumes rapid growth of output — indicates that the value of world trade in rice may decline by over 55 per cent between 1964—66 and 1980.[16] This does not imply, of course, that receipts from rice exports will fall by a half or more for every exporting country: some countries, particularly the underdeveloped ones, may be able to increase their share of the world market. But the shocking implication of the set II projections is that even if the developed capitalist nations and the socialist nations cease entirely to export rice, the foreign exchange receipts of the underdeveloped country exporters still would be less in 1980 than they had been in 1964—66.[17] Unless the underdeveloped rice exporting nations can cut their costs of production — and the high yielding varieties have yet to be employed widely in Thailand and Burma — a successful 'green revolution' could ruin their major export market and threaten the livelihood of millions of peasant cultivators, unless a policy of diversification is initiated early.

D. Trade Policies

We have been concerned so far with discussing the possible evolution of international trade in wheat and rice over the next ten years. Our analysis suggests that there may be a tendency for supply to increase faster than demand in both markets and particularly in the case of rice, one can imagine a continuing decline in world prices. These changing market conditions reflect in part the faster growth in production of foodgrains that has been achieved in some areas in recent years and in part the optimistic assumption that this growth will continue in future. The anticipated price reductions,

[16] Ibid., Table 21, p. 42.
[17] Rice exports from underdeveloped countries are estimated to have been $464 million in 1964—66. The value of world rice exports in 1980 (set II) is projected to be $357 million. (Ibid.)

however, constitute both a threat and an opportunity for further growth.

If lower world prices are translated into lower domestic producer prices, profits and incentives from rice and wheat cultivation may decline and the 'green revolution' may come to a halt, although there may continue to be shifts of production activity between efficient and inefficient farmers. On the other hand, if governments maintain domestic grain prices above the world level, subsidy payments may absorb a large part of government revenue, surplus stocks may accumulate (which will require investment in storage facilities), resources will be inefficiently allocated and the level of productive investment may decline. The result, once again, will be slower growth.

Lower food costs and prices also represent an opportunity, however. First, countries which import foodgrains will be able simultaneously to obtain a larger quantity and disburse a smaller sum. This should enable them to improve their standards of nutrition while economizing on scarce foreign exchange. The foreign currency resources formerly spent on purchasing food abroad will become available for purchases of other items, e.g. imports of raw materials or capital equipment, which may be essential for faster growth. Second, those countries which have pursued a policy of foodgrain autarchy and subsequently introduced the high yielding seeds will be able to obtain their domestic food supplies at a lower real cost. This should enable them to produce a given quantity of rice or wheat on a smaller acreage and thereby release land for cultivation of other crops and livestock. Total production should rise even if cereal output remains constant, the agricultural sector should become more diversified and, if necessary, domestic production could replace other commodities currently being imported.

Finally, even grain exporting nations need not necessarily lose. If the 'green revolution' leads to lower prices, as is possible, although it appears rather unlikely today, the commodity terms of trade of exporting countries will deteriorate. Everything else being equal, this will reduce national income. Everything else need not be equal, however. In particular, if the exporting countries are able to cut their costs by more than the fall in prices, e.g. by introducing high yielding varieties, their gains from trade will increase rather than diminish. That is, the commodity terms of trade may decline but the single factoral terms of trade may improve. If they do, national income will rise. Thus, whether a country benefits or loses from falling world prices and costs depends at least in part on the policies pursued.

Policies in developed capitalist countries

The developed capitalist countries have enormous influence in world grain markets. The United States, for instance, is in some years the largest exporter of both wheat and rice, while the enlarged E.E.C. will account for approximately 45 per cent of world agricultural imports. Evidently, decisions made in North America and the E.E.C. will largely determine the course of world trade in rice and wheat.

American and Canadian wheat policies are well defined. These countries, if necessary, can be expected to restrain production and exports in an effort to prevent a sharp decline in world prices. This policy should enable some underdeveloped countries to increase their share of the market. The market, however, will not expand very much unless the E.E.C. can be persuaded to alter its agricultural policies. At present the E.E.C. protects European producers through a system of variable levies and, as a result, wheat prices on the Continent normally are substantially higher than elsewhere. In 1968, for example, the producer price of wheat was about 50 per cent higher in the E.E.C. than in the United Kingdom — a country which has followed a policy of free trade in grains for many decades.

The incorporation of the U.K. into the E.E.C. increases the danger that the export market in wheat in Europe will shrink. It is in the interests of wheat exporters, therefore, to urge the E.E.C. to adopt a more liberal import policy. Britain, as a large importer, also would benefit from lower grain prices, and she can be expected to support arguments for freer trade. Of course, it is also in the interests of the Continental countries to reduce agricultural protection and allocate resources more efficiently, but the murmurings for efficiency may not be heard above the shouts of farmers for higher prices.

Japanese imports of wheat already are quite large and are certain to expand considerably as consumption shifts from rice to wheat. Even now, however, the country could absorb much larger imports than it does. Producer prices in Japan probably are the highest in the world (see Table 5.9) and this severely restricts its purchases from abroad. Japan should be encouraged to change its domestic price structure so that it reflects the fact that the country is an advanced industrial nation that has a comparative advantage in the export of manufactured goods.

Japan's rice policy is even more objectionable than its wheat policy. The support price of brown rice in Japan is nearly twice as high as the export price of high quality Thai rice. The effect of this policy has been to insulate the huge Japanese market from world commerce, to prevent Asian rice exporters from engaging in mutually profitable trade and to force the country to accumulate large surpluses. Some of these surpluses have been dumped on the world market, and thereby spoiled the market for other competitors; other surpluses have been used as animal feed, and thereby spoiled the growing market for imported feedgrains.

Rice stocks in Japan increased to 9.36 million tons in 1969, and in the following year they rose a further 13 per cent to 12 million tons. The large excess inventories in Japan, and the rapid growth of output in the U.S.A., induced these countries to engage in dumping, or as it is euphemistically called, to make concessional sales of rice. Disposal of rice under concessional terms has expanded very quickly in recent years. In the period 1964 to 1966 an average of 600,000 tons a year was sold in this way, while in 1970 concessional sales, almost all of which were by the United States and Japan, were 1.8 million tons, i.e. they were equivalent to about a quarter of the entire world rice trade.

Between 1960 and 1968 the Japanese government determined the support price of rice on the basis of hypothetical costs of production which took into account family labour valued at a wage comparable to that received by urban workers in manufacturing activities. Thus as wages in industry rose, the hypothetical cost of cultivation was increased and the support price of rice was raised. As a result the incentive of farmers to switch to other crops (or to industry) was reduced and resources became grossly misallocated. There is no doubt that Japanese farmers had a higher standard of living than would otherwise have been the case, but this occurred at the expense of urban consumers[18] and other Asian rice exporting nations.

In recent years, however, the Japanese have attempted to divert land from rice to other uses, to freeze producer prices at the 1968 level and to introduce a limited 'free' market in rice. In 1970 the government strengthened these measures by giving farmers a subsidy of $970 per hectare for not producing rice. At the same time, a target was set to reduce rice acreage by 11 per cent. The price support policy was changed yet again in 1971 when the government announced that its objective was to reduce rice production by 2–3 million tons between 1971 and 1972. It remains to be seen whether these measures will succeed. Moreover, even if rice production falls, it may not fall much faster than consumption, so that the country will continue to be self-sufficient.

Japanese international economic policy has come under increasing criticism from many Asian nations, and others. The country is the largest and fastest growing export market in the region, yet the Japanese have contrived to prevent their neighbours from participating fully in the gains from trade. Agricultural policy has been highly protectionist and consequently many potential exports, particularly, as we have seen, of rice and wheat, have been excluded. At the same time, the yen has been undervalued, and this has enabled Japanese businessmen to inundate Asia with inexpensive manufactured goods, to the detriment of infant industries throughout the region. Agricultural protection combined with an undervalued exchange rate has resulted in a surplus on trade account of the balance of payments.[19]

---

[18] Rice consumption also is subsidized in Japan, but this offsets only in part the higher producer prices.

[19] Between 1960 and 1970 Japan's exports to the non-socialist part of Asia extending from Burma to South Korea increased from 14 to 26 per cent of the region's imports, and in 1980 the Japan Economic Research Centre expects Japanese exports to account for 40.5 per cent of the region's imports. At the same time, the region's share of Japan's imports fell from 20 per cent in 1960 to 15 per cent in 1970, and this trend is expected to continue to 1980 when the share will be only 13.6 per cent. At present, Japan exports about 25 per cent more to the region than she imports from it.

Increasingly, this surplus has been partially offset by capital movements in the form of private direct investment in neighbouring countries. These investments have been concentrated in minerals and the domestic manufacturing sector. Japan, evidently, has preferred to invest in Asia rather than import from Asia, but many of her customers would rather sell rice and wheat to Japan than allow her to acquire an ever growing proportion of their stock of capital assets.

The Japanese government has begun to think again about its rice subsidy programme and Asian rice exporters should take advantage of this period of uncertainty to try to persuade Japan to reverse her policy. A more liberal rice policy should receive support from strong vested interests within the country. Lower rice prices would result in higher real wages in industry, and this should be attractive to urban labour unions. Similarly, lower farm prices would encourage more rapid migration of labour from the countryside and alleviate the shortage of industrial labour. In addition, a more liberal import policy would help to combat inflation. If indeed the policy is radically changed, it probably will be because of these domestic political considerations, but Japan's neighbours should make it clear that continued protection has its costs, not only in terms of allocative inefficiency but also in terms of international ill will. Conversely, if Japan were to reduce the area devoted to rice by a significant amount, this would help to stabilize the world price and earn her much good will.

Policies in underdeveloped countries

The underdeveloped countries fall naturally into two groups: those that have a comparative advantage in exporting food-grains and those that do not. Underdeveloped countries which can export wheat competitively, e.g. Argentina, should continue their efforts to cut costs by introducing improved varieties. If this is done, they can expect to increase their share of the world market and offset any lower prices which might emerge with greater volume and lower costs. Countries such as Mexico, however, which subsidize exports of wheat, should review their policy – as, in fact, Mexico is doing. If prices begin to fall, the financial and real cost of the subsidy could increase considerably and this could have adverse consequences for growth, as previously explained.

Burma and Thailand, the two largest rice exporting nations in south-east Asia, confront an awkward dilemma. At present Burma in particular is discouraging exports by, in effect, taxing rice. The original purpose of this policy was to raise revenue for the government while simultaneously taking advantage of their market power to increase the world price of their principal export. This policy, however, gradually has become less viable. First, it has encouraged other countries to begin to export rice or to increase their share of the market, notably China and the U.S.A. Second, it has encouraged importing nations to seek self-sufficiency in rice by planting the new high yielding varieties. Third, it has resulted in slow growth of foreign exchange and tax revenue. If rice prices were to begin to fall, it is obvious that the present policy could not be continued much longer.

One alternative for Burma and Thailand would be to persist in taxing rice exports and exploit to the bitter end their dwindling market power in this commodity while, at the same time, actively seeking new export possibilities. This, in fact, is the implicit policy Thailand followed until very recently. The high tax on rice farmers induced them to shift to maize and, in consequence, maize exports – particularly to Japan – have grown at an impressive rate. In 1960, Thai exports of maize were insignificant, while today they account for about 3 percent of world trade in this commodity. Even so, maize exports still are less important than rice and rubber in terms of value; in terms of quantity, however, maize exports exceed rice exports by about half a million tons.

Another alternative would be for Thailand and Burma to assert aggressively their comparative advantage in rice by cutting export taxes and prices, expanding production and regaining some of the markets lost to other competitors and to import substitution. This is a policy now being followed in Thailand. There are two difficulties with this strategy, however. First, if export duties are reduced abruptly, government revenue will decline and the authorities will be compelled to tax other sectors of the economy more heavily. This may not be easy, either for administrative or political reasons. Second, the loss of export markets may be irreversible, at least in the short run. One reason for this is that countries which have adopted a policy of import substitution in rice, e.g. Sri Lanka and Indonesia, may be reluctant to abandon their programmes when they appear to be on the verge of success. Another reason is that the new rice technology has been biased against countries such as Thailand and Burma which grow rice under conditions of uncontrolled river flooding. The high yielding seeds are best used where irrigation can be accurately controlled, and it so happens that many of these areas are in countries which import rice. Thus costs of cultivation in the importing nations are falling relative to costs in the traditional exporting nations. On the other hand, some of the new varieties can be cultivated in parts of Burma and Thailand; furthermore, there is no reason to believe that varieties could not be developed which are particularly suitable for Thai and Burmese conditions.

Despite the obstacles that would be encountered by a policy of vigorous price competition and export promotion, it is in the interest of Burma and Thailand to maintain their position in the rice export market, and if possible to enlarge it. There is little doubt that these two countries are low cost producers. The data in Table 6.9 suggest that Burmese paddy and rice export prices already are lower than those of other producers. In the case of Thailand, until 1969 about 35 per cent of the export price consisted of taxes. This was reduced to 21.5 per cent in 1970. If these remaining taxes were abolished the export price of high quality Thai rice would be lower than the wholesale price of ordinary rice in virtually every country.

Vigorous price competition from Burma and Thailand would force several high cost producers such as the Philippines and Pakistan to reconsider their policy of foodgrain autarchy. They should do this in any case. Taiwan, in fact, recently has decided to reduce rice acreage by 5 per cent and rice output by 2 per cent. Malaysia has reconsidered its policy of autarchy and now aims at 'only' 90 per cent self-sufficiency in rice in order to avoid accumulating unwanted surpluses in years of exceptionally abundant harvests. These tentative steps should be applauded, but the process should go much further. Countries which do not have a comparative advantage in rice (or wheat) should be encouraged to reallocate resources to other crops in which price and demand prospects are more attractive. There are various possibilities, of which two will be discussed.

First, world demand for feedgrains is likely to grow considerably faster than the demand for rice and wheat for human consumption. Maize, in particular, has relatively good prospects and world trade should grow by about 4 per cent a year for the next decade.[20] The share of the underdeveloped countries in the world market has declined in recent years and this trend could be reversed. In fact, the underdeveloped countries have switched from being a small net exporter of feedgrains to a net importer. Opportunities exist, therefore, both to import substitute feedgrains and to export them. The Japanese market, for instance, is expanding rapidly, but so far only Thailand really has taken advantage of this, although Indonesia, Cambodia and the Philippines have begun to expand production.

A second possibility would be to shift to intensive livestock production. The income elasticity of demand for meat is quite high: the U.S. Department of Agriculture estimates it to be about 0.65 for the world as a whole and FAO about 0.32.[21] In Africa and Asia the elasticity almost certainly exceeds unity, although it will be much lower in Latin America, where per capita meat consumption already is relatively high.[22] Not only does meat production represent a large and rapidly growing potential export market for underdeveloped countries, the introduction of livestock into a grain economy can help to stabilize domestic food consumption. In years of bumper harvests when grains are in excess supply the surplus can be used to feed livestock, while in years of poor harvest, most of the grain can be consumed by humans and some of the livestock can be slaughtered. In this way, expansion and contraction of the number of livestock

---

[20] See USDA, Foreign Agricultural Report No. 63, *Growth in World Demand for Feed Grains*, July 1970.
[21] Ibid., p. 8; FAO, *op. cit.*, Vol. II.
[22] USDA, *Growth in World Demand for Feed Grains*, p. 91.

can be used both to stabilize the price of grain and the supply of food.

In some countries the impact of the 'green revolution' may not be reflected in greater output of rice and wheat. The significance of the new technology in some regions may be that by reducing the amount of land required to grow a given quantity of foodgrains, farmers will be able to diversify, say, into maize and livestock or vegetables and fruit.[23] The essential point is that the 'green revolution' need not end with wheat and rice. Indeed, if sensible policies are pursued it cannot end there. The availability of high yielding seeds which lower costs of production, and hence relative prices, may encourage some countries to reduce grain output (and import rice or wheat from low cost sources abroad) and devote the resources thereby released to producing other things. It is paradoxical but true that an improved rice technology may result in less rice and more meat being produced.

[23] Demand prospects for vegetables and fruit are good, and this is another branch of agriculture in which the underdeveloped countries may be able to regain the share of the market they formerly enjoyed.

PART THREE

Political Objectives and Policy Instruments

CHAPTER 7

Agrarian Policy: The Political and Economic Context

A. Government Objectives and Political Constraints

Economists are accustomed to think in terms of choices. Indeed, it is often claimed that economics is essentially a study of the logic of choice. This assertion is clearly an exaggeration, however, since many members of the profession study topics that have little to do with problems of allocation under conditions of scarcity. Much of Keynesian economics, for example, is unrelated to considerations of this kind. Nonetheless, choice is what a large part of the subject is about, and it is quite natural that when an economist turns from an examination of what 'is' to recommend what 'ought to be', he assumes that there are policy options from which governments can choose. In addition, he normally assumes that the objective of government is to achieve the highest welfare possible for the society as a whole.

A brief acquaintance with conditions in underdeveloped countries is enough to convince a trained observer that welfare seldom is being maximized. The presence of excess capacity, unemployed labour, growing inequality and poverty, etc., all attest to the fact that resources are being badly allocated and the well-being of the majority of the population is being neglected. It does not follow from this, however, that government policies have been based on ignorance or foolishness. In fact it is hardly plausible that lack of knowledge alone is a sufficient explanation for what governments do.

171

Rather than assume that governments attempt to maximize social or national welfare but fail to do so, it might be
more fruitful to assume that governments have quite different objectives and generally succeed in achieving them.
Rather than criticising governments for failing to attain what
they did not set out to attain, or offering advice on how to
attain a non-goal, it would be instructive if more time were
devoted to analysing what governments actually do and
why.[1]

Implicit in the usual approach to policy issues is the
assumption that the government is apart from the rest of
society and above it. The government is viewed as disinter-
ested and omnipotent, a guardian of the national interest and
independent of class or sectional ambitions. Few analysts,
perhaps, believe that this is literally true, but they defend the
assumption as the only basis on which 'objective' and
'scientific', i.e., value free, policies can be formulated. Unfortunately, the defence is untenable. It is not the governments
which occupy the Olympian heights but those who aspire to
advise them.

The ends as well as the means of government policy
usually are largely determined by the government's sources of
support. In most states this support comes from local elites
and economic policy is designed to further their interests.[2] In

---

[1] Two decades ago Paul Baran called attention to the fact that 'faith in
the manipulative omnipotence of the state has all but displaced analysis
of its social structure and understanding of its political and economic
functions. . . .' (Paul A. Baran, 'On the Political Economy of Backwardness', *Manchester School of Economic and Social Studies*, January
1952, reprinted in Robert Rhodes, ed., *Imperialism and Underdevelopment*, 1970, p. 295.)

[2] Ilchman and Uphoff call the group which actively supports and
directly benefits from government action the 'core combination'. This
might be a family (Nicaragua), a monarchy (Iran) or a dominant class
(say, the landed elite) and their immediate allies. Linked to the 'core
combination' are those who share their 'ideological bias' but are
relatively passive in providing support. 'Stability groups' acquiesce with
government policy whereas extra-stability groups' actively — even
violently — oppose the government. Lastly, there are the 'unmobilized
sectors', of which agricultural labourers might be an example. (See
Warren F. Ilchman and Norman Thomas Uphoff, *The Political
Economy of Change*, University of California Press, 1969.)

some countries, e.g., Pakistan, a system of controls has been introduced;[3] in others, e.g., Malaysia, liberal economic policies have been adopted. Military regimes, e.g. in Brazil, have imposed their will in some countries, while in others, e.g. in India and parts of Africa, a single political party, in principle or in practice, has assumed responsibility for the destiny of the nation. In almost every case, however, regardless of the instruments of policy used or the form of political organization, the basis of government support is narrow and the area of action within which the state operates is severely constrained. Seldom has a government attempted deliberately to mobilize the groups that comprise the 'wretched of the earth', i.e. those who lack the privileges of power and the resources necessary for material progress.

Thus the willingness and ability to alter policies may not always be present. On the other hand, it would be unrealistic to assume that nothing ever changes or can be changed. In the short run, political conditions may be inflexible, but conditions will change in the course of time — presumably at various rates — and gradual transformations may be possible. Occasionally, a conjuncture of external events and internal social forces may materialize in which swift and radical changes become possible. Hence, what constitutes good policy advice depends in part on what one considers to be variable: policies which are unacceptable in one place at one point in time may be acceptable in another place or at another point in time.[4]

The purpose of most policy recommendations is to introduce marginal changes within a given socio-economic system Only rarely is it suggested that, say, property relations be altered, the distribution of income be radically changed, or the position and status of one group be improved relative to

[3] An analysis of economic policies in Pakistan in terms of the political groups which benefit from them is contained in Keith Griffin and A. R. Khan, eds., *Growth and Inequality in Pakistan*, especially the commentary to Part III. An analysis in the Latin American context can be found in the introduction to Keith Griffin, ed., *Financing Development in Latin America*, Macmillan, 1971.
[4] Exhortations to make 'constructive' criticisms and give 'practical' advice usually come from people who have short time horizons and assume no fundamental changes are possible or desirable.

that of another. While it would be wrong to despise small changes, it would be equally wrong not to consider whether fundamental changes in the nature of the system are required. Indeed, it has been argued that the maintenance of the existing agrarian system in many underdeveloped countries is incompatible with the elimination of rural poverty. This point of view has been powerfully expressed by Lenin:

> It goes without saying that if capitalism could develop agriculture which is everywhere lagging terribly behind industry it could raise the standard of living of the masses ... But if capitalism did these things it would not be capitalism: for both uneven development and a semistarvation level of existence of the masses are fundamental and inevitable conditions and constitute the premises of this mode of production.[5]

It is impossible to determine what is inevitable by reference solely to the facts, be they the facts of contemporary society or of history. But a study of the facts can tell us what has happened and is happening, and unfortunately in a distressing number of cases in underdeveloped countries the facts are consistent with Lenin's assertion.[6] Agriculture has lagged behind the rest of the economy, and despite the 'green revolution' the level of existence of the masses has yet to improve significantly. Those who have carefully studied recent events do not dispute this; indeed, it would be futile to do so, since the facts speak for themselves.

For example, in India, the largest non-socialist underdeveloped country, it is widely recognized that 'the green revolution belongs to the "kulaks"'.[7] Moreover, many people are beginning to believe that the reason for this is in the nature of the system, and thus a solution, presumably, lies in a change in system. Guy Hunter, for instance, notes

[5] V. I. Lenin, *Imperialism the Highest Stage of Capitalism*, Moscow, p. 59.
[6] This does not imply that all capitalist agriculture in underdeveloped countries results in poverty or that agriculture in all capitalist countries is incapable of overcoming rural poverty.
[7] John P. Lewis, 'Wanted in India: A Relevant Radicalism', *Economic and Political Weekly*, Special Number, July 1970, pp. 1219–1220.

that 'there are parts of India where any genuine share of control by small men is virtually impossible, partly from general ignorance and poverty, but also because the big men have so many strings to their bow of domination — caste, land ownership, their position as both creditors and political bosses'.[8] In this situation — and India is not unique, of course — it is difficult to imagine how rural poverty can be reduced significantly in the absence of a major structural transformation.

B. Agricultural Stagnation

As can be seen in Table 7.1, the majority of people in underdeveloped countries live and work in rural areas. The techniques of production that cultivators employ often are simple, if not primitive. Credit is scarce and expensive for the majority of inhabitants, and the land frequently is controlled by a small minority. The peasants frequently are illiterate and have limited access to knowledge and new methods of cultivation. Marketing, transport and storage facilities are inadequate. As a consequence of these conditions, the average standard of living in rural areas is very low, usually considerably less than $100 per head per year.[9] Debilitating disease is rampant. Infant mortality rates are high and life expectancy is less than 50 years. There is no doubt that the greatest concentration of poverty in the world is in the rural areas of underdeveloped countries.

Considerably more than half the labour force is engaged in agricultural activities; in Africa the figure is nearly 80 per cent and in many parts of Asia it is over two-thirds. In some countries, notably Uganda and Tanzania, only about ten per cent of the labour force is employed outside of agriculture. If one divides the underdeveloped world into five broad regions, as has been done in the table below, it can be seen that Latin America appears to be unique in having slightly less than half

[8] Guy Hunter, *The Administration of Agricultural Development: Lessons from India.*
[9] Even in Latin America, the richest of the major underdeveloped regions of the world, over two-thirds of the agricultural population, viz. about 70 million people, receive an annual income of less than $100 per person.

Table 7.1
Employment and Output in Agriculture

	Percentage of Labour Force in Agriculture	Output of Agriculture, Forestry and Fishing as percent of G.D.P.
South Asia	71	40+
East Asia[1]	64	33[2]
Latin America	49	21
Africa[3]	79	44
Near East	61	n.a.

Notes: n.a. = not available

[1] exclusive of Japan.
[2] average of Burma, Philippines, South Korea, Taiwan, Thailand and West Malaysia.
[3] exclusive of South Africa.

its active population in agriculture. The figure for Latin America as a whole is misleading, however, because the average is strongly influenced by the highly urbanized 'southern cone' countries of Argentina, Chile and Uruguay. Were we to exclude these three countries, the average for Latin America would be substantially higher.

Although agriculture accounts for most of the employment in underdeveloped countries, it does not account for most of the output. Indeed in no region does agricultural production constitute half of the gross domestic product, although it does in a few countries, notably in Africa, e.g. Ghana, Malawi, Nigeria. In general, as a rough rule of thumb, agriculture accounts for nearly twice as much employment as it does of income. This is but another way of saying that the average productivity of labour in agriculture is much less than half that of the other sectors of the economy.[10] There are important exceptions, of course. In Uruguay, for instance,

[10] Part of the difference, however, is a statistical artifact, since overvalued exchange rates and other policies which turn the terms of trade against agriculture result in an understatement of the value of agricultural production and an overstatement of the value of industrial production. The difference in value added per man would be somewhat diminished if world prices rather than 'distorted' domestic prices were used.

the average productivity of labour in agriculture is only slightly lower than the national average: the sector accounts for 18 per cent of employment and 15 per cent of output. At the other extreme is Zambia, where agriculture employs four-fifths of the work force but produces only ten per cent of domestic product. The reason for the enormous difference in the productivity of labour between agriculture and the rest of the economy in Zambia is, of course, the existence of the highly productive, capital intensive copper mines in the northern part of the country. In addition, it is probable that some agricultural output has failed to be recorded by the statisticians.

Trends in output and investment

The data in Table 7.1 strongly suggest that if one wishes to improve the standard of living of the mass of the population one must achieve rapid growth not just of GNP in general but of agricultural output in particular. It is in rural areas that the most numerous cases of poverty exist, and it is in these areas that the assault on poverty should begin. Unfortunately, despite widespread speculation that 'traditional agriculture' is becoming transformed, there is not much evidence yet of accelerated expansion of agricultural production.

Over the two decades which ended in 1970 both per capita food production and per capita agricultural production increased less than one per cent a year in the underdeveloped world as a whole.[11] Moreover, the rate of growth of both these aggregates was much slower in the 1960s than in the 1950s. Indeed, agriculture completely stagnated in the 1960s, i.e. during the much heralded Decade of Development and during the period (after 1965) when the 'green revolution' is reported to have begun. So far progress in the 1970s has been zero, largely because of drought.

The same broad tendencies appear if one disaggregates the data for the Third World and examines each major region separately. In Latin America there was some acceleration in the growth of per capita food production, but per capita agricultural production as a whole showed no tendency

[11] Also see the trend rates of growth presented in Chapter 1.

Table 7.2
Rate of Growth of Per Capita Food and Agricultural Output,
1948/52–1970
(per cent per annum)

	Per Capita Food Production 1948/52–1970	1960–1970	Per Capita Agricultural Production 1948/52–1970	1960–1970
Latin America	0.4	0.6	0.2	0.0
Far East (excl. Japan)	0.8	0.3	0.7	0.3
Near East (excl. Israel)	0.7	0.0	0.8	0.0
Africa (excl. South Africa)	0.0	−0.7	0.3	−0.5
All under-developed countries	0.6	0.1	0.6	0.0
Developed capitalist countries	1.1	0.9	1.0	0.6

Source: Compiled from data reported in FAO, *The State of Food and Agriculture 1971.* The figures in the table refer to end-to-end growth rates.

whatever to increase in the last decade. The situation in Africa is even worse: production per head of food and of total agricultural commodities declined sharply in the 1960s. This suggests *prima facie* that the majority of the African population suffered a decline in their level of consumption during this period. The region was becoming even more underdeveloped.

The performance in Asia, the centre of the 'green revolution', was only slightly better than in the other two regions. In the Near East there was a decline in the rate of growth, and during 1960–1970 there was a zero tendency for food and agricultural output per head to increase. In the Far East, once again, rates of growth appeared to fall, although production per head did increase about 0.3 per cent a year. Thus the regional data on growth rates do not suggest that there has been a breakthrough in agricultural development.[12] If anything, the rate of advance was declining and in general there was negligible progress in agriculture – the sector in which most people in underdeveloped countries must seek a livelihood.

The basic reason why agriculture has performed relatively badly is because it has been given relatively low priority by those responsible for economic policy. Development planning has in general been characterized by a pronounced urban bias.[13] One aspect of this neglect of the countryside is the low proportion of total investment that has been allocated to agriculture. In very few countries, for example, does the fraction of investment channeled to agriculture reflect its relative importance in national output – much less its contribution to employment. There are exceptions, of course. For example, in Venezuela and Israel the share of agriculture in total investment is greater than its share in GDP. In most countries, however, the share of investment allocated to agriculture is less than half its contribution to gross domestic product. For instance, a recent study of eighteen underdeveloped countries in the period 1960–1965 indicates that agriculture accounts for twelve per cent of total investment and nearly 30 per cent of total output.[14] A study of twelve countries in an earlier period produced virtually the same result.

No one would suggest, of course, that investment should be distributed among sectors in accordance with their contribution to domestic product. It is quite natural that industry and social overhead facilities should receive a more than proportional share of fixed capital formation, for these are activities whose relative importance is certain to rise as development proceeds. The problem in many underdeveloped

[12] Alternatively, if there has been a breakthrough, it has occurred so recently that it is not reflected in the data on growth for the 1960s. In other words, the existence of a breakthrough is at present more a matter of faith than of fact.

[13] For a detailed examination of the Indian case see Michael Lipton's contribution to P. P. Streeten and M. Lipton, eds., *The Crisis of Indian Planning*.

[14] E. F. Szczepanik, *Agricultural Capital Formation in Selected Developing Countries*, Agricultural Planning Studies No. 11, FAO, 1970.

Table 7.3
Agricultural Investment

	Weighted averages of	
	18 countries 1960–65	12 countries 1950–60
1 Agricultural investment as a per cent of total fixed investment.	12.3	11.5
2 Agricultural investment as a per cent of agricultural output.	7.4	6.9
3 Agricultural output as a per cent of GDP.	29.5	29.3
4 Gross marginal capital-output ratio		
(a) in agriculture	1.73	1.78
(b) in the entire economy	3.20	2.70

Source: E. F. Szczepanik, *Agricultural Capital Formation in Selected Developing Countries*, Agricultural Planning Studies No. 11, FAO, 1970, p. 2, Tables 1A and 1B.

countries, however, is that the concentration on non-agricultural investment has been excessive, and as a result there has been insufficient capital formation in rural areas. This, in turn, has led to slow growth of food and fibre production, rising agricultural prices, and either increased imports or decreased exports of agricultural products. Economic growth has been unbalanced to such an extent that the overall rate of advance has been slower than it need have been and the distribution of income has been more unequal than it might have been.

In the first half of the 1960s, in the eighteen countries mentioned in the study above, the rate of investment in agriculture was only 7.4 per cent. At the same time the incremental capital–output ratio for the economy as a whole was 3.2. Had this ratio been applicable to agriculture, the rate of growth in the sector would have been only 2.3 per cent a year, that is, probably less than the rate of increase of the population. Fortunately, the capital–output ratio in agriculture in the 18 countries that were studied was substantially lower than the average, and in consequence agriculture achieved a rate of growth of 4.3 per cent despite the low level of investment.

The comparatively low capital—output ratio in agriculture suggests that the neglect of the sector cannot be attributed to a low average rate of return on capital, although it must be recognized that the capital—output ratio is a rather crude concept and is not always a good indicator of profitability. Nonetheless, from the available evidence it appears that if a larger share of investment had been allocated to rural areas both the rate of growth of agricultural output and of GDP would have been faster. In other words, the concentration of investment in urban and industrial activities not only led to increased income inequality, it also resulted in slower growth. In this respect there was no conflict between equality and growth in most underdeveloped countries.

As one would expect, the low capital—output ratios in agriculture are associated with low capital—labour ratios. For this reason it is usually much cheaper to create employment in rural areas than in urban areas. A weighted average of seventeen countries in the period 1960—1965, for example, indicates that investment per additional agricultural worker was only $850.[15] In the industrial sector, in contrast, the incremental capital—labour ratio often is over $5,000. In other words, it costs five or six times as much to create a job in industry as it does in agriculture. Thus, if one is interested in creating employment — quite apart from improving the distribution of income or accelerating growth — a strong case can be made for concentrating resources in agriculture.

Not all countries, of course, have a low capital—output ratio in the agricultural sector. In Egypt, for example, the capital—output ratio in agriculture was 3.4 and this was higher than the overall ratio of 2.6. Moreover, the agricultural capital—labour ratio in Egypt also is quite high, viz. $2,210. Evidently, agriculture in Egypt has become rather capital intensive. The reason for this is that in recent years agricultural investment has been directed towards major construction projects which have long gestation periods. The most obvious example is the Aswan High Dam, which in 1960—1965 absorbed 28 per cent of total agricultural investment in the country. Conversely, directly productive

[15] Ibid., p. 38, Table 13.

investment in machinery, equipment and livestock has been small, namely 33 per cent, and this has led to a rather high capital—output ratio. Thus it is not inevitable that rural capital formation will generate more employment and output than investment in other sectors, but the available evidence suggests that this is quite likely in many underdeveloped countries.

Innovation and technical change

Rapid expansion in agriculture requires more than just a faster rate of capital accumulation, however. Methods of cultivation must be altered, new crops must be introduced, marketing facilities improved and agricultural supply industries expanded. In other words, investment, to be effective, must be accompanied by technical change. The reverse also is true, however: most technical advances cannot be incorporated into the economic system in the absence of capital accumulation. Thus investment and technical change are complementary or reinforcing.

Is rapid technical change possible in the rural areas of underdeveloped countries? Will impoverished and illiterate peasants take advantage of opportunities to innovate? For many years it was widely believed that the answer to these questions is 'no', but recent evidence shows quite clearly that under suitable conditions rapid change in rural areas is indeed possible.

Agricultural conditions in underdeveloped areas frequently are described as 'static' and 'traditional'. This is misleading. Change is always occurring, but in many instances the stimulus to change originates outside the rural community and tends to depress the standard of living of large sections of the community. Common examples are demographic increase which reduces land resources per head, expansion of the manufacturing sector which destroys local artisanal activities, and falling agricultural prices which reduce the net income from agricultural production. When these external pressures arise, peasants respond in a variety of ways — by migration, by increased labour intensity of cultivation, by shifting to

other types of handicrafts and to other crops, etc.[16]
Techniques of production and the composition of output
adapt to changing resource endowments and relative prices,
but the innovation is largely defensive in nature and usually
merely offsets in part the adverse consequences of the initial
stimulus. History shows that peasants are adaptable and they
do innovate, but the evidence also shows that innovation is
not a synonym for progress; on the contrary, it often is an
indication of regression and increased underdevelopment.[17]

The question, thus, is not whether peasants innovate, but
whether they are able to move from a defensive to an
offensive position and thereby achieve a breakthrough to
higher levels of productivity, income and accumulation. In
some instances such a breakthrough may be difficult to
achieve for structural reasons. Specifically, in regions where
farms are extremely small and cultivation is dependent upon
highly variable rainfall, average incomes will be extraordin-
arily low and in poor years the peasant and his family will be
exposed to the dangers of starvation. In such circumstances
the peasant may be preoccupied not with maximizing his
income but with maximizing his chances of survival. That is,
when risk and uncertainty are high, a small farmer may prefer
a technology and a crop pattern which combine a low mean
yield with low variance to alternative technologies and crops
which, although characterized by higher mean yields, are also
associated with greater variance.[18] This will be particularly
true if institutions for spreading risk are poorly developed.[19]

[16] In section C below we discuss cases in which certain groups in the
rural community suffer a decline in their wellbeing as a result of
changes internal to the agricultural sector. We also discuss possible
political responses to technical change.
[17] We do not wish to suggest that all external stimuli reduce the
wellbeing of the peasantry; the reverse can also occur, e.g. when new
crops are introduced or foreign markets become more accessible as a
result of improved transport facilities.
[18] See Michael Lipton, 'The Theory of the Optimising Peasant', *Journal
of Development Studies*, April 1968.
[19] See Chapter 3, Section B, where it is argued that in some regions, at
least, risk spreading institutions are quite common.

Thus, ideally, a new technology is more likely to be acceptable to impoverished peasants if it promises not only higher income in an 'average' year but also fewer 'bad' years: the mean should be higher and the variance lower. Unhappily, not all technological changes possess these characteristics, and one should not be surprised to discover that some farmers resist an innovation even though it can be shown to be 'profitable'. The new high yielding seeds of rice, for example, do not require more water than indigenous varieties[20] but they do require an assured supply of water, and in areas where farming depends on an uncertain rainfall these new seeds may not be adopted, or adopted only partially — despite the fact that the average yield and net income may be greater with the new seeds than the old. The risk of a total crop failure also is greater and those on the margin of subsistence may not be able to afford to run such a risk.

If it is government policy to encourage small farmers to adopt high yielding varieties in areas where the amount and timing of rainfall are uncertain, and where risk seems to be an inhibiting factor, either risk must be reduced, e.g. by providing supplementary irrigation facilities, or the burden of risk must be assumed by the government, e.g. by agreeing to provide credit at low cost for purchases of consumption goods during periods of hardship.[21] The basic point is that peasants are responsive to economic incentives and opportunities. Where innovation fails to occur one should not assume that peasants are perverse, irrational or conservative; instead one should search for the particular institutional or commercial obstacles which are frustrating constructive change.

This does not imply that sociological factors are never of importance in determining both which innovations are accepted and their rate of diffusion. On occasion they clearly

[20] In fact, some high yielding varieties require less water than the older varieties because their growing period is shorter.

[21] An alternative policy would be to establish a crop insurance scheme, but this cannot be done quickly. (See Bernard Oury, 'Crop Insurance, Creditworthiness, and Development', *Finance and Development*, Vol. 7, No. 3, September 1970.)

can be. For example, in many rural communities it is the custom for those who are most prosperous to share their relative abundance with friends and neighbours. Where rough equality in income prevails, such a custom acts as a form of cooperative credit, allowing those who encounter temporary difficulties, say, due to illness, to maintain their consumption, on the implicit understanding that when they experience unusually favourable circumstances they will not forget the needs of former (potential or actual) benefactors.

This custom, however, can act as a disincentive to any single farmer to increase his output substantially above the average of his community. Since the peasant is expected to distribute his 'surplus' among relatives and friends, he may not personally benefit very much from adopting an innovation. Hence pioneering efforts may be discouraged and individualistic, isolated change in some peasant communities may become rather difficult.[22] On the other hand, once a 'threshold' has been passed and, say, ten per cent of the households in a community have successfully used a new technology, the rate of diffusion of the innovation tends to accelerate markedly, and if conditions are appropriate, within a short period of time virtually the entire community will have altered its methods of production or cropping pattern, as the case may be.[23]

It would appear, thus, that there usually are good explanations why farmers do or do not innovate. If peasants sometimes appear to be unresponsive or hostile to proposed technical changes it is probably because the risks are high, the returns to the cultivator are low — for example, because of local custom or land tenure conditions — or because credit facilities and marketing outlets are inadequate and the necessary inputs — including knowledge — are missing.

[22] This phenomen was observed by F. Landa Jocano in his study of a rural barrio on the island of Panay, Philippines. See his *The Traditional World of Malitbog*, Community Development Research Council, Quezon City, 1969.
[23] The S-shaped pattern of diffusion is well demonstrated by Z. Griliches, 'Hybrid Corn and the Economics of Innovation', *Science*, 29 July 1960, reprinted in N. Rosenberg, ed., *The Economics of Technological Change*.

There are numerous indications that farmers in poor countries are no less responsive to price signals than farmers in rich countries. Research in West Africa, for instance, has shown that cocoa and palm oil producers will increase the quality of their output if price differentials become wider.[24] Similarly, it has been shown, in Pakistan and elsewhere, that cultivators will alter the composition of agricultural output in response to changes in relative crop prices. If, for example, the price of cotton in the Punjab rises relative to the price of sugar cane, maize and other food grains, the acreage devoted to cotton will increase at the expense of the other crops.[25] Lastly, research in central and northeastern Thailand has shown that farmers will introduce both a new technique — namely, new maize seeds, and a new crop — namely, kenaf — when market conditions make such innovations profitable.[26] Thus one can now be confident that farmers in under-developed countries can and do make radical changes in what and how they produce. Lack of innovation in agriculture, where it exists, is due not to poor motivation, but to inadequate opportunities.

On the interpretation of S-curves
It has been widely observed, in rich and poor countries alike, that the spread of an improved variety through time can be described in terms of an S-shaped curve. That is, innovation

[24] P. T. Bauer and B. S. Yamey, 'A Case Study of Response to Price in an Underdeveloped Country', *Economic Journal*, December 1959.
[25] W. P. Falcon, 'Farmer Response to Price in a Subsistence Economy: The Case of West Pakistan', *American Economic Review*, May 1964.
[26] J. R. Behrman, 'The Adoption of New Products and of New Factors in Response to Market Incentives in Peasant Agriculture: An Econometric Investigation of Thai Corn and Kenaf Responses in the Post-War Period', University of Pennsylvania, Department of Economics, Discussion Paper No. 45, February 1967. Also see R. L. Sansom, 'The Motor Pump: A Case Study of Innovation and Development', *Oxford Economic Papers*, March 1969, for an example of mechanization by peasants in South Vietnam. An important study using Indian data is D. Narain, *The Impact of Price Movements on Areas Under Selected Crops in India 1900–1939*, Cambridge University Press, 1965. Also see Raj Krishna, 'Farm Supply Response in India–Pakistan: A Case Study of the Punjab Region', *Economic Journal*, 1962.

occurs at an accelerating pace during the early stages, followed by a period of deceleration and the eventual attainment of a maximum. This general tendency seems to be more or less universal. What is not universal, however, is the extent of ultimate acceptance of an innovation. Hybrid maize in the United States, for example, is grown on virtually all of the land devoted to maize used for animal foodstuffs; improved varieties of rice occupy virtually all of the paddy fields in Taiwan. In contrast, only a third of the wheat grown in India is of the high yielding variety and only half of the paddy fields in the Philippines are cultivated with high yielding varieties of rice.

These contrasts arise not only between countries but also within a single country. Mexico is a particularly interesting illustration of this phenomenon because attempts were made simultaneously in the late 1940s to introduce high yielding varieties of wheat and maize. Yet only the new wheat technology was successful. This can be seen at a glance in the accompanying figure, in which a three year moving average of

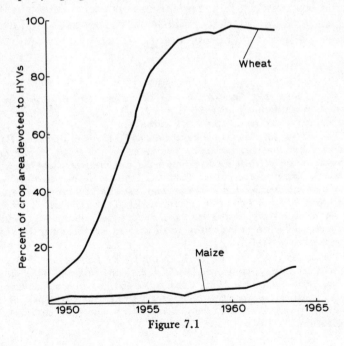

Figure 7.1

the percentage of total area of wheat and maize devoted to improved varieties is plotted over time. By the middle of the 1960s over 95 per cent of the wheat area in Mexico was planted to high yielding varieties, whereas only 13 per cent of the maize grown in Mexico is from hybrid seeds.[27]

What accounts for these differences in the depth to which technical change penetrates the countryside? Is it merely ignorance, a lack of awareness by farmers of the benefits of change? The answer would seem to be 'no', since in many parts of the world one can find adopters of a new technology and non-adopters living and working side-by-side. In such situations there are no obvious obstacles to the transfer of information or experience.

Is the answer to be sought, then, in terms of the dichotomy between subsistence and commercial producers? It is true, certainly, that large commercial farmers tend to adopt high yielding varieties quite readily whereas small subsistence farmers tend not to.[28] But it is equally true that not all farmers with a commercial orientation adopt new varieties; many, in fact, remain non-adopters. Thus it would appear that 'subsistence-mindedness' cannot account for the observed facts.[29] The psychology of the peasant, tradition,

[27] Dana Dalrymple, *New Cereal Varieties: Wheat and Corn in Mexico*, USDA, Washington, July 1969, Table 2, p. 9; also see the figure on p. 10 which is reproduced above as Figure 7.1.

[28] The reason for this, as we have indicated before, is that most HYVs require that material inputs be purchased and thus the farmer must have a source of cash income before he can innovate. Where cash is available from sources other than farming, e.g. from part-time wage employment, a subsistence farmer may use the new seeds — provided the taste, colour and cooking characteristics of the grain are not inferior to indigenous cereals. An example of this behaviour was found in Tanjore, India, where even very small farmers were using an improved variety of rice, ADT-27.

[29] For a contrary view see D. H. Penny, 'The Economics of Peasant Agriculture: The Indonesian Case', *Bulletin of Indonesian Economic Studies*, No. 5, October 1966. There is considerable internal evidence in Penny's article, however, which suggests that the mentality of the Javanese peasant has relatively little to do with the slow rate of innovation.

conservatism or a subsistence mentality do not appear to inhibit the spread of technical change.

Neither ignorance of new methods nor reluctance of farmers to accept new methods seems to be an adequate explanation why Mexican maize growers do not innovate while Mexican wheat farmers do, or why Taiwanese farmers quickly adopted improved rice varieties while Indian rice farmers have not. The likely explanation, as we have suggested before, lies not in motives but in means.

In some cases it can be demonstrated that high yielding varieties have not been widely adopted because they are not suitable to the local environment. Dwarf varieties of rice, for example, obviously are not appropriate in areas subject to deep flooding. In situations such as these it is easy to explain why technical change is limited. In other areas, however, the natural environment may not be hostile to change, yet one still finds that technical innovation does not penetrate very far. The most probable explanation in this case lies in the social and economic structure of the rural community. The introduction of high yielding varieties requires not only a sympathetic environment, it also requires several other inputs, e.g. irrigation, fertilizer, insecticides or credit. If access to these other ingredients of technical change is restricted to a minority of cultivators (who may own, of course, a substantial proportion of the land), the majority of farmers may be structurally unable to innovate and the S-curve, in consequence, will reach its maximum well below the 100 per cent mark.

Mexican wheat farmers tend to be rather large landowners and are able themselves to finance the purchase of inputs complementary to the high yielding varieties.[30] Hence innovation in the wheat areas is very widespread. Taiwanese rice farmers, on the other hand, tend to have small holdings, but the necessary inputs for cultivating high yielding rice are supplied through government supported agencies on a non-discriminatory basis, and hence each cultivator — however

[30] The precondition for introducing HYV wheat was the availability of water and this was supplied by massive public investment in irrigation facilities.

small he may be — has access to the necessary means of production. Mexican maize growers, however, are neither sufficiently large to be able to finance their own requirements for material inputs nor sufficiently strong politically to compel the government to supply the necessary services. As a result, they appear to be slow to innovate.

In summary, the height of the S-curve is a possible indicator of the ease of access of cultivators to the means of production: the lower is the peak of the curve, the more restricted is access, and vice versa. The hypothesis only applies, of course, in situations where the environment is not hostile to a particular technical innovation. In situations where the environment is not a constraint, an examination of S-curves may tell us something about the society in which technical change is occurring.

C. Is Technical Change Desirable?

It has been assumed implicitly so far in this chapter that technical change in rural areas is desirable and its relative absence in many parts of the world should be deplored. While this assumption may often be correct, it is important to recognize that 'change' is not synonymous with 'progress'. Indeed, whether any particular technical or institutional change is desirable depends on one's objectives and value judgements. Even if a new technology allows an economy to produce more output with its given resources, it does not follow that this technology is unambiguously desirable. The most one can conclude is that the new technology in principle would enable every member of the community to increase his consumption, but whether this potential is realized in practice depends upon the way the increased output is distributed. It certainly is possible for average output per head to increase while the consumption of certain groups falls.

Furthermore, even if everyone experiences increased consumption, it is likely that some groups will gain relatively more than others. In other words, any technical change is likely to affect not only the volume of production but also the distribution of income. When this occurs, one must consider both the distribution effects and the output effects when assessing the desirability of change.[31] In addition, there will be other consequences of innovation — e.g., on the distribution of wealth, social status and working conditions — and these should not be neglected when making normative judgements. There is no scientific way of answering the question posed in the title of this section; each case must be judged separately, and one must expect to encounter differences of opinion.

Cumulative movements and social differences

It is not difficult to find historical cases in which technical change created victims as well as beneficiaries. The enclosure movement in England is, of course, a classic example, but it is not unique. The expulsion of small farmers from the land in the 1930s in the southwestern part of the United States is eloquently described by John Steinbeck in *The Grapes of Wrath*. In Morelos, Mexico, new milling machines were introduced in the 1870s which were capable of extracting a much higher proportion of sugar from the stalk than the old presses. At the same time the development of the Mexican railroad system led to the creation of a national market. As a result of these two technical changes, costs of sugar production fell and effective demand rose; the profitability of sugar plantations consequently increased substantially. This provided an incentive to the Morelos planters to expand output and the size of their plantations, and they did this at the expense of the livelihood and land of the villagers in the region. The peasantry resisted, attempted to defend their own interests, and eventually rebelled. The struggle persisted for many years and the demand of the villagers for the restitution of their lands ultimately was achieved under the leadership of Zapata.[32]

A similar struggle over land can be observed today on the island of Mindanao in the Philippines. The local Muslim communities have come into conflict with two different groups of outsiders. First, there has been a large immigration of Christian settlers from other parts of the country, their

[31] For a theoretical discussion of this point see I. M. D Little, *A Critique of Welfare Economics*.
[32] See John Womack, Jr., *Zapata and the Mexican Revolution*, 1969.

motive for moving being largely to escape from the high population densities of Luzon and the Visayas. The Muslims, naturally, have resented being dislodged from their territory and have violently resisted. Second, there has been an invasion of large landowners. Large estates have been expanding in Mindanao by taking advantage of a constitutional provision which allows any citizen to lease from the government up to 2000 hectares of unoccupied land. This terrain, for reasons which are unclear, is supposed to be used for pasture. Aspiring landowners have expelled from the land both Christian settlers and the indigenous Muslims by employing the local police or their own private army. Once the land is 'cleared' the 'warlord' applies to the government for a lease. These are available for a nominal fee on 25 year terms, after which the land can be purchased. Very little of this land is in practice being used to graze livestock; most of it is devoted to growing rice or maize.[33]

Technical change clearly is occurring in Mindanao, but the benefits of this change have accrued to outsiders. The indigenous people have been deprived of their land, impoverished and killed. They have become the victims of what many have described as progress.

The possibility of a cumulative downward spiral of poverty in rural areas has become widely acknowledged in the fifteen years since Myrdal first enunciated the principle of cumulative causation.[34] Where growing poverty occurs, however, it usually is attributed to exogenous phenomena or forces external to the rural community. Rapid population growth combined with slow expansion of employment opportunities in industry may compel farmers to use increasingly labour intensive methods of cultivation in a context of sharply diminishing returns to human effort.[35] Alternatively, technical advances in industry may result in the destruction of

[33] Gerrit Huizer, 'Agrarian Unrest and Peasant Organizations in the Philippines', Institute of Social Studies, The Hague, Occasional Paper No. 17, February 1972.
[34] G. Myrdal, *Economic Theory and Underdeveloped Regions*, Duckworth, 1957.
[35] C. Geertz describes this process very well. See his *Agricultural Involution*, University of California Press, 1968.

traditional rural crafts and trades. This, in turn, might lead to considerable unemployment in the countryside and the conversion of a prosperous village into 'an agricultural slum'.[36]

There is no doubt that population growth and certain types of industrialization can and have transformed the peasantry into paupers. On occasion these external shocks can be devastating. It must also be recognized, however, that changes which occur within the rural sector itself can be equally devastating to the peasantry. That is, a high rate of investment in agriculture and rapid technological change are not always sufficient to prevent distress; indeed, they may be the cause of it. The experiences of Morelos and Mindanao show that this possibility is a real one.

Once the focus of analysis shifts from external stimuli to technical changes occurring inside the agrarian sector, one is required to specify rather carefully the social composition of the rural community. A model in which 'agriculture' confronts 'industry' will no longer suffice. Moreover, it is almost as misleading to envisage the rural community as composed of an undifferentiated mass of 'peasants' confronting 'landlords': the 'peasants' are not a homogenous class and they should be broken up into groups which have common interests.

Obviously the class composition of rural society is not uniform throughout the Third World. Some broad generalizations may be valid, however. At the top of the society one usually finds the large landowners, and the merchants, brokers and moneylenders who are allied to them. Then come the 'middle peasants', i.e. those who own or have assured access to sufficient land to enable them to produce enough for the subsistence of their family and perhaps also a small surplus. Next, there are the small peasants, minifundistas and tenants who cannot obtain a livelihood from their own land alone and are therefore forced to supplement their income by working as labourers for others. At the very bottom of the social structure are the agricultural labourers,

[36] H. H. Mann, *The Social Framework of Agriculture*, Frank Cass, 1968, p. 301.

i.e. those whose income depends entirely on wages. Thus we have distinguished a minimum of four groups or classes: landlords, middle peasants, small peasants and agricultural labourers.

Technical change in the agricultural sector will have a different impact on each of the four groups. For example, the introduction of labour saving machinery, such as a combine harvester, may be beneficial to landlords and possibly even to the middle peasants (if they can hire the machines), but it will reduce the employment opportunities and well-being of agricultural labourers. Alternatively, investment by landlords in irrigation equipment may increase the demand for labour, and hence result in higher incomes for the labourers; but increased supplies of agricultural produce may depress prices and this would tend to reduce the income of the middle peasantry and possibly also of the small peasantry. Other combinations of benefit and loss are possible, of course. The only point that is being made at this stage is that in formulating agricultural p.... it would be a mistake to assume that there is a harmo.... .nterests in the rural community.

Organized and unorganized interest groups
Government policies can be used to redress injustice, to mitigate harm or to bestow positive benefits on favoured groups. The classes and factions on which the government relies for support usually can anticipate that state action will be forthcoming in defence of their interests. But in any case, those who are hurt by technical change or government policy will, of course, try to protect themselves. The extent to which they will succeed depends in part on how well they are organized.

In most countries the landlords are organized into various groups: national farm associations look after the interests of the class as a whole, while regional organizations and societies concerned with specific crops or livestock have more narrowly defined tasks. In some instances, banks have been established specifically for large farmers.[37] In addition, the large landowners usually have close links with (or participate directly in) urban financial, commercial and industrial undertakings. They may also play an active role in the established political parties. In other words, there are a variety of channels through which landlords can exercise influence on behalf of their interests and ambitions.

The middle peasants, on the other hand, have virtually no influence outside the agricultural sector. They may belong to a farm association but their influence inside such an organization is likely to be small in comparison to that of the landlords. In some countries institutions specifically designed to cater to the needs of small farmers have been established, but they have met with relatively little success. The small peasants and landless labourers have even less power than the middle peasant. Rural labourers and tenants seldom are organized either in political parties or trade unions, and indeed in some countries they are prevented by law from becoming so. These groups, thus, are in a highly vulnerable position.

We have argued in an earlier chapter[37] that the peasantry in general — particularly the labourers and small peasantry, but also the middle peasantry — is subjected to monopolistic exploitation by those who have privileged access to the means of production. There is a social system which corresponds to this economic system and which has developed parallel to it. This social system has been called by some writers the 'culture of repression'.[39]

There is a variety of institutions and practices which have been devised to repress the mass of rural inhabitants: the

---

[37] In Iran, for example, the Agricultural Development Fund was established in 1968 for the purpose of financing large-scale agricultural development projects on mechanized farms as well as large agro-businesses. The Fund makes long-term loans at 7.5 per cent interest; the minimum amount that can be borrowed is 5 million rials, i.e. $67,000. In Brazil, the Banco do Brazil lends only to those who are at least as large as the 'minimum profitable agriculturalist', and the smallest loan it makes is 50 times the annual earnings of an industrial worker.

[38] See Chapter 2.

[39] Allan Holmberg, 'Some Relationships Between Psychobiological Deprivation and Culture Change in the Andes', Cornell University, 21–25 March 1966, mimeo.

concentration of resources in a few hands, debt peonage, slavery, serfdom, pass laws (e.g., in South Africa), paternalism, caste differentiation, racial discrimination, linguistic divisions, murder and terror. Usually repression has succeeded and the status quo has not been threatened, but occasionally the unorganized peasantry has attempted to become organized or has erupted in spontaneous revolt — in response to foreign invasion, a loss of land or civil rights, intolerable exploitation, frustration resulting from failure to share in new sources of income and wealth, or natural calamities. Francisco Juliao attempted to organize peasant leagues in the Northeast of Brazil; Jacinto Lopez and the UGOCM tried to organize the peasants of Northwest Mexico when it became clear that the government's irrigation schemes were essentially for the benefit of large landowners. Both of these movements were suppressed by the authorities. When it becomes impossible to organize legally, illegal movements usually emerge. In fact, violent eruptions of the rural proletariat and middle peasantry have occurred throughout history.[40] Well known examples are the Sakdal and Huq movements in Central Luzon, Philippines in the 1930s and 1940s respectively; Emiliano Zapata in Mexico; the late 19th century peasant rebellions in Bolivia; and the rural uprising in Burma in the 1930s.

Although none of the movements cited above were wholly successful in obtaining their objectives, several did manage to impose some changes or to induce the government to alter its policy. This is perhaps most apparent in the land reforms of Bolivia and Mexico, which were introduced during and after a revolution. In other cases the government was persuaded to pass legislation which appeared to favour the rural masses, but the legislation either was never properly enforced or contained so many loopholes that it was ineffective. The land reform law of the Philippines is a contemporary example. In yet other countries the landlord class and their domestic allies were intransigent and were able to obtain support from

[40] Eric Wolf, *Peasant Wars of the Twentieth Century*, New York, 1969, emphasizes the role of the middle peasant in providing leadership for guerrilla movements and the need for a secure regional base or frontier area.

a foreign power to restore the status quo (as in Guatemala in 1954) or to prevent it from being altered (as in South Vietnam at present).

In conclusion, any change — be it of a technical nature or not — which has an impact on the wellbeing of large numbers of people in rural areas is likely to create a reaction from those who believe their interests have been damaged. If the reacting groups are well organized there is a good chance that they will succeed in reducing or eliminating the ill effects of change, either by persuading the government to modify its policies or by working through private organizations and altering their collective behaviour. If the affected groups are poorly organized, however, it is unlikely that an established mechanism will exist through which their grievances can be conveyed to government and pressure exerted to change policy. Attempts to become organized may be viewed by those in authority as a challenge to the legal order, and if so, they will be suppressed. This, in turn, will force the unorganized peasantry to try to solve their difficulties in other ways, e.g., by migration, by passive resistance and non-cooperation, by various forms of violence, etc. There is no certainty that any of these responses will be fully successful, but each is likely to lead to further reactions from other groups. Ultimately, politics will change even if policies do not.

CHAPTER 8

Policy Options

In the previous chapter we argued (*i*) that technical change is not identical to progress, and that the latter has little meaning unless values are specified; (*ii*) that scant progress has occurred in the agricultural regions of most under-developed countries, in the sense that inequality has not diminished and the income of small peasants and the rural landless labour force has increased in general only slightly, and in some areas not at all; (*iii*) that because of the narrow class or factional support on which most governments depend, the range within which policies can be varied normally is rather restricted; but (*iv*) that those groups which are harmed by technical change can be expected to try to protect their interests by operating either through existing institutions or, if necessary, outside the established law. Thus the role of public policy in the processes of growth and development must be kept in perspective. Although in principle acts of government policy can be powerful, in practice they may not always be so — not because government policies are intrinsically weak, but because the capacity and willingness of governments radically to alter previous decisions is limited.

A. Styles of Rural Development

In discussing policy one must beware of the fallacy of eclecticism, that is, in the words of Marshall Wolfe, 'the assumption that countries can borrow freely bits and pieces of policies that are alleged to have been successful in other settings'. Although governments seldom are consistent in everything they do, their objectives, programmes and policies tend to have a certain coherence or internal logic which makes it difficult for them to benefit from the experience of other nations where objectives and policies may be radically different. This does not imply that the government of no

198

country can borrow from any other, but it does imply that borrowing is likely to be most successful when it is from a similar country.

Intuition tells us that, say, Pakistan could and would borrow development policies more readily from India than from China, despite her political hostility toward India and her friendship toward China. Similarly, North Vietnam would be more likely to emulate Chinese policies than those of the Philippines. In a sense, the Chinese 'style' of development is incompatible with that of Pakistan, and the Cuban style is incompatible with that of, say, Guatemala. Of course, countries differ primarily in degree, not in kind; policies, objectives and ideologies are scattered along a spectrum in multi--dimensional space. Nonetheless, three distinct strategies or approaches to development in general and rural problems in particular can be detected: we shall label these the technocratic strategy, the reformist strategy and the radical strategy.

These three strategies define three points on a spectrum — viz. the extremes and the middle — and thus do not constitute a taxonomy. It is for this reason that few countries can be placed firmly under one category or another; most occupy neither an extreme position nor the mid-point, but are distributed (probably skewed right) along a continuum. It is important to recognize that the classification we propose rests on social and political considerations, namely the intended beneficiaries of agrarian policy.[1] Evidently, it would be possible to classify strategies on a different basis, such as the interesting economic (or technological) taxonomic classification of rural strategies into uni-modal and bi-modal favoured by such authors as Bruce Johnston and Eric Thorbecke.[2] We choose not to follow them, however,

---

[1] Solon Barraclough has devised a three-fold classification of rural development strategies which is very similar to ours. He labels them (*i*) mechanization strategies, (*ii*) reformist strategies and (*iii*) strategies of deep structural change. See his 'Rural Development Strategy and Agrarian Reform', paper presented to the Latin American Seminar on Agrarian Reform and Colonization, Chiclayo, Peru, 29 November— 5 December 1971.

[2] See, for example, Bruce Johnston and John Cownie, 'The Seed-Fertilizer Revolution and Labor Force Absorption', *American Economic Review*, September 1969.

because we wish to trace the connections which flow from politics, through policies, to economics and technology.

Our three strategies differ in their objectives (or the priorities they attach to various objectives), in the ideology which is used to mobilize support and action, in the dominant form of land tenure institution (and in the pattern of property rights), as well as in the way the benefits of the economic system and growth process are distributed. These differences in objectives, ideologies, institutions and distribution constitute differences in style. Differences in style, in turn, are related to the classes or 'core combination'[3] on which the government depends for support.

Most underdeveloped countries have pursued a strategy for rural development which is located toward the technocratic end of the spectrum.[4] The prime economic objective has been to increase agricultural output, either by incorporating more conventional inputs such as land, as in Brazil, or by encouraging farmers to adopt an improved technology, as in the Philippines. The economic system has been justified essentially in terms of a liberal capitalist ideology: emphasis is placed on competition, free markets and widely dispersed private property as sufficient conditions for achieving the objective. In practice, property ownership is highly concentrated and this is reflected in the dominant form of land tenure institutions, viz., latifundia, plantations, large corporate farms and various types of tenancy arrangements. The benefits of technical change and higher output accrue, at least in the first instance, to the landowning elite and other men of property. Inequality of income, far from being deplored, is welcomed, since it is assumed that the rich will save a large proportion of their extra income and thereby contribute to faster accumulation and growth. In other words, the concentration of income and wealth is one of the

[3] See Warren F. Ilchman and Norman Thomas Uphoff, *The Political Economy of Change.*
[4] Moreover, much of the advice tendered by international institutions presupposes a technocratic strategy. See, for example, the comments of an economist employed by the World Bank: Barend de Vries, 'New Perspectives in International Development', *Finance and Development,* September 1968.

ways whereby the output objective is expected to be achieved.

The reformist strategy, on the other hand, is basically a compromise between the two extreme positions, and governments which adopt this style of development run the risk of committing the fallacy of eclecticism. Reformist governments tend to vacillate in their choice of policies and one frequently encounters inconsistencies between what a government proclaims and what it actually does. Nonetheless, this style of rural development places priority on redistributing income to some sections of the community (particularly the middle peasantry) and accordingly attributes lower priority than the technocratic strategy to increasing agricultural output. Attempts are made to reconcile greater equity with faster growth by changing agrarian institutions. Quite often, however, the reforms are partial, fragmented and incomplete, and concentrated in certain regions to the exclusion of others, with the consequence that this style creates a dualistic or bi-modal agricultural sector. This is very clear in Mexico, where a policy of redistributing land in favour of the peasantry was followed in the populous areas in the south while a policy of encouraging capital intensive farming on large holdings was pursued in the irrigated areas of the north. Similarly, in Egypt, the original thrust of the reform movement was to encourage labour intensive farming on cooperatives and small holdings, but more recently there has been a shift in favour of more capital intensive techniques on larger 'new farms'.

The ideology associated with this style of rural development usually is nationalist and occasionally is populist. The dominant land tenure institutions tend to be family farms, but if the dualism is pronounced one may find small cooperatives and minifundia confronting large capitalist farms or neo-latifundia. In practice the beneficiaries of the strategy often are the middle peasants on family farms and large 'progressive' farmers on substantial holdings. Several of the 'progressive' farmers who benefit from a reformist strategy may be of urban origin, e.g. retired army officers, civil servants or politicians. The redistribution of income that occurs, thus, is largely from the upper income groups to the

middle; those in the lowest deciles of the income distribution
may receive higher earnings, e.g. because of greater employment
opportunities, but they are unlikely to improve their
relative share — or to increase their political influence.

Finally, the objective of the radical strategy is first and
foremost to achieve rapid social change and a redistribution
of political power. Next in priority comes a redistribution of
wealth and income (in that order) and, lastly, higher production.
In short, the objectives are greater mass participation,
economic equality and faster growth. No conflict is seen
between the first two objectives, indeed they are merely
different aspects of the same thing, and these, in turn, need
not conflict with the third. If there is a conflict, however, the
growth objective would give way to the quest for social,
political and economic equality.

The radical strategy is supported by the ideology of
socialism. Agrarian socialism, particularly its Asian variant, is
based on the assumption that it is possible to mobilize an
untapped resource potential, namely, human labour. This
involves extending the number of days worked, increasing the
intensity of effort and raising the efficiency and inventiveness
of labour.[5] This can be done, however, only if social and
economic inequalities are reduced, since equal sacrifices are
incompatible with a system of unequal rewards. Rough
equality is achieved by abolishing private property in land
and establishing collectives, communes or state farms. These
institutions, evidently, tend to favour small peasants and
landless labourers.

Implicit in this strategy is a profound scepticism of the
desirability of relying on unregulated market forces for
development. Considerable emphasis is placed on the immobility
and specificity of resources and great importance is
attached to exploiting unique local opportunities. In contrast
to the first two styles of development, the radical strategy,
especially as applied in China, places relatively little emphasis

[5] Cf. the following dictum of Chairman Mao: 'the changeover from
individual to socialist, collective ownership in agriculture and handicrafts
... is bound to bring about a tremendous liberation of productive
forces'. (*Quotations from Chairman Mao Tse-Tung*, Peking, Foreign
Languages Press, 1966.)

on national agricultural planning, the manipulation of macro-economic aggregates or price signals. Instead more attention is concentrated on the locality; solutions to problems are sought at the local level rather than in general, national policies. Motives and attitudes, even morality, are believed to be capable of being changed (witness the search for a 'new socialist man'); moreover, institutional arrangements are treated as variables and considerable experimentation with alternative means of organizing production and consumption is permitted; and if a particular locality encounters a difficulty, local initiative rather than outside assistance is expected to be relied upon.

The three styles of rural development represent, therefore, three distinct approaches to the agricultural sector and to the people who live and work within it. The major characteristics of these three styles are summarized in Table 8.1. A study of countries which have adopted different styles of development should be highly instructive, e.g., in determining the social and economic consequences of a particular technical change, but it is doubtful if governments following one style can or would wish to borrow policies used by countries following either of the other two styles.

B. Salient Features of the Green Revolution
A technology is in the process of being created which will enable some tropical countries – or some farmers in some regions of tropical countries – to increase the yields from foodgrains by 50 per cent or more. This new technology is commonly thought to have caused a 'green revolution'. The 'revolution' consists of the application of a package of inputs, the most prominent of which are the new high-yielding seeds. Thus the core of the new technology is based on biological research. At present the new high-yielding seeds are largely for wheat and rice, but improved varieties of other crops have also been developed, notably, maize, sorghum (jowar) and millet (bajra). There is no reason to doubt that this process of plant improvement will continue for as far ahead as anyone may care to look.

In addition to higher yields per crop, this technology has several advantages. First, in the case of rice, it permits shorter

Table 8.1
Styles of Rural Development

Development strategy	Objectives	Major beneficiaries	Dominant form of tenure	Ideology	Representative countries
Technocratic	increase output	landowning elite	large private and corporate farms, plantations, latifundia, various tenancy systems	capitalist	Philippines, Brazil, Ivory Coast
Reformist	redistribute income (and wealth); increase output	middle peasants, 'progressive' farmers	family farms, cooperatives	nationalist	Mexico, Egypt
Radical	social change; redistribute political power, wealth and output	small peasants and landless labourers	collectives, communes, state farms	socialist	China, Cuba, Algeria

cropping cycles and thereby enables the farmer to economize on water. Moreover, in the case both of wheat and rice, the amount of water required per unit of output is reduced. Second, the short cycles sometimes permit multiple cropping, and thus in effect economize on land. Third, under optimal conditions the new technology utilizes much more labour per unit of land and thus can increase farm employment.[6] Finally, in principle, the new technology is rather easily disseminated since it is scale-neutral and does not require a major transformation of agricultural practices. These advantages have led some observers to predict an end to the foodgrain problem in underdeveloped countries and the beginning of an era of worldwide surplus production.[7]

Such optimism, however, cannot at present be justified by the facts. No miracle has occurred or is likely to occur. Indeed, the new seeds have several serious disadvantages. First, the high-yielding varieties tend to be more delicate than indigenous plants and require a great deal more care on the part of the cultivator. Second, the new seeds at present available are in general less resistant to drought and flood, and thus require sophisticated irrigation and water control facilities. The new short stemmed varieties of rice, for example, cannot be used in many parts of Thailand, Bangladesh and South Vietnam because of excessive flooding. Third, the high-yielding varieties are somewhat more susceptible to disease and infestation by insects, and thus require protective applications of herbicides and pesticides. The severe outbreak of tungro in the Philippines in 1970 and 1971 underlines the importance of plant protection.

Fourth, the new seeds often — but not always — are more productive than local varieties even in the absence of fertilizers, but the differences are not very great unless substantial amounts of fertilizer are applied. For example, when no fertilizer is applied, Sonora-64 (a high yielding variety of wheat) has a yield of about 2232 kilograms per hectare in

[6] This issue is explored in some detail in William H. Bartsch, 'Employment Effects of Alternative Technologies and Techniques in Agriculture', *International Labour Review*, forthcoming.
[7] See, for example, L. R. Brown, *Seeds of Change: The Green Revolution and Development in the 1970s*, 1969.

India, while C-306 (a local variety) has a slightly higher yield of 2355 kg. However, if 100 kg. of elemental nitrogen are applied per ha., the yield of Sonora-64 rises to 4600 kg. while that of C-306 increases to only 3689 kg. Similarly, local rice planted in the wet season in India has a yield of approximately 2500 kg. per ha., in the absence of fertilizer, whereas IR-8 produces 3000 kg. The difference increases substantially, moreover, when fertilizer is applied. When the dose is 100 kg. of nitrogen per ha., the yield of IR-8 rises to 4566 kg. while that of the local variety increases to about 3500 kg. In other words, the difference in yield doubles.[8]

The response of seeds to fertilizer cannot occur in the absence of water, and for this reason irrigation and fertilizers (and perhaps pesticides as well) may be complementary in some countries. Consequently the 'package' of material inputs that accompanies the new seeds may compel massive investment in industries supplying fertilizer and plant chemicals, and expenditure on irrigation works and equipment. Alternatively, many of the necessary material inputs could be imported, if it is cheaper to do this than produce them locally, but this implies a need to earn more foreign exchange or reduce imports of other items. Storage, transport, distribution and marketing facilities must also be provided, and farmers must have access to credit and technical information. Hence, from the point of view of the economy as a whole, the widespread extension of the 'green revolution' is likely to be expensive in terms of fixed and working capital, and the opportunity cost of this capital (and of scientific personnel) may be high.

The investments required by the 'revolution' need not be undertaken simultaneously, however. Some facilities may exist already and not be fully utilized; the provision of other facilities can be postponed until a later period. The complementarities may be partial, not rigid, and if so, this will

[8] Estimates of yields were obtained from fertilizer response functions reported in R. Barker, 'Environmental Factors Influencing the Performance of New High Yielding Varieties of Wheat and Rice in Asia', mimeo, n.d., Table 2.

permit sequential investment. Fertilizers are highly complementary to the new seeds and must be provided first.
Fertilizers, in fact, are a *sine qua non* of the 'green revolution'. Then comes irrigation, although it may be possible in
some cases to delay investing in drainage facilities. Next, pest
and disease control become essential and, lastly, mechanization (especially the provision of sprayers, mechanical weeders,
etc.). Such a sequence of investment would enable a country
to spread the costs of transforming tropical agriculture over
an extended period of time, and thereby economize on scarce
capital, but such a strategy also implies that the full benefits
of the 'revolution' in terms of output will be delayed.

The complementarity among the various inputs which
comprise the 'green revolution' are such that many governments have concentrated their effort on particular regions
(usually the more prosperous ones) and particular farmers
(usually the larger ones). This tendency is particularly no-
table in countries pursuing a 'technocratic' style of development, but it is also visible in countries which have followed a
'reformist' style. In Mexico the rapid expansion of wheat
output has been largely confined to large commercial farms
in the northern part of the country. In Pakistan, the wheat
and rice revolution has occurred largely in the prosperous
areas of the Punjab, as well as in the other irrigated zones of
the Indus basin; almost nothing has occurred in Baluchistan
and the NWFP. In the Philippines, Central Luzon was given
priority in the Rice and Corn Self-Sufficiency Programme,
1966/67—1969/70, and thus regional inequality was accentuated, since Luzon was already the most prosperous and
advanced agricultural region in the country.

In India the 'revolution' is a bit more widespread, but it
has penetrated most deeply in the Punjab and the other
wheat growing areas in the north. These are precisely the
areas which were most prosperous and where capitalist
farming was most advanced prior to the introduction of the
new technology. Between 1949/50 and 1968/69 wheat production in India increased 4.2 per cent a year, whereas rice
output increased only 3 per cent. Thus the phenomenon of
wheat expanding faster than rice antidates the advent of the

'green revolution'.[9] Similarly, the wheat growing areas of India have experienced more rapid agricultural growth than the rest of the nation throughout the post-independence period. Between 1952/3 and 1964/5 agricultural output in the Punjab grew 4.56 per cent a year, for example, as compared to 2.27 per cent in Kerala, 1.94 per cent in West Bengal and 1.17 per cent in Assam. The 'green revolution' in India clearly has accentuated on-going trends toward regional inequality; it has not reversed them.

These examples from the four countries where the 'revolution' has had the greatest impact suggest that the spatial distribution of the benefits and costs of technical change has not been even. The 'green revolution', from a technical point of view, is largely a biological and chemical revolution, but from a socio-economic point of view it has largely become transformed into a commercial revolution. This is a consequence not only of the nature of the technology but also of the government policies which have been used to disseminate it. In practice the new technology has been successful primarily in the context of commercial agriculture. Moreover, the 'revolution' tends to strengthen whatever commercial agriculture already exists, often at the expense of peasant farming. That is, the new technology tends to accelerate the spread of capitalist agriculture but does not necessarily initiate it, although it has done so in a few areas. For example, mechanization may accelerate the tendency for the number of agricultural wage labourers to increase, but the tendency itself exists independently of the 'revolution'. Similarly, government policies which discriminate in favour of large farmers (e.g. by subsidizing inputs to them) have the effect of increasing the return on their land, and this provides a strong incentive to them to acquire land from small farmers who are unable to obtain the necessary inputs and hence are

[9] As we explain below on page 246., high yielding varieties of wheat have spread more widely throughout the world than high yielding varieties of rice for both agronomic and environmental reasons. Even within the wheat regions of India, however, the more prosperous districts and states (e.g. the Punjab and Haryana) have done better than the less prosperous areas (e.g. U.P. and Bihar). The same is true of the rice regions of India.

unable to innovate. But the tendency for small peasants to lose their land may be present in any case, e.g. merely as a result of rising population densities consequent upon demographic increase.[10] It is also true, of course, that the new technology is not very suitable for subsistence, non-market farming because it is intensive in cash inputs and in some cases requires fairly elaborate production and marketing facilities.[11] Thus for all these reasons the 'revolution' tends to occur in regions where large scale commercial agriculture already exists and, within these regions, on farms owned by large landowners.

In conclusion, the new technology is discriminatory, particularly when it is combined with policies typical of countries following a 'technocratic' style of rural development. The technology has a differential impact. It is neutral neither as regards geographical area nor as regards social class. On the contrary, unless governments pursue a 'radical' or, at least, 'reformist' strategy, the 'green revolution' tends to increase economic inequality and this, in turn, may aggravate social

[10] Population pressure would tend to result in a rising man—land ratio in agriculture and a smaller size of farm — and this would be true of the average and for big and small farmers separately. Nonetheless, the impact is unlikely to be uniform on all classes. The children of large landowners usually have employment opportunities outside agriculture (e.g. in manufacturing or commercial activities, the professions or the civil service) and thus there is less need to break up a holding upon the death of the owner. The sons of small peasants, in contrast, either must remain in agriculture on a divided holding or, say, migrate to the cities and join the ranks of the unemployed or the underemployed workers in the services sector. The former will be the more attractive alternative as long as the combined income from land and family labour exceeds the expected wage earnings in urban areas. The process of sub-division of land, however, eventually results in holdings which are too small to support a peasant household, and at this point the peasant must either (*i*) sell his land, (*ii*) lease-in land to supplement his holding, or (*iii*) lease-out his land and obtain employment elsewhere to supplement his rental income. For the peasantry as a whole, options (*ii*) and (*iii*) tend to be transitional, leaving only (*i*) as the ultimate solution.

[11] This point is carefully developed in S. Ishikawa, *Agricultural Development Strategies in Asia: Case Studies of the Philippines and Thailand*, Asian Development Bank, 1970.

conflicts which already exist. It would be foolish to disregard its possible political implications.[12]

Innovation and inequality

Although the impact of the 'green revolution' on total agricultural production has been relatively slight, the introduction of high yielding varieties has led to an increase in domestic supplies of some foodstuffs in several countries. If this continues, increased output is likely to result eventually in a decline in the relative price of foodgrains. At the moment, however, the governments of several countries, e.g. Pakistan and India, are supporting domestic grain prices at levels which exceed world prices by a considerable margin. In the Philippines the price of rice relative to the price of all other commodities fell from 1967 to 1970 and then rose very sharply indeed in 1971, so that by the end of the period the relative price of rice was higher than at the beginning.[13] Moreover, even when the relative price of rice in the Philippines was falling, the domestic level of rice prices still was substantially above world prices. Because of the high domestic support policies urban consumers have yet to benefit from increased food output. Exceptions to this generalization are Sri Lanka and Taiwan where rice is rationed and delivered at a subsidized price to all (Sri Lanka) or some (Taiwan) urban inhabitants.[14] In the other countries, nonetheless, the urban areas are potentially major beneficiaries of the 'green revolution'. Potential benefits could be transformed into actual benefits merely by allowing domestic prices to fall to those prevailing in the world grain market.

[12] See Chapter 3, Section B and Chapter 7, Sections A and C. Few social scientists have written about the politics of the green revolution. A good example of one who has is F. R. Frankel, 'India's New Strategy of Agricultural Development: Political Costs of Agrarian Modernization', *Journal of Asian Studies*, 1969. Also see her *India's Green Revolution: Economic Gains and Political Costs*, 1971.

[13] Mahar Mangahas, 'Philippine Rice Policy Reconsidered in Terms of Urban Bias', Institute of Economic Development and Research, School of Economics, University of the Philippines, Discussion Paper No. 72–8, 2 May 1972.

[14] Everyone in Sri Lanka, in both urban and rural areas, is entitled to subsidized rice.

The rural sector as a whole, on the other hand, will experience a deterioration of its commodity terms of trade if grain prices are allowed to fall. This would be of relatively little consequence to those farmers who have introduced the cost-cutting innovations, since their factoral terms of trade will have improved and their profits increased. They clearly will be better off, although they can be expected to lobby politicians for the continuation of the price support programme — as is happening in India today.

The innovating farmers have enjoyed not only high prices for their products but also low prices for their inputs. But if it is really necessary for a country to subsidize both output and inputs for a long period in order to permit the successful introduction of the new technology, it is debatable whether that country has a comparative advantage in wheat and rice. In fact, from the point of view of allocative efficiency, it might be better to discontinue the policy of import substitution in foodgrains and rely instead on foreign suppliers.[15] Of course, as we have stressed before,[16] it is doubtful if most governments in underdeveloped countries attribute a high priority to achieving efficiency.

In many cases the cost of innovation has been heavily subsidized by the government, and this has supplemented price supports and further increased the incomes of large so-called 'progressive' farmers. For example, in India, and elsewhere, irrigation works are financed by the government out of general revenues and water is provided to farmers at a nominal price. As a result, the tax-payers bear the cost of innovation and a small number of farmers reap the benefits.

Consider, too, the case of Pakistan, a country which in the 1960s pursued a technocratic style of rural development *par excellence*. Pakistan maintained a substantial support price for wheat. In addition, fertilizer was sold at 50 per cent of landed cost and agricultural machinery was sold at a price well below landed cost! The plant protection service was provided by government free of charge to those who had

[15] See Chapter 6, Section D for a discussion of international trade policies.
[16] See Chapter 7, Section A.

access to the bureaucracy. All current agricultural inpu
were exempt from tariffs and import restrictions an
furthermore, they enjoyed the benefit of an overvalue
exchange rate. Lastly, agricultural income was exempt fror
direct taxation and the land tax was allowed practically t
wither away.[17] The exchange rate and import control syster
was used to provide a handsome subsidy to the purchase c
tractors. In fact for a while tractors were cheaper in Pakista
than in the United States. These policies, of course, led to
misallocation of scarce foreign exchange and the creation c
technological unemployment in rural areas; at the same tim
they inflated the profits and rents of large farmers in th
Punjab. The beneficiaries of the system were hailed a
progressive; the losers were simply ignored.

The growth in inequality in rural areas stems in large pa:
from the fact that small, poor peasants who have restricte
access to credit, technical knowledge and the material mear
of production are unable to innovate as easily or as quickly a
those who are landed, liquid and literate. Ownership of lan
or even a secure tenancy, provides an outlet for savings, a
incentive for investment and an asset on which credit can b
obtained. Liquid assets, especially cash, constitute the wor
ing capital needed to purchase commercialized inputs. Mor
over, liquidity enables a farmer more easily to bear risk an
to time his sales and purchases to maximum advantag
Finally, literacy gives farmers access to further knowledg
although it certainly is not the only — or even perhaps th
most important — means of obtaining information. Thos
farmers who already possess resources in the form of lan
capital and knowledge are able to grasp the opportuniti
created by the 'green revolution' and further improve the
position. But those who are landless and illiterate will tend t
lag behind and perhaps become further impoverished.

There is evidence from all over the underdeveloped worl
that it is the largest and most prosperous farmers wh
innovate and the middle-sized farmers who imitate.[18] I

---

[17] Total direct agricultural taxes as a percentage of agricultural incom
fell from 1.7 per cent in 1959/60 to 1.0 per cent in 1969/70.
[18] Some of the evidence is discussed in Chapter 3.

ome cases the smallest and very poor farmers subsequently
ntroduce the new seeds and adopt a commercial pattern of
roduction and marketing, but in many cases they do not.[19]
Ladejinsky reports that in the Indian Punjab it takes
Rs.10,000—12,000 for a farmer with 7—10 acres to switch to
ne of the high yielding varieties of wheat.[20] In Rajasthan
hose who adopted the new wheat varieties tended to have
arger farms, to make greater use of irrigation pumps and to
be more literate.[21] Again, in Andhra Pradesh, size of holding,
alue of assets and literacy were correlated with innovative
ctivity.[22] A study of the response to improved seeds among
ice farmers of South India as early as 1965 was conducted
by N. S. Shetty. His results indicate that it is the wealthy,
anded and educated farmers who first adopt the new
echnology and the poor who lag behind. Nothing that has
merged from the vast amount of research which has since
been conducted contradicts his conclusions. His findings are
presented in Table 8.2, and the cluster of characteristics
which distinguish the innovators from imitators and laggards
can readily be seen.

Small peasant landowners who are excluded from the
green revolution' can be subjected to considerable hardship.
here is a danger that ultimately they will become squeezed

---

[19] In a discussion of an earlier version of this study M. Yudelman, now
f the IBRD, dismissed this issue by commenting that 'it is just a
roblem of lags'. The remark implies that the increase in inequality is
he result of a purely mechanical (and inevitable) process which cannot
should not?) be altered by conscious public policy. If one accepts Mr.
Yudelman's statement one is accepting that inequality will never
liminish; the best one can hope is that once the lags are overcome
nequality will cease to increase. Given the technocratic style of
development which Mr. Yudelman seems to advocate, his analysis is, of
ourse, correct and in no way conflicts with our own.
[20] W. Ladejinsky, 'Ironies of India's Green Revolution', *Foreign Affairs*,
970. In view of our comments in the preceding footnote it should be
ecorded that Mr. Ladejinsky also is employed by the IBRD. Indeed he
s a most ardent and distinguished advocate of agrarian reform.
[21] S. S. Acharya, 'Comparative Efficiency of H.Y.V.P.: A Case Study of
Udaipur District', *Economic and Political Weekly*, 1969.
[22] G. Parthasarathy, 'Economies of IR8 Paddy: Factors Influencing its
Adoption in a Tank Irrigated District', *Economic and Political Weekly*,
969.

Table 8.2

Characteristics of Innovators, Imitators and Non-Adopters in South India, 1965

	Innovators	Imitators	Non-adopters
Sample number	24	172	69
Assets per capita (rupees)	22,535	4,326	2,976
Area cultivated (acres)	8.0	3.3	2.5
Percent of cultivated area that is rented	26.4	54.7	79.8
Education of farmers (years)	9	4	2
Extension contacts (score)	6.4	3.1	2.0

Source: N. S. Shetty, 'Agricultural Innovation: Leaders and Laggards' *Economic and Political Weekly*, 17 August 1968; quoted in D. Turnham, *The Employment Problem in Less Developed Countries: A Review of Evidence*, O.E.C.D., June 1970, p. 148.

between their high costs and the falling prices of their output, and if this happens their incomes will decline absolutely. Many may be forced to sell their land to the larger farmers and this will lead to greater inequality in the distribution of land and an increase in the landless rural work force. In economic terms, commercialization of agriculture will be accompanied by increased specialization and division of labour. In sociological terms, it will be accompanied by increased social differentiation and the gradual polarization of the community into two broad classes, one of which possess the means of production and derives its income therefrom, and another which owns little property and derives its income from the sale of labour services.

Small farmers are being subjected to increased economic pressure almost everywhere, not just in Asia. For instance, in Guatemala, modern technologies in maize production are being applied on large farms in the Pacific coastal lowland areas, not in the highlands where the majority of small maize growers eke out a living. Similarly, in Mexico, 'sorghum, supposedly a crop for dry areas with highly variable rainfall, is being grown by the highly commercialized farmers in the better rainfall areas and often under irrigation'.[23] If this intense, usually subsidized, competition continues, independent small farmers will slowly become dependent on large landowners and some may be converted into landless labourers.

A rise in the number of landless workers, say, as a result of population increase or tenants and small peasants losing their land, will tend to depress rural wage rates and increase poverty in this section of the community. The decline in wages will be accentuated if the 'green revolution' is accompanied by labour-saving innovations. We have already mentioned the subsidy to tractors in Pakistan. Technological unemployment resulting from the mechanization of agriculture is unlikely to remain in rural areas; ultimately it will move to the cities and further increase the amount of underemployment in petty services. Thus rural innovation may lead to greater misery for many workers in urban areas — despite the fact that food prices may be lower.

The polarization to which we have referred can be observed already in India, in the form of a dramatic rise in rural landlessness. Between the census years 1961 and 1971 the number of agricultural labourers in the male rural labour force rose from 15.3 per cent to 24.9 per cent. That is, the proportion increased by well over 60 per cent. In the Punjab, the region where agricultural growth and technical change have been most rapid, the rise in landlessness is even more extraordinary. In fact, the proportion of labourers in the male rural work force more than doubled, from 9.2 per cent in 1961 to 19.8 per cent in 1971. A similar change occurred in U.P., and less spectacular changes have occurred in Bihar, Madras, Andhra Pradesh and West Bengal.[24] Evidently, throughout India, and indeed throughout much of the Third

[23] E. J. Wellhausen, 'The Urgency of Accelerating Production on Small Farms', in D. T. Myren, ed., *Strategies for Increasing Agricultural Production on Small Holdings*, Puebla, Mexico, August 1970, p. 7.
[24] See J. Krishnamurty, 'Working Force in the 1971 Census: Some Exercises on Provisional Results', *Economic and Political Weekly*, Vol. VII, No. 3, 15 January 1972.

World, capitalist farming systems are in the ascendancy and cultivators are coming to rely increasingly on hired labour.

There is little inherent in the use of high yielding seeds, however, which increases landlessness and reduces the demand for labour. On the contrary, the spread of irrigation and the increase of multiple cropping which the 'green revolution' ideally permits should raise labour requirements and wage rates. In India, again, the scanty evidence suggests that money wages in the agricultural sector probably have increased,[25] although it is not certain that they have risen fast enough to keep up with the increase in the cost of living. In fact, between 1960/61 and 1968/69, agricultural income per worker in agriculture declined, even in money terms, in Uttar Pradesh, Assam and West Bengal. Between 1959/60 and 1968/69, real wages of agricultural labourers declined one per cent in Gujarat, five per cent in Maharashtra, 19 per cent in Assam and 22 per cent in West Bengal, whereas they rose from 10 per cent in the Punjab to 32 per cent in Andhra Pradesh.[26] A more recent study of the Punjab and Haryana — two states where the 'green revolution' has been most successful — indicates that real wages rose in 1968/69 and 1969/70 after a long period of virtual constancy.[27] Even here, however, we cannot conclude that the standard of living of agricultural labourers rose in the absence of information on changes in the number of days worked per year and on the extent to which cash payments have replaced payments in kind. For India as a whole there is little doubt that the standard of living of the bottom strata in rural (and urban) areas has declined.[28]

The demand for labour will increase relatively slowly if large farmers are given non-labour inputs at subsidized prices.

[25] R. N. Soni, 'The Recent Agricultural Revolution and the Agricultural Labour', *Indian Journal of Agricultural Economics*, 1970.
[26] R. K. Lahiri, 'Impact of HYVP on Rural Labour Market', *Economic and Political Weekly*, 26 September 1970, p. A-114.
[27] James W. Gough, 'Agricultural Wages in Punjab and Haryana', *Economic and Political Weekly*, 27 March 1971.
[28] See, for example, V. M. Dandekar and N. Rath, *Poverty in India*. The Indian data can be compared with those from Sri Lanka and the Philippines by consulting Chapter 2, especially Table 2.7.

If credit, herbicides and especially machinery are provided at less than their opportunity costs, factor proportions on the larger farms will be suboptimal, inefficient techniques of production will be adopted and employment may increase less rapidly than the labour force.[29] Innovation, instead of raising the standard of living of the poor, may actually reduce it. In principle, of course, these problems can be avoided by appropriate policies, e.g. those which encourage selective mechanization designed to overcome genuine bottlenecks and which thereby permit higher employment. In practice, however, these policies seldom are implemented, because it is not in the interests of the social forces which control the government to do so. This point is well put by Erich Jacoby, a man who acquired enormous experience over many years while working for FAO:

> Under present conditions, however, the new varieties will further diminish employment in agriculture since the large commercially managed estates will combine the use of the new varieties with the introduction of modern labour-saving equipment which, in its turn, will inevitably lead to the ejection of tenants and dismissal of workers. There is little hope that in countries such as the Philippines, Thailand and even India this trend can be counteracted by *selective mechanization*, since the large landowning interests who dominate the legislation and administrative machinery are accustomed to react generously to the demands for 'sound' farm management.[30]

We do not wish to imply, of course, that agricultural innovation should be resisted. On the contrary, it must be actively encouraged. But at the same time measures must be

---

[29] Subsidies to irrigation water and fertilizer, however, might encourage employment in certain circumstances.

[30] Erich Jacoby, *Man and Land*, Andre Deutsch, 1971, p. 70. Jacoby's point is essentially that for political reasons one will not be able to select some machines and not others. There is a further point, however, that some machines, e.g. tractors, can be used for several operations, and it is unrealistic to assume that the use of a machine can be selectively restricted to some operations and activities but not others. (I am grateful to William Bartsch of I.L.O. for pointing this out to me.)

adopted to ensure that the benefits are widely shared. If the political will were present, one simple way of doing this would be to tax either the land or the income of innovating landlords.[31] This, regrettably, is almost never done. In most states of India and in Pakistan, for example, incomes originating from agricultural activities are exempt from income tax. Moreover, land taxation has ceased to be an important source of revenue. In fact, in India the level of the land tax is a matter for each individual state to decide, and since state politics are almost invariably controlled by the landlord class, the land tax has practically disappeared in most states. As a result, in both these countries – and in Sri Lanka – the section of the rural community in which incomes are rising most rapidly, viz. among the large farmers, is contributing nothing to government revenue[32] A similar situation exists in the Philippines. The land tax is negligible and the income tax is low and easily evaded. In fact, as Professor Ishikawa notes, 'No one can look at the Philippines tax system without being shocked by its serious regressive nature'.[33] Thus in the three Asian countries which are in the vanguard of the 'green revolution' the most prosperous people in rural areas are subsidized but not taxed; policies have been introduced which ensure that they receive the benefits of agrarian change while those who are less prosperous incur its costs. The consequences are greater inequality and, in some instances, greater misery.

It must be recognized, however, that the inequitable tax and subsidy systems merely accentuate a tendency towards inequality that probably would be present in any case. This is because in countries where labour is relatively abundant

[31] A land tax would in principle be better than an income tax since it need not be a disincentive to increased production. Either form of taxation, however, is a more efficient and equitable way of extracting resources from agriculture than any of the actual methods discussed in Chapter 5.

[32] In India the urban areas have become increasingly resentful of subsidizing agricultural prices while largely exempting landlords from taxation, and it may not be possible for the landed interests to resist the demands for agricultural income taxes much longer.

[33] Op. cit., pp. 58–59.

improved techniques tend to raise profits and rents,[34] but not wages, so that unless property is evenly distributed the destribution of income becomes worse. There are two broad solutions to this problem. First, workers and small peasants can be organized in an attempt to obtain higher incomes without altering the distribution of wealth. Minimum wage legislation, the encouragement of rural trade unions and the promotion of various types of cooperatives are examples of policies which come under this heading — and which usually are misguided (if well intentioned) and fail. Alternatively, one can eliminate the causes of income inequality by redistributing productive wealth. In economies which are primarily agrarian, such a policy implies a redistribution of land. The first solution is essentially a 'liberal' solution, while the second is essentially 'radical'. The two approaches are not entirely competitive — indeed government policy could well contain elements of both — but they do entail rather different consequences for the direction and pace of socioeconomic change. The two approaches, in other words, imply different styles of rural development.

The basic issue which confronts all governments is whether to attempt to redistribute income while leaving the distribution of wealth intact, or to attempt to redistribute wealth directly. The former requires the government to maintain continuous pressure on wealth-holders, since they can be expected to try to regain the income produced by their assets, whereas the latter requires a single assault. A policy of redistributing wealth implies the destruction of a class by severing its connection with the means of production, whereas a policy of redistributing income merely weakens a class by appropriating part of the surplus which its assets generate.

---

[34] A subsidy to food prices obviously will increase the derived demand for land and hence rents. On the other hand, insofar as the 'green revolution' takes the form of economizing on land by raising yields, rents should fall. This decline, if it occurs, it unlikely to be uniform, however. In fact, rents should rise in the areas most suitable for the introduction of high yielding varieties and fall only in the 'marginal' areas.

C. Lines of Policy

There is no doubt that under appropriate circumstances the 'green revolution' can make an important contribution towards increasing agricultural output in underdeveloped countries. The new technology, however, is neither necessary nor sufficient for achieving more rapid growth. Moreover, as we have seen in earlier chapters, it has become reasonably clear that the introduction of high yielding varieties of foodgrains has often been associated with increased economic inequality and greater social differentiation in rural areas. Thus the 'revolution' creates as well as alleviates problems, and thereby raises issues of public policy.

In the discussion which follows we shall assume that the objectives of government agricultural policy are to promote greater equality, accelerate the growth of production and ensure the efficient allocation of resources within the sector. We know from our previous discussion that many governments do not in fact pursue all these objectives, and that some governments have additional objectives. Thus our assumption will not always correspond to reality. Nonetheless, the goals we have selected are those to which many governments have aspired in their published pronouncements, and it may be useful to examine alternative means that could be used to reach declared ends. One implication of this approach is that it becomes clear that governments which in practice do not will the means, do not truly will the ends.

The main policy issues are grouped under six headings: (1) the ownership and use of land, (2) factor prices, (3) agricultural surpluses and non-agricultural growth, (4) output prices and marketing, (5) government expenditure, and (6) science policy.

The ownership and use of land

The major cause of inequality in the distribution of income in rural areas is inequality in the ownership of land. This is true not only because land is the most important means of production but also because ownership of land is highly correlated with ease of access to institutions (e.g. banks and the bureaucracy) and the resources they provide (e.g. credit and technical assistance). As we have argued in Chapter 2, the distribution of land ownership is grossly unequal throughout the underdeveloped world. In Paraguay, for example, 1.02 per cent of those active in the agricultural sector own over 86 per cent of the land. In India, where a 20 acre farm is considered to be large, nearly 38 per cent of rural households in 1961/62 either owned no land or had less than one half acre; in Kerala, one of the poorest states, the proportion was 59 per cent. A study of rural poverty in India found a high positive association between the per cent of the rural population in a state below the 'poverty line'[35] and the degree of concentration of land holdings, as measured by the Gini coefficient.[36] A similar relationship was found between rural poverty and the proportion of households with less than one acre.

In addition to its effect on the extent of poverty, land concentration also affects the distribution of political power (nationally and locally), the class structure of the society and the general cohesiveness of the rural community. These, in turn, influence the way the benefits of a particular technical change are distributed as well as the direction that will be taken by subsequent innovations. This is brought out very well in a comparative study by Carl Gotsch of the impact of tubewell installation in Pakistan and the Comilla District of Bangladesh.[37]

In Pakistan only 4 per cent of the tubewells as of 1969 were installed on small farms, the great majority, viz. 69 per cent, being placed on farms larger than 25 acres. This investment in modern technology, by giving the dominant landowners even more control over scarce resources, increased the political power of faction leaders in the community and tended 'to undermine further any possibility of organizing agricultural institutions that could aid small

---

[35] This is defined as the expenditure level on food necessary to obtain 2250 calories per day per person.
[36] R. Sau, 'On Rural Poverty: A Tentative Hypothesis', *Economic and Political Weekly*, Vol. VI, No. 52, December 1971, p. 2563.
[37] See Carl Gotsch, 'Technical Change and Distribution of Income Benefits in Rural Areas', *LTC Newsletter*, No. 35, December–March 1972, Land Tenure Center, University of Wisconsin.

farmers'.[38] In Comilla, in contrast, several cooperatives have been organized to install and manage tubewells and the distribution of the benefits of technical change among the members of the cooperatives has been equitable. Equally important, 'the tubewell has been a powerful instrument in solidifying ... community organizing activities ... and in providing the middle and small peasant group with sufficient resources to break the economic hold of the large farmer-trader-moneylender group. In addition, the green revolution in Comilla has supported a variety of other development programs with positive distributive effects (primary education, health, adult literacy, training for women, etc.) built on a solid base of increasing agricultural productivity'.[39]

Thus the long-run consequences of technical change depend very much upon the institutional context in which it occurs. If one is interested in augmenting equity (both political and economic) there is a strong case for implementing a land reform. 'Liberal' policies of the type mentioned earlier are clearly inferior to a 'radical' solution: they do not attack the root of the difficulty, they often are slow to take effect and they usually make some problems worse. (Minimum wages, for instance, encourage the substitution of capital for labour and hence aggravate the employment problem. Similarly, the promotion of cooperatives in areas where land is unequally distributed usually is of benefit only to the more prosperous farmers.)[40]

Land reform also is necessary on grounds of efficiency.[41] Factor markets in underdeveloped countries are highly imperfect. Land is monopolized by a few families, particularly in North Africa, the Middle East and Latin America, but also in some Asian nations such as the Philippines. This alone is sufficient in many cases to give landowners monopsony power in the local labour market, since in a predominantly agricultural country those without land have no alternative

[38] Ibid., p. 16.
[39] Ibid., p. 17.
[40] See two publications by UNRISD: Orlando Fals Borda, ed., *Estudio de la Realidad Campesina: Cooperación y Cambio* and Raymond Apthorpe, ed., *Rural Cooperatives and Planned Change in Africa.*
[41] See Chapters 2 and 4.

but to offer their labour services to powerful landlords. Serfdom and debt slavery are unnecessary in most instances, although they can still be found. Credit, too, is relatively cheap to the large landowners and dear to everyone else, particularly to tenants with insecure leases. Similarly, control over water rights by landlords can be viewed as an imperfection in the market for this input.

As a result of these market imperfections relative factor prices will vary considerably from one locality to another. Indeed the price of a single factor of production may be very different in one area from another. Consider, for example, the wages of labourers engaged in transplanting rice in Java in 1971/72. In the village of Sidomuljo, East Java the wage was US$0.11 per day; in Tjidahu, West Java it was US$0.20; in Ngandjat, Central Java it was US$0.21; in Pluneng, Central Java it was US$0.26 and in Kahuman, Central Java it was US$0.36.[42] That is, even on a single densely populated island an arbitrary sample of five villages indicated that the wage rate for a specific task could vary by as much as 200 per cent. Evidently, the extent of market imperfection is enormous.

More important, the imperfections are such that large landowners face a very different set of relative prices from those confronted by small-holders and tenants. Land and capital are abundant and cheap relative to labour for the big farmers, whereas the reverse is true for the small. Thus the big farmers tend to adopt techniques of production with relatively high land-labour ratios and small cultivators and tenants adopt very labour intensive techniques. These differences in techniques are a reflection of allocative inefficiency, namely, a failure of the large farmers to economize on the scarce factor of production — land, and to use intensively the plentiful factor — labour. Moreover, it has been shown, from Guatemala[43] to India,[44] that the

[42] Data were kindly supplied by Randolph Barker of IRRI, Los Baños, Philippines.
[43] Keith Griffin, 'Problems of Diversification in a Coffee Economy: The Case of Guatemala', in P. P. Streeten, ed., *Unfashionable Economics.*
[44] N. D. Abdul Hamed, 'Tenancy and Resource Use in Peasant Agriculture — A Case Study', University of Sussex, mimeo., February 1971.

misallocation of resources is due to the fact that different types or classes of farmers face different relative factor prices.

A striking feature of the agricultural systems of virtually all poor countries is that yields per acre rise as average farm size declines. That is, the smaller the farm, the greater the average productivity of land. Conversely, the larger the farm, the greater the average productivity of labour. Since land is usually the factor in most acute shortage, the farms with the highest yields per acre are normally the most efficient. Even in countries where the average farm is very small, such as in India, it has been demonstrated that those farms which are smaller than the average are economically the most efficient.[45]

An obvious implication of this is that a land reform which resulted in smaller units of management in agriculture would both reduce inequality and increase total output. In Brazil, for example, it has been estimated that a land reform could raise agricultural production by about 20 per cent.[46] Similarly, it has been estimated that a redistribution of land in Colombia might raise output by 17 per cent.[47] These, of course, are static or once and for all gains which arise from an improvement in the allocation of resources. It is also possible to argue, however, that in certain circumstances an agrarian reform would lead to an acceleration in the rate of growth of output, i.e. to cumulative gains.

It sometimes is claimed, for example, that small farmers living near a subsistence level are inhibited by the risk of harvest failure from undertaking an innovation. Earlier we expressed a certain amount of scepticism about this proposition,[48] but it is conceivable that a land reform which increased the average size of mini- and micro-fundia, or organized production in collectives and state farms, might

---

[45] E. J. Lau and P. A. Yotopoulos, 'A Test for Relative Efficiency and Application to Indian Agriculture', *American Economic Review*, March 1971. Also see M. Paglin, 'Surplus' Agricultural Labor and Development', *American Economic Review*, September 1965.
[46] W. R. Cline, *Economic Consequences of a Land Reform in Brazil.*
[47] Keith Griffin and John Enos, *Planning Development*, Chapter 6.
[48] See Chapter 3, Section B.

succeed in reducing risk and could perhaps thereby eliminate an obstacle to rapid technological change.

Another way in which agricultural growth could be accelerated would be by combining a land reform with a programme of rural public works. By now it is widely accepted that in many underdeveloped countries it is technically possible to increase the rate of rural capital formation by mobilizing underemployed labour, especially during periods of pronounced seasonal unemployment. In practice, few countries apart from China have attempted to mobilize labour on a massive scale. Small projects have been started in several nations, e.g. Algeria, Tunisia and in East Pakistan before it became independent, but they have never become a major instrument of development.[49] In India there is much discussion today about mounting a major rural public works programme.[50] One reason why few countries apart from China and North Vietnam have succeeded with this policy is that few governments have been able to raise the tax revenues necessary to finance a large investment programme. Thus real resources in the form of unemployed labour have remained idle because governments have been unable to amass the financial resources required to pay the wage bill.[51]

The financial constraint could be overcome if it were possible to employ labour at less than the going wage rate, i.e. if it were possible to persuade workers to contribute their labour on a semi-voluntary basis. This clearly will not happen if the capital assets created by the works programme are used to increase the income and wealth of only a small number of people. No one, for instance, will work for nothing -- or for

[49] See Keith Griffin, 'Algerian Agriculture in Transition', *Bulletin* of the Oxford University Institute of Economics and Statistics, November 1965; E. Costa, 'Manpower Mobilization for Economic Development in Tunisia', *International Labour Review*, January 1966; R. Sobhan, *Basic Democracies Works Programme and Rural Development in East Pakistan.*

[50] See, for example, B. S. Minhas, 'Rural Poverty, Land Redistribution and Development', *Indian Economic Review*, April 1970.

[51] Another reason that is often advanced is administrative difficulties, but this can be exaggerated. It is not obvious that the organization of a dam constructed of cement, for example, is easier than one constructed of earth.

less than the market wage — in order to dig a well for a large private landlord. Those who advocate tacking on a mass public works programme to an agrarian system in which large private holdings predominate are committing what we have previously described as the fallacy of eclecticism. The two policies are inconsistent and contradictory because they pertain to two quite different styles of development. On the other hand, if the agrarian system is such that the workers themselves are the direct beneficiaries of the fruits of their efforts, it may be possible to organize them on a semi—voluntary basis for rural investment projects. As long as land is unequally distributed it will be difficult to undertake massive labour intensive projects, but once property relations are altered, it should be both technically and politically possible to accelerate sharply capital formation in rural areas.

Economists and politicians of a 'technocratic' persuasion would dispute this. They would argue, on the contrary, that a more egalitarian distribution of income and wealth in rural areas would conflict with faster accumulation and growth because it inevitably would reduce private savings. There are two things to be said about this assertion. First, even if household savings decline this may be offset by greater public savings generated through taxation or by greater collective effort in the manner described in the preceeding paragraphs. In most of the countries following a technocratic style of rural development the bulk of the economic surplus is appropriated by a small minority who, because of their political power, are able to ensure that their incomes are lightly taxed. If incomes were more equitably distributed, however, and if political power were more widely diffused, the tax base would be broader and the political obstacles to reducing consumption via taxation for the sake of accumulation would be much diminished; at the same time, the incentive to reduce leisure in order to engage in labour intensive investment projects would be much increased. The consequences of these two effects on total capital formation cannot easily be calculated, but from what little we know of China, their importance can be considerable.

Second, it is far from certain that a reduction in inequality will in fact be accompanied by a sharp decline in household savings.[52] Recent evidence suggests that excessive emphasis in the past has been placed on the level of income as the determinant of the proportion of income that a rural household saves. In several parts of Asia studies have shown that peasant cultivators — even very poor ones — save a substantial portion of their income.[53] The reason for this is not entirely clear, but one promising hypothesis is that in economies (or parts of economies) in which financial institutions are poorly developed household savings are strongly influenced by investment opportunities. That is, the saving and investment decisions coincide, and households save in order to undertake a specific investment project. One of the things that follows from this is that if land were more equally distributed, more households would have a profitable outlet for their savings and consequently the rate of rural capital formation might increase. A further corollary is that if the profitability of rural investment increases, say, as a result of an improved technology, small peasant landowners can be expected to increase their savings along with everyone else.

The 'green revolution' represents an admirable opportunity to test these hypotheses, particularly in those parts of the world where the technology associated with the high yielding varieties of foodgrains has become accessible to all farmers, large and small alike. This condition is best satisfied in some of the wheat growing regions of India, and we are fortunate to have available a recent study of rural savings from this area.

A team from the Punjab Agricultural University examined the savings and investment behaviour of 72 holdings from Ludhiana District in the Punjab and 108 holdings from Hissar District in Haryana.[54] These farms were studied over a

---

[52] It is even less obvious that there would be a decline in household savings invested in socially productive activities.
[53] Some of the evidence is summarized in Keith Griffin and A. R. Khan, eds., *Growth and Inequality in Pakistan*, commentary to Part Four.
[54] A. S. Kahlon and Harbhajan Singh Bal, *Factors Associated with Farm and Farm Family Investment Pattern in Ludhiana (Punjab) and Hissar (Haryana) Districts: (1966–67 through 1969–70)*, Department of Economics and Sociology, Punjab Agricultural University, Ludhiana, n.d.

Table 8.3

Net Savings as a Percentage of Total Income in Two Wheat Districts of India, 1969—1970

Size of holding	Ludhiana District, Punjab	Hissar District, Haryana
Small	16.72	34.18
Medium	26.48	35.51
Large	25.14	31.26
Average	24.19	33.57

Source: A. S. Kahlon and Harbhajan Singh Bal, *Factors Associated with Farm and Farm Family Investment Pattern in Ludhiana (Punjab) and Hissar (Haryana) Districts: (1966—67 through 1969—70)*, Department of Economics and Sociology, Punjab Agricultural University, Ludhiana, n.d., p. 116.

Note: Small holdings are defined as 0—3.5 ha. in Ludhiana and 0—4 ha. in Hissar; medium holdings are 3.5—6 ha. and 4—8 ha. in the two districts, respectively; and large holdings are those above 6 and 8 ha.

period of four years beginning in 1966—67 and terminating in 1969—70. In other words, the period of study extends from the early years of the 'green revolution' in the area to the recent peak of innovative activity. During this period of rising investment opportunities net savings rose from 14.25 per cent of income in Ludhiana to 24.19 per cent. In Hissar, which at the beginning of the study was not as developed as Ludhiana, the rise in the savings ratio was even more dramatic, namely, from 11.53 to 33.57 per cent.[55] Thus the data from these 180 holdings are consistent with our hypothesis that savings in rural areas are at least in part a function of investment opportunities.

What about our contention that small farmers may on occasion save proportionately as much as large? Once again the data from these two wheat growing districts of India do not contradict our hypothesis. The farms in the sample were divided into three size categories — small, medium, and large — and savings ratios for each category were calculated. The results are presented in Table 8.3. It can be seen that in neither district was the savings ratio on large farms the

[55] Ibid., p. 233.

highest, and in Hissar it was the lowest. The small farmers, on the other hand, had the lowest savings rate in Ludhiana but a very high rate in Hissar. Medium size farmers, however, had the highest rate of savings in both districts. There is nothing in this evidence, therefore, that indicates that inequality of landed wealth or of agricultural income is conducive of a high rate of savings, or that a redistribution of land necessarily would lead to a fall in the rate of accumulation. Those who wish to defend status, privilege and wealth must seek other grounds for doing so.

Factor prices

We have stressed repeatedly that methods of cultivation and the pace of innovation are strongly affected by the ease of access to the means of production and by relative factor prices. It has been argued that factor markets in rural areas are seriously 'distorted' and that factor prices fail to reflect social opportunity costs. A land reform, as suggested above, will help to correct some of these distortions, but a change in tenure arrangements will not suffice to remove all distortions. Agrarian reform, moreover, may not be politically acceptable to most governments. Thus, for both these reasons, we should consider alternative policies which might improve the allocation of factors of production, although it should be recognized that in the absence of land reform several of the policy alternatives we examine are mere palliatives.

At present it is differences in relative factor prices which largely account for the fact that larger landowners — either directly or through their tenants — innovate more quickly than smallholder peasants. For example, in most countries the amount of credit available in rural areas is inadequate, and what little credit that is available through organized institutions tends to be rationed among those with secure titles to land and supplied at a relatively low rate of interest.[56] The majority of the rural population must seek

[56] Moreover, there is some evidence from India that the larger farmers have a higher default rate with cooperative credit institutions than do small farmers. See, for example, Daniel Thorner, *Agricultural Cooperatives in India: A Field Report*, Asia, New York, 1964.

credit in the unorganized capital market and pay a high price
for it. On grounds of equity, efficiency and growth this
situation should be corrected. The rate of interest in the
organized credit market in rural areas should be substantially
raised in order, first, to encourage more saving in the
countryside and, second, to encourage commercial banks to
shift part of their lending activity from industry to agriculture. Equally important, additional credit should be supplied
from government sources. The effect of these two measures
would be to put pressure on the unorganized credit market to
reduce interest rates paid by those who must have recourse to
this source. Once the total supply of credit available to the
agricultural sector has increased, the government should
adopt policies whose purpose is to ensure that small peasants
have access to the organized market on terms which are not
inferior (and perhaps even superior) to those enjoyed by large
landlords.[57]

In principle, similar policies should be adopted to ensure
that small owner-operators have equal or preferential access
to irrigation water, technical assistance and all the other
inputs which are vital to the success of the 'green revolution'.
At present they are discriminated against in virtually all
factor 'markets' — either in terms of price, or because of the
way scarce resources are allocated by rationing, or because of
restricted access to the bureaucracy.

A line of policy based in part on the conscious manipulation of factor prices rests on the assumption that producers
do respond when relative costs change. There is abundant
evidence that this assumption is true. India, for example, has
recently imposed new tariffs and excise taxes on tractors; this
has caused a sharp rise in their price and already the volume
of tractor imports has declined. Similarly, the devaluation of
the peso in the Philippines in 1970 was followed by a rise in
the local currency price of tractors and fertilizer and a
reduction in the quantity of both that was imported. More
generally, Randolph Barker and three of his colleagues have
shown that the degree of mechanization in four Asian
countries is sensitive to relative factor prices.[58] They calculated the price of mechanical horsepower relative to the cost
of farm labour, and then compared this ratio with average
horsepower per agricultural worker. As one would expect,

they found that the higher the factor price ratio the lower the horsepower-labour ratio. Their results have been converted to index number form and are summarized below:

	Factor price ratio	Horsepower-labour ratio
Philippines	100.0	100.0
Thailand	85.7	122.9
Taiwan	73.5	145.8
Japan	17.7	2187.5

---

[57] The argument can be illustrated diagramatically. In the organized credit market we assume that interest rates are fixed at a level of i_s (as a result of laws against usury, the policy of state sponsored rural banks, etc.) and that rationing is used to close the excess demand gap of AC. In the informal market, however, we assume supply and demand for credit are equated at a rate of interest of i_1. If, first, additional credit from government sources were channelled into the organized market this would (a) reduce the excess demand in that market to BC and (b) lead to a shift to the left of the demand curve in the informal market, thereby lowering interest rates there. Second, if i_s were allowed to vary in accordance with market conditions, this would lead (c) to a rise in the rate of interest in the formal market to i_e and the elimination of rationing plus (d) to a further shift of the demand curve and a decline in the rate of interest in the informal credit market to i_2.

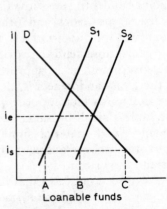

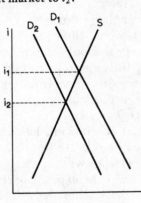

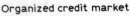

Organized credit market   Informal credit market

[58] Randolph Barker, William H. Meyers, Christina M. Crisostomo and Bart Duff, 'Employment and Technological Change in Philippine Agriculture', mimeo., I.L.O., Geneva, Switzerland, October 1971. See especially Table 6.

It is sometimes thought that the new high yielding varieties of foodgrains are characterized by economies of scale, and that this explains why it is the owners of large holdings who are the most active in adopting the new technology. This hypothesis in general is not correct, as is evident from the fact that frequently large holdings are broken up into many small tenancies. Seeds, fertilizers and pesticides are complementary but highly divisible; even the smallest peasant can use them, as experience in Taiwan indicates. Some types of irrigation facilities are indeed rather indivisible, and hence the scale factor is important, but large dams and canals are invariably financed by the government, and thus economies of scale in irrigation cannot explain why small peasant owners lag behind landlords. Pumping machinery and even sprayers can be rather 'lumpy', but these can be supplied through cooperatives organized for the purpose or obtained by hiring. Examples of both methods of organizing the supply of lumpy inputs are common, especially the practice of relatively prosperous villagers hiring out pieces of capital equipment to their neighbours.

The technical inputs required by the 'green revolution' are essentially 'scale-neutral', but the institutions required by the new technology often are not. Extension agents concentrate on the large farmers; credit agencies concentrate on low risk borrowers; those who sell fertilizers, pesticides and other chemical inputs concentrate on cultivators who are likely to buy the largest quantities. State organizations tend to provide services to those from whom the government seeks approval, and in most instances these are the large landowners. Unless there is 'scale-neutrality' in the institutions which support the 'green revolution', i.e. to repeat, unless small peasants have equal access to knowledge, finance and material inputs, innovation will inevitably favour the prosperous and the secure at the expense of the poor and the insecure.

Almost all of the evidence we have seen indicates that the average productivity of land and capital are higher on small holdings than on large, while the average productivity of labour is higher on large holdings than on small. Since land and capital are scarce relative to labour, we have concluded that average total factor productivity is greater on the small farms than on the large, and we have assumed further that what is true of the average is true on the margin as well. The implication of this analysis is that small farms should generally be encouraged relative to large farms by transferring resources from the latter to the former.

This simple policy conclusion does not necessarily remain valid, however, if some factors of production are immobile. Assume, for example, that the political system is such that it is impossible to transfer land and capital from one group of farmers to another. In this case the only mobile factor would be labour, and an improvement in resource allocation would require that labour be shifted to farms where on the margin its productivity is highest, i.e. toward the large farms. In other words, although total factor productivity may be higher on small holdings, this ceases to be relevant to policy if not all factors are mobile. Given immobility of some factors of production, efficiency requires that the remaining factors be encouraged to move where their marginal product is highest and this might imply subsidizing farms where total factor productivity is low.

A policy of subsidizing the cost of labour to large landowners — even assuming it is administratively feasible — is decidedly a 'second best' solution, of course. In the first place, the policy does not enable the rural sector to maximize output from its given resources; it merely allows production to be somewhat higher than it might otherwise have been. That is, the policy reduces but does not eliminate inefficiency. Secondly, the policy is inegalitarian. It increases the profits of large landowners (by lowering costs) and thereby subjects small owner-operators to greater competitive pressure.[59] Whereas a redistribution of land and capital in favour of the peasantry would lead to greater equality, a redistribution of labour in favour of landlords would result in greater inequality. (Some members of the rural proletariat would

[59] In theory the correct prescription for this problem is to tax the profits of landlords and use the receipts to subsidize the cost of labour. In practice, however, this is likely to be extremely difficult, since large landowners can be expected to use their political power not only to prevent a redistribution of land but also to prevent their incomes from being taxed.

benefit, of course, but they represent a minority of the rural
poor.) Thus 'second best' policies and piecemeal reforms may
improve allocative efficiency but they may also aggravate
social problems. Moreover, third, to the extent that a policy
of subsidizing rural wages strengthens the landowning elite,
the likelihood of undertaking a major transformation of
agrarian institutions is diminished, and in the long run this is
contrary to the interests of the majority of the agricultural
population.

Agricultural surpluses and non-agricultural growth
In several of the countries where the 'green revolution' is now
occurring, notably India, Pakistan and the Philippines, the
growth of agricultural production has been adversely affected
by the general policies pursued by governments anxious to
encourage industrialization. A majority of underdeveloped
countries, especially during the first two decades after the
end of the second world war, have provided strong incentives
to import substitute manufactures, particularly consumer
goods. High tariffs were erected to protect nascent industries,
import quotas and other direct controls were used to direct
resources towards manufactures, exchange rates became
grossly overvalued and in at least one case, viz. Pakistan, a
scheme for the compulsory delivery of food grains was
implemented.

The effect of these policies was to turn the terms of trade
against agriculture, to reduce the profitability of investment
and innovation in rural areas, and to discourage production
for the market, particularly the export market. The relative
stagnation of agriculture which has characterized so many
underdeveloped countries is due in large part to the overall
growth strategy pursued by governments. It has now become
painfully obvious that any strategy which hopes to transform
agriculture from a technically stagnant sector to one in which
rapid innovation occurs must pay particular attention to the
relative commodity prices which farmers confront. If, say,
exchange rate and commercial policy are such that agriculture is an unprofitable activity, it is unlikely that biological
research will be able to alter this situation fundamentally.

One of the consequences of turning the terms of trade
against agriculture is that the income of the peasantry is

reduced. The landed élite, however, need not be harmed since they can diversify their assets and shift the focus of their economic activities to the urban sector. Once they acquire a stake in manufacturing and commerce as well as in agriculture they acquire a vested interest in the status quo. The reason for this is that there is a close connection between the income of the peasantry and the urban wage rate. Low peasant incomes usually result in low wages and high profits outside of agriculture. 'The fact that the wage level in the capitalist sector depends upon earnings in the subsistence sector is sometimes of immense political importance, since the effect is that capitalists have a direct interest in holding down productivity of the subsistence workers.'[60] The importance of this point increases substantially once the landed élite have merged with the industrial capitalist class, because then all property owning groups have an interest in turning the terms of trade against agriculture. This tends to perpetuate low productivity and stagnation in the rural sector and low wages combined with high profits in the urban sector.

Eventually, however, the system will begin to collapse. This will occur when the subsidy required for the support and expansion of the industrial sector is greater than the resources which can be squeezed out of agriculture. When that point is reached, policy will have to be switched to favour agriculture, regardless of the nature of the regime in power.

This does not imply, of course, that the sole concern of policy should then be to promote agricultural development. On the contrary, as long as the non-agricultural sectors are small it will be desirable to extract a surplus from agriculture in order to increase investment and growth in some activities in other sectors. In the non-socialist countries agriculture usually is squeezed by ensuring that most of the agricultural surplus is concentrated in the hands of a few large landowners and then relying on them to make a substantial portion of their output available in urban markets.[61] The

[60] W. A. Lewis, 'Economic Development with Unlimited Supplies of Labour', *Manchester School of Economic and Social Studies*, May 1954, p. 149.
[61] The various ways in which a surplus has been extracted from agriculture are discussed in Chapter 5.

combination of agrarian monopoly and markets relatively free of direct government intervention has permitted a certain amount of industrialization in many underdeveloped countries, but the rate of industrial capital formation has been disappointing.

The direct contribution of the agricultural sector to government revenue and public savings has been low in most non-socialist underdeveloped countries.[62] In fact several important countries, most notably Pakistan and many states of India, exempt income originating in agriculture from income taxation. This practice is hard to defend in terms either of equity or growth. The exemption is of negligible benefit to the peasantry but is of considerable benefit to the rich. First, it enables large landowners to avoid contributing to the general costs of financing development. Second, it provides an incentive to urban industrialists and members of the professions to acquire land from impoverished peasants, since by investing undeclared industrial profits and professional fees in land they can turn 'black', i.e. taxable, money into 'white'. If countries wish to pursue a technocratic style of rural development the least they should do is restore the land tax and use it as an instrument of accumulation. Land taxes were employed very effectively by Japan and colonial governments throughout South Asia to appropriate a large part of the agricultural surplus. The governments of the newly independent Asian countries have committed a major technical error in allowing this instrument virtually to disappear, although there are good political reasons why this has happened. The effect, of course, has been to strengthen the old and new landowning élite.

In most socialist countries, in contrast, the landlord class has been abolished and the state has assumed direct responsibility for extracting a surplus from agriculture. This has been achieved by organizing production in very large units – as state farms, collectives or communes, and then requiring these units to deliver specific quantities of com-

---

[62] The most important exception is countries which impose heavy taxes on peasant export crops.

modities at prices fixed by the planning authorities.[63] These arrangements have been remarkably successful in facilitating a high rate of capital accumulation in industry, but the cost has been high.

First, the predominance of large farms has resulted in allocative inefficiency. The land-labour ratio has been too high on the collective farms and too low on small holdings and private plots. Thus the pattern that is common in the non-socialist underdeveloped countries has been reproduced in the socialist countries. In consequence, there is a considerable difference in output per acre between small and large farms, and because large farms occupy most of the land, average yields are low.

Second, the policy of collectivization has imposed a considerable burden on the material wellbeing of the peasantry. The Russians were ruthless in extracting a surplus from agriculture and were quite willing to tolerate low incomes in rural areas. The Chinese, on the other hand, could not afford to be quite so ruthless because incomes in rural areas could not be squeezed too much without running a risk of famine. In any case, a policy of squeezing the peasantry was contrary to the Chinese style of rural development.

Finally, the policy in socialist countries of extracting a surplus through collectivization has resulted in a relatively slow rate of growth of agricultural production. In the Soviet Union agricultural performance was terrible during the early planning period. The grain harvest of 1935 was still below output in the exceptionally favourable year of 1913, and in the period 1928–1935 the number of cattle declined by about 29 per cent and the number of sheep and goats by 58 per cent. Conditions in China were not nearly so bad, but during the First Five Year Plan period (1952–57) agricultural output increased only about 1.7 per cent a year, i.e. roughly in line with the population. More recently, however, the rate of growth of the agricultural sector in China has increased substantially.

[63] In Taiwan, land has been equitably distributed in small holdings and a marketable surplus has been extracted by regulating the terms on which rice is bartered for fertilizer. This system is discussed in Chapter 5, Section B.

One of the tasks of those who make policy, particularly in countries which wish to follow a revolutionary style of rural development, is to devise a system which avoids the inefficiencies of large collectives, and yet is able to obtain resources from rural areas for use elsewhere without creating unacceptable inequalities. In capitalist economies, as we have seen, it is the private landlord who usually appropriates the surplus and transfers it to urban areas via unregulated, or partially regulated, markets. In socialist countries the collective amasses the surplus and transfers it to the state via compulsory delivery schemes. An alternative strategy would be to terminate the institution of private property in agricultural land and replaced it by public or communal ownership. The object of 'nationalizing' the land would be to replace the landlord by the state (or the local community). As owner of the land the state would be entitled to a rent, and a level of rents could be fixed so as to obtain the amount of resources necessary to fulfil government objectives. Farm management, on the other hand, need not be the direct responsibility of government, although state farms could be introduced if these were thought desirable. Relatively small farms could be created and run either as a cooperative or as a family enterprise. In this way efficiency and equality in rural areas could be assured without having to run the risk that too large a fraction of output would be consumed and the rate of accumulation thereby reduced.

A growing number of countries has restricted private ownership of property in land, and this has proved to be quite compatible with small scale operational holdings. The socialist countries are not unique in attributing importance to state or communal ownership of land, although their practice of organizing production in enormous state or collective farms is distinctive and more akin to large capitalist farms in North America than to the peasant systems of most of the Third World.[64] The land tenure system in Malaysia is

[64] It is not widely known that the U.S. government owns more than half the land in some western states. The total amount of land owned by the government is approximately 760 million acres, of which 707 million acres are leased to private individuals and corporations for livestock grazing.

based on the assumption that the federal and state governments possess all land rights, and these are distributed to individuals in various ways. The *ryotwari* system in south India was based on similar principles, although rights in land use were heritable. In Mexico, a third of the land is vested in village *ejidos*, and cultivation usually is done on individual plots, although collective farming also exists. In Algeria, the land formerly owned by French colonists has been nationalized and most production decisions are taken by the workers and their elected management committee. Traditionally in much of Africa the land was collectively owned by the tribe but farmed individually, the rights to use land being allocated by the chief. In Chile, new experiments with several types of communal or collective systems of ownership and management have been conducted. Israel, of course, has had considerable experience with the *kibbutz*.

As the examples above indicate, there are many ways of organizing the agricultural sector which do not require individual ownership of land. Unfortunately, relatively few scholars have taken the trouble to examine the social and economic implications of alternative systems of ownership, and consequently there is insufficient evidence on which to base firm generalizations. Raanan Weitz, however, has spent many years studying the *kibbutz* and *moshav* in Israel as well as farming systems in several other countries, and he has come to the conclusion that farms 'should be given to the farmer on lease only, while legal ownership remains permanently in the possession of the rural community'.[65] Of course, what governments *ought* to do depends on their objectives and the style of rural development they wish to pursue; all one can say is that if governments wish to introduce a communal form of property, there is evidence that such a system can work.

Output prices and marketing

We began the previous section by arguing that a great many underdeveloped countries adopted economic policies which

[65] Raanan Weitz, *From Peasant to Farmer*, Columbia University Press, 1971, p. 165.

had the effect of turning the terms of trade against rural areas. The purpose of the policy was to encourage growth in non-agricultural activities in urban areas, and while it succeeded in doing so to a certain extent, the policy also resulted in a slow growth of agricultural production. This, in turn, created severe difficulties — including near-famines in some countries — and governments have been forced to respond.

The typical response, however, has not been to turn the terms of trade sharply in favour of agriculture, but to raise the price of particular items that were in short supply. Most prominent among these items has, of course, been foodgrains. Indeed in some countries, e.g. Mexico, the Philippines and Pakistan, it is difficult to tell to what extent the rise in foodgrain output is attributable to an improved technology (which lowers costs) and to what extent it is due to high domestic prices. If the introduction of high yielding seeds reduces total costs of grain production, it will raise farm profits and lead to increased output. It should not be necessary, therefore, for governments to support the 'green revolution' by maintaining the domestic price of any particular commodity above that prevailing in the world at large. On the contrary, a sensible objective of government policy would be to ensure that lower costs are passed on to the community in the form of lower food prices.

We have noted on several occasions that large farmers often benefit from what are in effect subsidized material inputs. If these same farmers now receive a subsidy to output as well, the consequences for income distribution and resource allocation will be serious. A policy of high support prices, first, will raise the cost of living for urban consumers, increase inequality in the cities — which in most countries already is much greater than in rural areas, accentuate demands for higher money wages and, possibly, lead to a cost-push inflation.

Secondly, support prices will induce producers to alter the composition of agricultural output. For example, there is evidence that rice production in Pakistan has been encouraged at the expense of cotton exports, and wheat acreage in India has expanded at the expense of the more nutritious high protein pulses. Given that 'the average Indian today receives 8 per cent less protein than in 1960',[66] a high support price for wheat seems unwise as well as unnecessary. In the Philippines too the local price of rice is considerably higher than the world price. The government has a monopoly of international trade in rice and is able to affect the domestic price through variations in the quantity of grain imports. The same is true in Sri Lanka. The issue that has to be resolved, however, is whether a rise in the price of foodgrains gives farmers an incentive to produce in accordance with a country's comparative advantage, and if not, whether this matters. Our views on this issue have already been expressed[67] and there is no need to repeat them. But in general it seems doubtful that there is any special reason to raise the price of grains relative to other food crops and agricultural commodities; what is needed is a rise in the price of agricultural commodities as a whole relative to the price of non-agricultural commodities.

Lastly, high support prices for selected foodgrains may result in large domestic surpluses and severe marketing problems. That is, if local prices are high enough domestic production may exceed consumption even after all previous imports have been replaced. In many countries it may be desirable to build up domestic stocks of food in order to ensure an adequate supply in years of bad harvests, but there can be little justification for following policies which result in persistent surplus production.

India already had about 9 or 10 million tons of wheat stocks in early 1972, and there was no indication that in the absence of droughts the rate of accumulation of inventories would diminish. Yet only about 5 million tons are needed to protect foodgrain supplies from possible harvest failures; anything in excess of this is surplus to normal requirements. Some wheat was given to Bangladesh shortly after the country became independent, but even so, India still had

[66] Alan Berg, 'Nutrition as a National Priority: Lessons from the Indian Experiment', *American Journal of Clinical Nutrition*, November 1970, p. 1397.
[67] See Chapter 6, Section D.

until recently a substantial disposal problem. One possible way of disposing of any surplus wheat that may exist, which has been suggested by Professor Dandekar and others, would be to use it to finance public works projects.[68] Unemployed labour could be paid in kind (namely, in wheat), in cash or in a combination of the two, and the labour force thus mobilized could be used to undertake a large number of projects of value to rural areas. These would include the construction of secondary roads, village schools and clinics, irrigation and drainage ditches, etc. In this way idle labour and unproductive inventories could be converted into productive capital.

Government expenditure

Although producing surplus grain in order to finance a rural works programme is a rather clumsy way of accelerating capital formation, any policy which results in more investment in the agricultural sector is likely to be an improvement over previous policies. In the previous chapter we argued that agriculture has frequently been neglected and received too small a share of total capital formation. A massive public works programme could help to redress the balance. Furthermore, we argued that the social return on investment in agriculture was often higher than the return in other sectors of the economy. To the extent that this is true, a strong case can be made in general terms for reallocating more investment resources from urban to rural areas.

More specifically, the spread of the 'green revolution' will require substantial investment in irrigation and transport. Much of this will have to be financed by the public sector. It will also require large investments by public and private enterprise in marketing and storage facilities, as well as in industries supplying agriculture with the necessary chemical and mechanical inputs. The private sector can be expected to respond to profit opportunities, and if the policies we have suggested are implemented, one can be confident that ad-

---

[68] Another possible way which has occasionally been used is to dump surplus grains on the world market. Mexico has disposed of some wheat in this way and for a while Japan was, in effect, dumping rice.

equate incentives will be present and that private and social cost-benefit calculations will converge. Public investment, however, usually responds not to market signals but to political decisions. It is important, therefore, that governments that wish to promote growth and equality in rural areas should review their public expenditure policies to ensure that agricultural innovation is not obstructed by inadequate supporting institutions (e.g. credit, technical assistance, education) or capital facilities (e.g. irrigation water and transport). It is the job of the scientists to discover an improved technology, but it is the responsibility of government to ensure that the technology is widely disseminated, and that the technology is not given a class bias as a result of policy. At present, few governments have adequately discharged this responsibility.

Science policy
Progress in agricultural science, however, has been much more encouraging. Of course, a great deal more remains to be done, but new research institutes are being established all over the world and one can be fairly confident that our knowledge of tropical agriculture will continue to increase. Indeed research on food crops in underdeveloped areas is still a fairly recent phenomenon. The first international institution — which later became The International Center for the Improvement of Maize and Wheat (CIMMYT) — was established in Mexico in 1944 and its first high yielding wheat seed was released three years later, in 1947. The International Rice Research Institute (IRRI) was founded at Los Baños, Philippines in 1962 and its first high yielding variety of rice (IR-8) was released in 1966. Another centre (CIAT) exists in Colombia, where research is being conducted on cassava, forage crops, beef cattle and pigs. CIAT also has a small rice research programme. The newly operational International Institute for Tropical Agriculture (IITA) in Ibadan, Nigeria plans to concentrate on developing productive alternatives to shifting cultivation. Their work will focus on maize, cow peas, rice and cassava. An International Potato Research Center (IPRC) has just been established in La Molina, Peru, and a centre for research in the semi-arid tropics (ICRISAT)

is about to begin in India. ICRISAT is expected to do work on sorghum, millet, pigeon peas and chick peas. Lastly, an Asian Vegetable Research and Development Center has been planned for Taiwan. This centre will specialize in leafy and fruiting vegetables, roots, tubers and bulbs, and it will pay particular attention to developing disease and insect resistant varieties for the humid tropics.

The cost of establishing and running a research institute is relatively modest and is not beyond the financial capacity of any country that gives a high priority to agricultural development.[69] As a rule of thumb, the capital cost of a research centre is between $3.5 and $7 million. The new centre in Taiwan, for example, has a capital budget of $3.7 million, including all equipment. The expected running costs of the centre are $1.5 million a year. IITA, on the other hand, is much larger: its capital costs were $18.5 million and its running costs are $6.5 million a year. In the ten years since IRRI was established five high yielding rice seeds have been released. This is an average of one every other year, and the cost has been about $5 million per seed.

It would be wrong to imagine that international research centres could or should be a substitute for national efforts. Their role is to be a pioneer in new research activities, to gather information and material, to maintain a seed bank, and to provide a minimum amount of coordination. National research organizations will be necessary to undertake location-specific research. At the very least this means adapting seeds released by the international institutes to local conditions. In addition, national institutes should develop improved varieties of their own. The admirable research on rice conducted in the long established centres in Taiwan and Sri Lanka are examples of what can be done.

National research centres cannot be content with discovering new knowledge, they must also disseminate it to local cultivators. That is, research should be closely linked to extension. The research institute should run several dem-

[69] The estimates in this paragraph were kindly supplied by Dr. Robert Chandler, the Director of IRRI and the Director-designate of the Asian Vegetable Center in Taiwan.

onstration farms in various parts of the country, and farmers should be encouraged to visit these frequently — not only so that they can learn what is happening at the institute, but also so that the scientists can learn what are the problems of the farmers. Similarly, extension agents could be trained on the demonstration farms, so that those who go out to visit the cultivators are aware of the latest research results and have seen them applied under conditions which hopefully are not too different from those which ordinary farmers confront. In this way a close connection between theory and practice, research and application can be established, and this should help to accelerate the pace of technical change and thereby raise the rate of return on research effort.

The costs of agricultural research, as we have seen, are low and the expected returns are high. It would be premature to attempt a definitive estimate of the rate of return on expenditure on plant breeding, but already enough is known to indicate that money spent on research is money well spent. In an exploratory study at Yale University, Robert Evenson and Yoav Kislev found positive correlations over time between the rate of increase of wheat and maize yields and the stock of knowledge as measured by the number of relevant scientific papers published. On the basis of this study they concluded that 'the rate of return to investment in research in wheat and maize has been of the order of magnitude of 30% to 100% per annum'.[70]

The rate of return might not be so high, however, if the focus of research switches from raising yields to, say, increasing the protein content of foodgrains or reducing the susceptibility of high yielding varieties to disease.[71] In the case of rice, for example, the high yielding varieties that are

---

[70] Robert E. Evenson and Yoav Kislev, 'Research and Productivity in Wheat and Maize', Progress Report, mimeo, Yale University, April 1972, p. 40. Estimates of the rate of return on research expenditure in Mexico, 1943—1963, were 750 per cent in wheat and 300 per cent in maize. (L. Ardito Barletta, *Costs and Social Returns of Agricultural Research in Mexico*, Ph.D. thesis, University of Chicago, 1966, cited in Y. Hayami and V. W. Ruttan, *Agricultural Development*, 1971, p. 41.)

[71] See Chapter 3, Section C for our suggestions regarding 'biological engineering'.

now being used have encountered a fairly high incidence of pest and disease problems. On the other hand, there apparently is no conflict between breeding for high yields and for genetic resistance to disease. IR-20, for instance, is a dwarf variety (i.e. is 100—120 cm. tall) which produces high yields and refrains from lodging; it also is resistant (but not immune) to rice blast, the stem borer, tungro and the tungro vector (i.e. the green leaf hopper). Moreover, even newer varieties are coming along which can resist other pests and diseases, e.g. IR-26. In contrast, attempts to increase the protein content of rice represent a difficult breeding problem. The main difficulty is that there is a negative correlation between protein content and yield. Average protein content is about 7.5 per cent and a reasonable objective would be to raise this to 10 per cent, but even if the biologists succeed (and some progress has been made with IR-480) it remains to be seen what will be the effect on yield, and whether a low yield—high protein grain would be acceptable to farmers and consumers.

Problems also arise in trying to breed for a variety of environmental conditions. The high yielding wheat seeds have been much more successful in Asia than the improved rice seeds. A major reason for this is that about 65 per cent of the wheat acreage in Asia benefits from some form of irrigation, whereas only about 20 per cent of the rice land is irrigated. It is only on this 20 per cent that the use of the new rice seeds would result in a 'significant yield increase'. On the 50 per cent of rice land which is rainfed the new varieties will produce yields which 'are not likely to be significantly different from local varieties'.[72] Moreover, the use of the new seeds in deep water areas (10 per cent of the land) and in upland rice zones (20 per cent of the land) would result in lower yields than can be obtained with indigenous varieties.

Research is underway to try to develop rice plants that will perform well in the non-irrigated areas. Some success has been achieved with higher yielding varieties suitable for rainfed conditions. Similarly, research in Thailand on deep water rice is encouraging. A dwarf variety has been crossed

[72] Randolph Barker, 'The Evolutionary Nature of the New Rice Technology', IRRI, mimeo, September 1971, p. 3.

with a 'flooder' which can grow as much as four inches a night for several nights in a row, and thus the plant can keep its head above water as the depth of the flood basin rises. Varieties of this type are now being tested in Thailand and Bangladesh. On the other hand, little progress has been achieved in developing a high yielding variety of rice which is resistant to drought.

In fact the problem of drought is very widespread and is not limited to a few rice growing regions. North Africa, the Near East and much of Black Africa south of the Sahara are semi-arid zones where the importance of rice is slight. In Black Africa, for example, more than half the total cereal area, i.e. 30 million hectares, is devoted to sorghum and millet. In parts of the Mahgreb half the land is idle at any one time: the typical rotation is wheat (or another cereal) followed by a year of fallow, so that a piece of land produces a crop only once every two years. In areas such as these it is unclear what science policy should be. It probably would be a mistake, however, to assume that there is a single solution. At least until a solution becomes clear, research should be exploratory, e.g. trying simultaneously to produce drought resistant cereals, devise new methods of irrigation, improve fodder crops, and breed better animals (especially sheep) for arid climates.

Science is a powerful instrument at the disposal of those who formulate policy. There is no doubt that it can be used to reduce poverty and inequality in rural areas and to raise the rate of growth of agricultural output. Whether it will be so used depends in large part on what are the objectives of the government and these, in turn, depend in part on which groups in the community the government relies on for support. Technology alone provides few answers to the problems that beset the underdeveloped world, although potentially it has much to contribute. Science can make it possible to increase the welfare of the impoverished mass of the population, but it cannot guarantee that the welfare of the masses will in fact be increased.

D. Conclusion
What is the nature of the world in which we live? The great majority of people who offer economic advice to govern-

ments assume, first, that we live in a self-equilibrating system and, second, that there is a basic harmony of interests among the individuals and groups who comprise the system. When interests diverge it is assumed that they can be reconciled relatively easily through minor policy adjustments, and when the system moves out of equilibrium it is assumed that automatic forces tend to restore it to the previous position. This vision of the world is strongly entrenched in economic thought. It is reflected in Adam Smith's benevolent 'hidden hand', which reconciles private self-interest with the general welfare, and in Alfred Marshall's theory of markets, which expounds the calculus of an optimising, self-adjusting economy.

Our view of the world is rather different. It is akin to that of Karl Marx, who saw class conflict where others imagined harmony, of Thomas Malthus, who feared a cumulative downward spiral as a result of the tendency of population to expand faster than food production, and of David Ricardo, who foresaw that mechanization could create unemployment and hardship. Our point of departure for an analysis of policy options is the assumption that interests are in conflict, that this conflict seldom can be eliminated, and that therefore the correct choice of policy is largely a value judgement that depends upon which groups one wishes to favour. We assume, furthermore, that there is no immediate, necessary or inevitable tendency for a 'countervailing power' to arise when one group finds itself at a disadvantage vis-à-vis another, and thus the possibility of cumulative movements is not ruled out. Naturally, those who are harmed by change will attempt to respond, but there is no guarantee that the response will be successful: the indigenous communities of Mindanao, for example, are in great danger of being destroyed by the forces unleashed by technical change.

Conflict can be found at many different levels, and we have divided the various groups in society in several different ways to reflect this fact. At one level there is a conflict between nations. This is an aspect of the 'green revolution' to which we have devoted relatively little attention. It did arise, however, in connection with the tendency of several countries to use the new varieties as an excuse or opportunity to import substitute foodgrains at the expense of traditional rice exporting nations.[73] There are other contexts, of course, in which international conflicts of interest can be present, e.g., a conflict between countries which wish to export agricultural machinery and agro-chemicals and those that wish to safeguard domestic employment.

The international dimension of conflict is not without interest,[74] but the evidence we have collected appears to indicate that most of the conflicts arising from the 'green revolution' are domestic in origin. A fundamental division in society is between those who own property and those who do not. The former have a common interest in keeping wage rates low and this can most easily be secured by adopting policies which restrain the rate of increase of the productivity of labour in the agricultural sector.[75] Although a policy of low productivity in agriculture would tend to go counter to the interests of landlords, in many countries the problem has been overcome by landlords diversifying their assets and becoming industrialists as well. The 'marriage of steel and rye' is a common phenomenon.

In Asia, for instance, the authors of a recent United Nations report note that 'the three groups [bureaucrats, entrepreneurs and professionals] are by no means discontinuous, and are in fact often found to be closely linked to one another — and to the traditional *élite* — by birth, intermarriage or economic interests'. The report then adds that these close links among groups with power inhibit institutional change: 'this inhibition is most obvious in the generally feeble enthusiasm shown for broad agrarian reforms, by the new and old *élites* alike'.[76] Similar comments about the close connections of kinship and economic interests among the rural and urban upper classes would be equally relevant to Latin America and Africa.

---

[73] See Chapter 6.
[74] Many broad issues are raised in an interesting way in Harry M. Cleaver, Jr., 'The Contradictions of the Green Revolution', *Monthly Review*, June 1972.
[75] See p. 235 above.
[76] United Nations, Department of Economic and Social Affairs, *1970 Report on the World Social Situation*, 1971, p. 11.

Nonetheless, there are many occasions when the interests of the agricultural sector as a whole conflict with those of non-agriculture. This is especially true when the rural areas are squeezed in order to extract resources which can be used for investment and consumption elsewhere. There are three devices which have been used to do this — by monopolizing land, by intentionally turning the terms of trade against agriculture and by imposing direct controls. Each device has different implications for resource allocation and income distribution, and these are explored in a separate chapter.[77]

The interests of agriculture and industry need not conflict, of course. Indeed in some cases growth in the one encourages growth in the other. For example, the 'green revolution' has provided an enormous stimulous to small manufacturing firms in Ludhiana, India to supply agricultural implements to wheat farmers in the Punjab. Similar growth of agriculture related industries, particularly of firms producing diesel engines and irrigation pumps, can be observed in Lahore and other cities of Pakistan.[78] Linkages between the two sectors are even more developed in Taiwan, however. Indeed Taiwan is the only underdeveloped country in Asia where agro-industries have achieved an advanced stage of growth, both in supplying inputs to the agricultural sector and in processing the sector's output. In addition, other industries have developed to provide consumer goods to the rural population. There are various reasons for this success. First, a high priority was given to agriculture in the 1960s and thus a potential demand for manufactured inputs was created. Second, an agrarian reform was implemented which resulted in lower rents, abolition of absentee landlordism and a more equitable distribution of land and, hence, of income;[79] this, in turn, created a broader market for industrial consumer

---

[77] See Chapter 5, particularly Section B.

[78] Hiromitsu Kaneda and Frank C. Child, 'Small-Scale, Agriculturally Related Industry in the Punjab', Department of Economics, University of California, Davis, Working Paper No. 11, September 1971. For a more general discussion see Bruce F. Johnston and Peter Kilby, *Agricultural Strategies, Rural—Urban Interactions and the Expansion of Income Opportunities*, OECD, forthcoming.

[79] The land reform in Taiwan was imposed by Nationalist Chinese officials who retreated to the island from the mainland. The National-

goods in rural areas. Third, Farmers Associations were strengthened and these ensured that farmers would have no difficulty in marketing their products or obtaining material inputs. Thus obstacles to the physical flow of commodities between the two sectors were reduced. Fourth, within industry, emphasis was placed initially on small and medium sized firms which used labour intensive techniques of production. The rapid expansion of these industries was associated with rapid growth of employment opportunities in urban areas and reduced pressure on the countryside to retain labour. In consequence, real wages rose quickly in both sectors, the absolute number of people engaged in agriculture began to decline in 1968—69, income inequality was reduced and the urban-rural wage differential practically vanished — the only country in Asia, and perhaps in the whole of the Third World, where this has occurred.[80]

Taiwan, thus, indicates what is possible, but in most underdeveloped countries economic policy has created a conflict of interests between agriculture and industry. This clash of interests between sectors, however, is subordinate to a clash of interests between classes.[81] Within agriculture, an analysis conducted in terms of a simple division between landlords and peasants will suffice for many purposes.[82]

---

ists had no commitments to Taiwanese landowners and thus were able to eliminate their political and economic power. In fact, it was essential for the Nationalists to do this in order to reduce the hostility to them of the mass of the local population.

[80] The top decile of households in Taiwan in 1964 received about 26 per cent of all family income. (Government of the Republic of China, Directorate-General of Budgets, Accounts and Statistics, *Report on the Survey of Family Income and Expenditure and Study of Personal Income Distribution in Taiwan*, Taipei, 1966.)

[81] I do not wish to imply that class conflict is the only source of conflict in rural areas, but merely that it is the most important from the point of view of policy. Clearly there are also conflicts between regions, between villages (over location of roads, allocation of school buildings, etc.), between religious and linguistic groups, between individuals, and so on.

[82] See Chapter 2, where this division is used to discuss techniques of cultivation used by small and large farmers.

That is, a basic distinction that has to be made is between those whose income is derived almost entirely from rent or profit and those who (implicitly or explicitly) derive much of their income in the form of returns to labour. Different policies can have quite different consequences for the two groups. This became clear when we discussed, for instance, factor prices and policies toward mechanization, as well as the issues connected with land reform.

We have argued that technical change in rural areas leads to greater specialization and division of labour and to greater social differentiation. In other words, in the course of the 'green revolution' our assumption that the rural community can be divided into two groups — landlords and peasants — tends to become undermined. The peasantry ceases to be a homogeneous class (if it ever was) and the analysis has to be conducted in terms of a more sophisticated model.[83] The minimum degree of elaboration is a division of the rural community into four classes: the landed élite, middle peasants, small peasants and agricultural labourers.[84] The purpose of this division is to allow us to take into account the fact that conflict of interest arises not only between the landed élite and the peasantry as a whole but also within the peasantry.

Middle peasants have three defining characteristics: first, they derive most (but not necessarily all) of their income from cultivation; second, their production on the farm exceeds the subsistence requirements of the household and thus a surplus is available for disposal on the market; third, their need for labour exceeds the amount available from within the household and consequently they must employ workers from off the farm. These three characteristics often will be found together, although there is no need to insist

[83] See Chapters 3 and 7.
[84] The division of the rural community into four classes is a conceptual device; it is not intended to be a literal description of any particular country. Clearly, if one were doing an empirical study in a specific area, the facts of the local situation would have to be taken into account. Depending on the issues being examined, one probably would want to place traders and intermediaries in a separate group — although many middle peasants also are small, part-time middlemen.

that the absence of one invalidates the concept. Small peasants and minifundistas, in contrast, have little land, often are unable even to produce the subsistence requirements of the family, and thus are forced to derive a significant proportion of their income from hiring themselves out for wage employment and engaging in other off-farm activities. Many small peasants are self-employed. The class of small peasants gradually merges into the class of landless agricultural labourers. This group, of little significance in Southeast Asia, is quite large in South Asia and in parts of Latin America. They derive their entire income from wages (received in cash or partly in kind) and may be employed either as permanent workers on a single farm, as seasonal workers in a single locality subject to lengthy periods of idleness or as roving migrant workers with no fixed abode.

Conflicts of various sorts can arise within the peasantry, of which the following are merely examples. First, agricultural labourers and small peasants are net buyers of foodgrains and thus have an interest in policies which help to keep the price of food cheap. The middle peasants, being net sellers, have an interest in maintaining high food prices and, hence, would favour price support programmes and similar measures. Second, the bottom two classes depend on wage employment for all or part of their livelihood and thus have an interest in policies which create additional work opportunities and higher wages. The middle peasants, however, hire labour and therefore have an opposing interest in low wages. Agricultural labourers would favour a rural public works programme, while middle peasants would not; the labourers would benefit from policies which enabled workers to become strongly organized, whereas the middle peasantry would lose from such policies. Similarly, there would be a conflict of interest over minimum wages, the terms on which credit is provided for agricultural mechanization, and even the desirable degree of capital intensity in urban areas. What unites the middle and small peasantry is their common interest in acquiring more land from the landed élite, but in many other respects their interests differ. The landless labourers, on the other hand, are interested not in land but in higher wages, job security and better working conditions. Their interests are in evident conflict with those of the middle peasantry, but on several issues the interests of labourers and small peasants coincide. Thus, once again, different policies can have very different implications for the various classes that comprise the rural community.

Many of the policies that governments have adopted have been not only inegalitarian, they have also reduced the level of output and its rate of growth. In effect, governments have been arbiters of a 'negative sum game'. That is, the gains of those who have benefited from public policy have been less than the losses of those discriminated against. This, of course, is an inevitable consequence of any policy which results in allocative inefficiency. An example of such a policy is the common practice of protecting industry and turning the terms of trade against agriculture. The losses suffered by the rural community may be substantial, whereas the additional profits reaped by industrialists may be rather small in comparison, particularly if the technical efficiency of the protected activities is rather low – as is often the case. Similarly, within agriculture, policies which subsidize labour displacing mechanization may increase the profits of landowners much less than it reduces the income of the workers; this will occur whenever factor proportions fail to reflect opportunity costs.

Unfortunately, the policies that preceeded and have accompanied the 'green revolution' in many underdeveloped countries have aggravated several of the problems these countries face. Supplies of some commodities have increased, but the rate of growth of total agricultural production has shown little tendency to rise. In India, for example, wheat production has increased substantially, but agriculture as a whole has not prospered. At the same time, inequality has become worse (e.g. in India), poverty sometimes has increased absolutely (e.g. in parts of Java), and employment opportunities have failed to keep up with population growth (e.g. in Sri Lanka); in some cases technical change has led to such sharp social conflict that the peasantry (or part of it) has had to try to defend itself with violence (e.g. in Mindanao, Philippines). The high yielding varieties of foodgrains that have been developed – and those which are still in the pipeline — could in principle be used to alleviate many of these problems. But with the important exception of Taiwan, this has not occurred. The reason lies not so much in inadequate technology as in inappropriate institutions and poor policy. The explanation for the latter, in turn, lies not in the ignorance of those who govern but in the powerlessness of most of those who are governed.

Index